"Beginning with earth (dirt), air (sky), and water, Bass weaves an engaging story of interconnectedness ending in the revelation of the divine in the here and now. I thoroughly enjoyed the texture and twists of insights opening the stunning truth of emerging faith in our midst."

—Sister Simone Campbell, author of *A Nun on a Bus*

"It is so delightful to endorse a book that says what you want to say—but then says it so much better! The reversing of engines that Diana Butler Bass describes in *Grounded* was first announced by Jesus himself, of course. How strange that it should seem so new and even revolutionary two thousand years later."

—Richard Rohr, O.F.M., founder of the Center for
Action and Contemplation and author of *Falling Upward*

"Diana Butler Bass's thoughtful mandate amounts not so much to a dismissal of the church, but a summons to renewal that can be both faithful and contemporary. Her accent champions a connectedness to the actual context in which we live."

—Walter Brueggemann, Columbia Theological Seminary

ADVANCE PRAISE FOR *Grounded*

"I have forever been grateful for Diana Butler Bass's razor-sharp mind, but upon finishing *Grounded,* I found myself in love with her mystical heart and gorgeous storytelling. We need to believe that God is *here,* with us, in dirt and water and our suffering and homes and neighborhoods. God is definitely in this book."
—Glennon Doyle Melton, author of *Carry On, Warrior*

"*Grounded* is a wise and beautiful book. It is, in fact and in places, almost an anthem to the sacred unity of the physical and the spiritual in the formation of human faith and in the maturation of the human soul. To sink into its pages is to come home again, however briefly, to the sure knowledge of what is."
—Phyllis Tickle, author of *The Great Emergence*

"An absolutely gorgeously written book about real faith in the real world."
—James Martin, SJ, author of *Jesus: A Pilgrimage*

"I've long respected Diana Butler Bass for her intelligent approach to the religious conversation, and never more so than in the pages of this book. *Grounded* made me love this beautiful world more deeply, and made God's presence more visible everywhere I looked."
—Shauna Niequist, author of *Savor* and *Bread & Wine*

"'There is nothing worse than sleeping through a revolution,' Diana Butler Bass says. Her new book, *Grounded,* will not only help you wake up, it will equip you to be an enthusiastic participant in what I believe is the deepest and most important movement taking shape in our lifetime."
—Brian D. McLaren, author of *A New Kind of Christianity*

GROUNDED

GROUNDED

FINDING GOD IN THE WORLD
A SPIRITUAL REVOLUTION

DIANA BUTLER BASS

HarperOne
An Imprint of HarperCollins*Publishers*

HarperOne

Excerpts on pages 191–92 from *Being Home: Discovering the Spiritual in the Everyday*, by Gunilla Norris. Copyright © 1991, 2001 by Gunilla Norris, Paulist Press, Inc., New York/Mahwah, N.J. Used with permission of Paulist Press. www.paulistpress.com.

Unless otherwise noted, all biblical quotations are taken from the New Revised Standard Version, copyright 1989, National Council of Churches of Christ in the U.S.A.

HarperCollins books may be purchased for educational, business, or sales promotional use. For information please e-mail the Special Markets Department at SPsales@harpercollins.com.

HarperCollins website: http://www.harpercollins.com

FIRST EDITION

Designed by Janet M. Evans

Library of Congress Cataloging-in-Publication Data is available upon request.

ISBN 978–0–06-232854–0

15 16 17 18 19   RRD(H)   10 9 8 7 6 5 4 3 2

For Richard

A few lines from Wendell Berry:

Make a story
Show how love and joy, beauty and goodness
shine out amongst the rubble.

Thank you for writing a life with me.

The whole universe is God's dwelling. Earth,
a very small, uniquely blessed corner of that universe,
gifted with unique natural blessings, is humanity's home,
and humans are never so much at home as when
God dwells with them.

> —*U.S. Conference of*
> *Catholic Bishops,*
> Renewing the Earth *(1991)*

Everything is related, and we human beings are united
as brothers and sisters on a wonderful pilgrimage, woven
together by the love God has for each . . . and which also
unites us in fond affection with brother sun, sister moon,
brother river and mother earth.

> —*Pope Francis,*
> Laudato Si *(2015)*

CONTENTS

Genesis

What we need is here.
—*Wendell Berry*

I am sitting in the center of a labyrinth at Mount Calvary, a monastery in Santa Barbara, California. The labyrinth, a walking path for prayer, is painted on a concrete patio in a garden behind an old building that now serves as a retreat house. At the edge of the labyrinth are native plants and flowers, including a bright purplish bush called woolly blue curls, where a hummingbird—oblivious to my presence—feeds. Crows, sacred to the Chumash people, who once inhabited this place, fly from the gnarled branches of live oaks to the heights of eucalyptus trees as they caw and search for food. There is abundant bougainvillea, fragrant lavender and rosemary, bright mountain lilac, and coastal sunflower. Along the stone pathways are statues of the Virgin Mary and saints, often paired with benches for those who wish to sit in prayer-filled solitude. A creek, actually a dry bed due to California's extended drought, runs along the base of the hillside below, where, I suspect, rattlesnakes make their home.

This is a contemplative place. But, oddly enough, it is not terribly quiet. Across the creek, schoolchildren play, cheering for their teams. Not far away, someone stands in back of a building talking on her cell phone. The museum nearby will open soon, and workers are making ready for the day. The sound of traffic on Los Olivos Street is muffled by the trees and shrubs but still obvious. Joggers on the road chat with one another during their morning run. Tourists talk behind the wall that separates the monastery from the mission next door. Neighborhood gardeners mow lawns and blow leaves.

Mount Calvary has not always occupied this particular place. Years ago, I often visited its original location—fifteen mostly vertical acres of mountaintop above Santa Barbara with sweeping views of the Pacific Ocean. When sitting on the porch on a clear day, you looked out toward the Channel Islands and down upon the city. There were distant sounds, voices traveling across the canyons or the faint rumble of the freeway far below, like indistinct prayers rising to the skies. Mostly, it was quiet—stunningly so—the immediate silence broken mostly by birdsong, bells, or monastic chant. So high up, that otherworldly place felt a bit like heaven.

But Mount Calvary's mountaintop paradise is no longer. In November 2008, the California winds blew hot, and a wildfire destroyed it all.

As the flames engulfed their home, the terrified monks fled downhill to the city. The sisters of St. Mary's Convent, an order whose house sits behind the Santa Barbara Mission in a busy residential area, took them in. At St. Mary's, the sisters and brothers lived together, sharing monastic community. Eventually, the monks received an insurance settlement for the old Mount Calvary and faced the decision of whether to rebuild on the top of the hill. After much prayer, they opted to sell the scorched site in favor of finding a different location. The sisters, with only a few women remaining in their small community, offered their property to the brothers. Thus, St. Mary's Convent became the new Mount Calvary, and the brothers took up permanent residence in the city.

From the labyrinth, I look up and see the peak where the monks used to live. When they gazed down from the heights above, this spot would have been just a speck in their commanding perspective; a person sitting where I sit would have been invisible to them. Now they live in the world, with everything right around them, no longer above it. They have become part of the view, not distant observers of it. Up there, they would not have heard the children, joggers, or tourists or noticed the persistent hummingbirds and noisy crows. Whereas once Mount Calvary offered retreatants the capacity to see widely and dream vast dreams of God, the new monastery invites guests to feel the world more deeply and experience the intimacy of Spirit.

If I think about what was lost, about the beautiful old monastery, I feel sad. I miss the majestic views, the vistas of mountain and ocean, with the towering sense of being above the world. But here, in the center of the labyrinth, peace prevails. The morning fog is lifting. I kick off my shoes. The sounds provide a kind of gentle companionship, reminding me that I am not completely alone with my prayers. Sitting on the ground, I feel warm solidarity with the world of nature and the worlds of all those traveling nearby. And I feel that other presence as well, the heartbeat of love at the center of things, the spirit of wonder or awe that many call God. Any sense of monastic isolation has been overcome with a sense of intimate connection with all that is around, things seen and things less tangible. I, like the monks, am not above. Here, I am with the world. And I find that God is with me.

Maybe coming off the mountain is not a bad thing after all.

Where Is God?

Not so long ago, believers confidently asserted that God inhabited heaven, a distant place of eternal reward for the faithful. We occupied a three-tiered universe, with heaven above, where God lived; the world below, where we lived; and the underworld, where we feared we might go after death. The church mediated the space between heaven and earth, acting as a kind of holy elevator, wherein God sent down divine directions and, if we obeyed the directives, we would go up—eventually—to live in heaven forever and avoid the terrors below. Stories and sermons taught us that God occupied the high places, looking over the world and caring for it from afar, occasionally interrupting the course of human affairs with some miraculous reminder of divine power. Those same tales emphasized the gap between worldly places and the holy mountains, between the creation and an Almighty Creator. Religious authorities mediated the gap, explaining right doctrine and holy living. If you wanted to live with God forever in heaven, then you listened to them, believed, and obeyed.

During the last century, the three-tiered universe and its orderly certainty crumbled. The Great War caused its philosophical and political foundations to wobble, and the whole thing collapsed after the even greater war, World War II, when the Nazis and the Holocaust and the bomb shattered history. God, like the monks from Mount Calvary chased by the roaring inferno, fled down the mountain seeking shelter in the midst of the city.

Oddly enough, most people did not seem to notice at first or, perhaps, were in a state of denial. There were prophets and writers who tried to explain what had happened. Dietrich Bonhoeffer, the Lutheran pastor awaiting execution in a Nazi prison, understood that the three-tiered universe with its majestic God had been swept away by the war and argued that a new "religionless" Christianity must emerge from history's ashes. Elie Wiesel, a Jewish humanist and survivor of the death camps, who daily experienced the horrors attending the end of the world as it was being incinerated at Auschwitz, summed it all up with a plaintive questioning cry, "For God's sake, where is God?"

Some postwar theologians and philosophers understood and began to proclaim the "death of God." Regular people did not take them seriously, however. Soldiers wanted to get home to their sweethearts, back to houses with picket fences in small towns, back to family, church, and business. There had been so much death; it was too awful to consider that God might have been a wartime casualty as well. Getting back to normal was the key task for mid-twentieth-century people, even if normal was irretrievably gone. Revivals of religion swept through Western nations to restore order and familiarity, first in the 1950s and then again in the 1970s. The faithful baptized legions of postwar offspring, built bigger and taller temples than ever before, and exercised more influence and political power than Christianity had known since the days of Pope Innocent III—all as a testimony to God's victory over the forces of evil and the triumph of true religion.

It could not last. In the decades that followed, it became increasingly evident that you cannot revive a God for a world that no longer exists. Venerating a God of a vanished world is the very definition of fundamentalism, the sort of religion that is inflicting great pain and violence on many millions of people across the planet and is leading to the rejection of religion by millions of others. Conventional theism is at the heart of fundamentalism and depends on the three-tiered universe. But we now live in a theologically flattened world—we have discovered that we are fully capable of creating the terrors of hell right here and no longer need a lake of fire to prove the existence of evil—and we have found that the ranks of saints and angels seem to have thinned and that no deity will be sending miracles to fix the mess we are in.

Is there another option between fundamentalism and a deceased God? I think so. If hell has moved in next door to us, perhaps heaven has as well. Bonhoeffer and Wiesel, who saw so clearly what was happening, asked the right question long ago: "Where is God?" That question—and how it is being answered—points toward a surprising spiritual revolution.

In the last decade, it has become increasingly obvious that people no longer fear asking the question, as events have conspired to make the problems of God's presence—or absence—clearer. In December 2012, a troubled teenager shot twenty-six people, some teachers but mostly small children, at Sandy Hook Elementary School in Newtown, Connecticut. The horror of this event shocked the world. In the days that followed, there were questions on radio, television, and the Internet, in magazines and newspapers: How could this have happened? What can be done to prevent it from happening again? Would new gun-safety laws safeguard our communities? Could the president and Congress agree on such legislation?

Amid these questions, however, another question, one not asked by pundits but by regular people, came to the fore: "Where was God at Sandy Hook?" The conversation took place in blogs and social media, in sermons and public memorials, in coffeehouses and around dining-room tables. Some people proclaimed that God was in heaven, waiting to welcome the victims with open arms; others declared that a distant, judging God permitted such violence as a blood sacrifice for national sins; a few opined that God had directed the heroic acts of teachers who saved their students or the police who arrived on scene. And then, of course, there were those who insisted that God had nothing to do with any of it, because God either does not intervene in human affairs or does not exist at all. Sandy Hook held up a spiritual mirror to our time, revealing a theological argument regarding God not often visible in public.

If the question was surprising, it is perhaps astonishing that a consensus emerged from the discussion. By far the most often repeated answer, and apparently the most comforting, was that God was "with" the victims. God was *with* them? *With* us?

During past times of profound public tragedy, such as the Battle of Gettysburg, the sinking of the *Titanic,* or the attack on Pearl Harbor, very few people thought to ask, "Where is God?" Most assumed that they knew where God was: in heaven, up in the divine throne room. Instead, our ancestors asked: "Why did God let this happen?" or "What is God trying to teach us?" or "What does God want us to do in response?" The older questions sought to discern God's intentions when terrible things occurred, not to query the location of the divinity.

We have heard this question with sad frequency in recent years. "Where is God?" arose from the rubble of the World Trade Center; from the inundated villages of tsunami-ravaged Thailand and Indonesia; from New Orleans, as the levees breaking swept all that was familiar out to sea; from African hamlets where the dead mount from Ebola; from the hidden, abused, and lost victims of human trafficking and slavery; from killing fields in any number of nations where war seems endless; and from native peoples watching their homelands sink into the earth or ocean due to melting tundra or rising seas. "Where is God?" has echoed from every corner of the planet in recent years in circumstances so dire that many wonder whether we have been abandoned and left to fend for ourselves. The case could be made that the first years of the twenty-first century could be called the "Age of Anxiety" or the "Age of Fear"; there are far too many reasons to believe that human history has tipped toward ultimate destruction. Hope is at a premium, but the supply is perilously short. Fear is both cheap and plentiful.

"Where is God?" is one of the most consequential questions of our times. Some stubbornly maintain that a distant God sits on his heavenly throne watching all these things, acting as either a divine puppet master or a stern judge of human affairs, ready at a moment's notice to throw more thunderbolts or toss the whole human race into an eternal lake of fire. But this is a vision of God whose time may be up, for such a divinity looks either increasingly absurd or suspiciously like a monster. And people know that, for a substantial number of them now say that "God is not," thus eliminating a divine throne-sitter completely and leaving responsibility for the global mess squarely on human shoulders. Humanism, agnosticism, atheism, and posttheism are all on the rise—perfectly logical choices with which thoughtful people should at least sympathize.

Yet while some have concluded that it is indeed the case that we humans are alone, others have looked at these same events and suggested a much different spiritual possibility: God is with us. It is a wildly improbable turn of theological events to claim that God is with victims of war, terrorism, or natural disaster, with the valorous who run toward burning buildings or navigate flooding streets, and with those who mourn and doubt and even despair. As Bonhoeffer said, "Only a suffering God can help." God is with us in and through all these terrible events.

Jewish scholar Abraham Heschel referred to this God as the God of pathos, who loves the world profoundly, feels with creation, and participates in its life. This means, of course, that God is with us not only in times of misery and anguish. Human beings have a tendency to ask important questions when tragedy strikes, but God is also in the midst of joy, when we forget to ask, and in life's more mundane experiences. In the years since Heschel wrote, a cultural language of divine nearness has come to surround us—God can be found at the seashore, in a sunset, in the gardens we plant, at home, in the work we do, in the games we watch or play, in the stories that entertain us, in good food and good company, when we eat, drink, laugh, and even make love. People who identify as "spiritual but not religious" or religiously unaffiliated use a vocabulary of theological intimacy, as do many who identify with more traditional faiths. Although some still worship a distant majesty and others deny divine existence, many millions of contemporary people experience God as far more personal and accessible than ever before.

There is much evidence for religious decline across the West, and much attention is paid to the growth of fundamentalist religions, especially in the Global South and developing world. But, in some ways, theories of decline or growth are not really the point. Roiling around the planet is a shifting conception of God. In a wide variety of cultures, God has become unmediated and local, animating the natural world and human activity in profoundly intimate ways. Of course, this has always been the path of mystics in the world's religions, what I often call the "minor chord" of faith. Now, however, the personal, mystical, immediate, and intimate is emerging as the dominant way of engaging the divine. What was once reserved for a few saints has now become the quest of millions around the planet— to be able to touch, feel, and know God for one's self.

This is an unexpected challenge for all the world's great faiths. Religion is changing because its deepest questions, those regarding the relationship between God and the world, are being asked in new ways. For the last several centuries, the primary questions regarding God and the world were of dogma or practice: *Who is God? What must I do to be a good person or to be saved?* Every religion answered such questions differently, and human beings typically accepted what their natal faith taught them. Religious institutions passed on particular traditions and served as mediating structures between that which was holy and that which was mundane. But faith questions now center on finding God—*Where is God?*—and figuring out what discovering the sacred here means—*How does God's presence enliven our actions in the world?* Simply put, the informational queries of *who* and *what*, along with their authoritative answers, have been traded for the experiential and open-ended concerns of *where* and *how*.

Not only have the questions changed, but the way we ask them has changed as well. We no longer live isolated behind boundaries of ethnicity, race, or religion. We are connected in global community. We search the Internet for answers; we ask our Buddhist or Hindu neighbors; we read our own sacred texts and the texts of others; we listen to preachers from the world's religions. Answers are no longer confined to the opinions of a local priest, mullah, rabbi, or guru. The answers depend on us figuring this out together. This shift in religious consciousness is a worldwide phenomenon, a sort of divine web in which we are tangled. Although atheists and humanists might look upon this askance, as a return to superstition, it is equally legitimate to read the shift as a reenchantment of the world, a spiritual revolution of astonishing scope. And everyone is caught up in the web.

In 1974, anthropologist David Buchdahl argued that a culture's understanding of God was central to its larger practices of social and political life. And when a culture's God is under stress or undergoing revision, the whole system is strained. Buchdahl claimed, "A change in the conception of God is a cultural event of some magnitude, especially because the character of a culture is heavily influenced by the notion of God that predominates within it."[1] If that is true, and I believe it to be so, it is no longer a singular reality—for Buchdahl was speaking of "a culture"—but this is now happening among many cultures, a planet-wide transformation of the way human life is shaped and organized. On the face of it, the question "Where is God?" might appear to be an arcane theological notion, but it is, in reality, a profound contemporary global inquiry. Depending on how it is answered, "Where is God?" could be a social and political question with sweeping consequences for the future. To relocate God is to reground our lives.

Where is God? God is here. How shall we act upon that? Well, that is up to us.

God With(in) the World

Here in the labyrinth, I struggle to find words to describe what I feel. Up on the mountaintop, I knew the language to describe God: majestic, transcendent, all-powerful, heavenly Father, Lord, and King. In this vocabulary, God remains stubbornly located in a few select places, mostly in external realms above or beyond: heaven, the church, doctrine, or the sacraments. What happens in the labyrinth seems vague, perhaps even theologically elusive.

Like countless others, I have been schooled in vertical theology. Western culture, especially Western Christianity, has imprinted a certain theological template upon the spiritual imagination: God exists far off from the world and does humankind a favor when choosing to draw close. Sermons declared that God's holiness was

11

foreign to us and sin separated us from God. Yes, humanity was made in God's image, but we had so messed things up in the Garden of Eden that any trace of God in us was obscured, if not destroyed. Whether conservative or liberal, most American churches teach some form of the idea that God exists in holy isolation, untouched by the messiness of creation, and that we, God's children, are morally and spiritually filthy, bereft of all goodness, utterly unworthy to stand before the Divine Presence. In its crudest form, the role of religion (whether through revivals, priesthood, ritual, story, sacraments, personal conversion, or morality) is to act as a holy elevator between God above and those muddling around down below in the world.

Despite my familiarity with conventional theology, I do have experience of another sort of language for God, for throughout my life something odd kept happening to me. God showed up. The first time God showed up I was very small, three, maybe four. My parents and I were playing in the surf at a beach. An unexpected wave ripped me away from my father's hand, pushing me under its crest. As I rolled beneath the waters, my eyes opened and I saw the sun, bright but oddly indistinct at the same time, its light diffused all around me, drawing me toward its source. Everything was blue, gold, and white. Water, sand, and sun: all was suddenly one. It was beautiful and terrifying. I felt suspended, without any real sense of either time or space. Then suddenly my father reached into the water and pulled me to the surface, where I both cried and choked. Many years later, my mother told me that I had nearly drowned.

And it has often been the same since. God, the spirit of wonder, or Jesus—it is often hard to label exactly—shows up in prayer; while walking on paths, hiking in the desert, or sitting in the sunshine; in the animals that cross my way; and in my dreams. For whatever reason, my soul has a mile-wide mystical streak. My friends regularly joke that, had I been born during the Middle Ages, I would have been condemned as a witch (and that is not really funny, for hundreds of thousands of people were killed by religious authorities for this very thing). When younger, I feared talking about it; my church did not help me understand it. But now I know that it is not that terribly unusual. Much of contemporary memoir is a literature of spiritual experience, including accounts of near-death experiences and profound encounters resulting from nature, service to others, or engaging in the arts. Half of all American adults, even some who call themselves atheists or nonbelievers, report having had such an experience at least once in their lives.[2]

The language of mysticism and spiritual experience cuts a wide swath through the world's religious traditions, and it presents an alternative theology, that of connection and intimacy. In Christian tradition, Jesus speaks this language when he claims, "The Father and I are one" (John 10:30), and when he breathes on his followers and fills them with God's Spirit (20:22); it appears in the testimony of the apostle Paul, who converts during a mystical encounter with Christ on a road; and it fills the effusive poetry of John the Evangelist, whose vision of God is nothing short of one in which the whole of creation is absorbed into love. When the Bible is read from the perspective of divine nearness, it becomes clear that most prophets, poets, and preachers are particularly worried about religious institutions and practices that perpetuate the gap between God and humanity, making the divine unapproachable or cordoned off behind cadres of priestly mediators, whose interest is in exercising their own power as brokers of salvation. The biblical narrative is that of a God who comes close, compelled by a burning desire to make heaven on earth and occupy human hearts.

One need not be a mystic or have had a near-death experience to understand this; it need not be the result of years of technical

13

training in some spiritual practice of enlightenment. This has become a prominent contemporary way of speaking about God that reflects a wisdom found in ancient scriptures, a spiritual vocabulary articulated by biblical heroes, saints, reformers, and the humble poor through the ages.[3] And this impulse toward spiritual intimacy is found not only in the Abrahamic faiths, but in Buddhism, Hinduism, and native religions. Far too many people who understand God in these ways probably do not know how rich the tradition is that speaks of God with us, God in the stars and sunrise, God as the face of their neighbor, God in the act of justice, or God as the wonder of love. The language of divine nearness is the very heart of vibrant faith. Yet it has often been obscured by vertical theologies and elevator institutions, which, I suspect, are far easier to both explain and control. Drawing God within the circle of the world is a messy and sometimes dangerous business.

In the middle of the twentieth century, theologian H. Richard Niebuhr wrote a bestselling and influential book about the problem of God's location entitled *Christ and Culture*.[4] Using Christian history and language, he identified five potential ways that God, that is, "Christ," related to the world, that is, "culture." According to Niebuhr, God might be seen as being (1) *against* the world, (2) *of* the world, (3) *above* the world, (4) paradoxically *in tension with* the world, or (5) *in a perpetual struggle to transform* the world. Although the book is almost seven decades old and much is dated, teachers and preachers still summon these categories to explain God and the world. Four of the five categories (*against, above, in tension with,* and *transforming*) emphasize God's distinctiveness, underscoring the idea of a distant divinity, and make the world a problem to be fixed or an obstacle to be overcome. Only one category (and the type Niebuhr most strongly ridiculed), *of,* portrayed God as close and the world of human experience, history, nature, and culture as a meaningful stage of divine action. When it comes to Christian theology, distance has been God's default location. Thus, *Christ and Culture* concisely summarizes Western religion—a worldview shaped from a divine mountaintop looking out and down, not from the center of the labyrinth looking around and up.

But this is changing. In the twenty-first-century world, top-down institutions and philosophies are weakening—and that includes top-down religions. People are leading their own theological revolution and finding that the Spirit is much more with the world than we had previously been taught.

This new understanding is far more than God being *of* the world (in Niebuhr's sense). One would have to be blind or morally bankrupt to think that God was *of* many things in our world: violence against women and children, slavery, terrorism, racism, social inequity, religious fundamentalisms, poverty, environmental degradation, and warfare. The problem of evil is real. (It is worth noting, however, that human beings create the vast majority of what we deem evil. Evil is not God's problem as much as it is ours.) But there is a widespread sense that God is *with us, within* creation, culture, and the cosmos. If anything, recent decades have revealed not a dreadful, distant God, but have slowly illuminated that an intimate presence of mystery abides with the world, a spirit of compassion that breathes hope and healing. And with it faith is shifting from a theology of distance toward a theology of nearness, from institution to unmediated experience.

The change in tone is obvious in the sermons of the well known, such as Desmond Tutu, the Dalai Lama, or Pope Francis, as well as the works of lesser-known writers, poets, artists, and spiritual guides, the insights of clergy from a wide range of traditions, and the prayers of everyday people. The field of vision has been redirected toward a quotidian God, whose holiness is revealed in worldly things, and toward divine simplicity, whose connections are woven through all that is. The most significant story in the history of religion at this time is not a decline in Western religion, a rejection of religious institutions, or the growth of religious extremism; rather, it is a changed conception of God, a rebirthing of faith from the ground up.[5]

We're Grounded

If you pay attention, you can hear this shift in conversations everywhere. On a flight from Washington, D.C., to Los Angeles, a successful executive was seated next to me. After she told me about her work, she asked, "What do you do?"

I replied that I write about religion and spirituality.

She laughed. "'Religion' isn't a very popular word, is it?"

I agreed.

"I used to be religious," she explained. "I grew up Catholic, but left the church over the sex-abuse scandal. The church doesn't make much sense in the world as it is now. But I still believe in God. I'd say I'm a spiritual person."

"Lots of people tell me that they are 'spiritual but not religious,'" I said, laughing a little. "What do you mean by that? Who is God to you?"

She shared with me how she found God in nature, in her relationships with family, friends, and neighbors, and in the work she does in the world. She told me how God was present to her through doing justice (serving hungry people at a local shelter), contemplative worship (occasional attendance at an evening jazz service at an Episcopal Church), and offering hospitality toward those in need (caring for those who were doubting, ill, or grieving among her own friends). Intelligent and obviously compassionate, she understood her own work as a vocation to create a more just and inclusive world. Sensing I would know what she was talking about, she threw in a few theologians and Catholic saints, like Thomas Aquinas and Dorothy Day, to explain her perspectives on spirituality and social justice.

"Why don't you join the church with the jazz service?" I asked.

"I've thought about that," she confessed. She also shared that she sometimes felt guilty about not attending church anymore. "But 'joining' an organization strikes me as a strange way to relate to God. And the institutional church is so broken, so hypocritical. It has wounded so many people. I just can't do that again with any honesty." She paused, seeming to wonder if she should continue. "But these other things—the Spirit all around, caring and praying for people, working for a better world—they ground me."

Her tale was similar to many stories in circulation about leaving religion behind in favor of spirituality. But it had a twist. She felt grounded by God. So there we were, at thirty-five thousand feet, talking—perhaps somewhat ironically—about what grounded us.

The English noun "ground" refers to the surface of the earth; the verb "to ground" has multiple senses: "to prohibit or prevent" (such as grounding a plane in a storm or punishing one's teenager), "to give a firm theoretical or practical basis," and "to instruct someone thoroughly in a subject." In Christian theology, the word "ground" conjures a very particular image. In 1916, a young German military chaplain named Paul Tillich was stationed on the front lines of World War I. The war undid all Tillich's youthful confidence in the world and in faith. He wrote to a friend, saying that he spent more time digging graves than sharing the sacraments. "I have constantly the most immediate and very strong feeling that

I am no longer alive," he confessed. "I am experiencing the actual death of this our time."[6] Tillich experienced the end of the old world, the same "death" Bonhoeffer and Wiesel would write of during the next war; he felt "that a certain God had died on the battlefields of Europe. . . . One could no longer easily preach about the benevolence of God or issue promises of peace from the heights of the mountaintop."[7]

After the war, Tillich made it his work to find dependable theological ground. Eventually, he proclaimed that God is the "Ground of all Being," the "centered presence of the divine"; the "whole world" is God's "periphery."[8] Human life may be finite, destined for dirt and death; but the ground and all that came from it and was connected to it, claimed Tillich, was drenched with the divine, the source of infinite holiness. Tillich did not mean that God was literally soil—he stressed that God is not an object—but God, the numinous presence at the center of all things, is what grounds us.

This insight appears in many of the world's faith traditions. Most tribal religions are based upon the absolute connection of God (or gods) and the earth. Buddhists see "the world as it is" as the stage of spiritual activity. For Hindus, Brahman is the source of all life, represented by the sacred word *Om;* the world itself is the expression of Brahman's dream. Judaism, Christianity, and Islam share a creation story in which the earth is the embodiment of God's breath and insist that God is present everywhere and in all things. Some contemporary Jewish scholars argue that the Hebrew scriptures describe a God with a "fluid" or "plural" body manifesting itself throughout the earth, in whose name, "I AM," resides all being.[9] Indeed, the primary hope of the ancient Hebrews was for "Immanuel," or "God with us," the God who dwells with humankind in love and justice. Christians refer to God's embodiment as "incarnation," God made flesh in Jesus, who is called Immanuel, and believe that God is present through the Spirit sent into the world after Jesus's death and resurrection.

Separating the material from the spiritual is, perhaps, one of the saddest philosophical missteps of Western culture. Our ancestors understandably wanted to break the chains of superstition and follow the exciting new paths opened by science and democratic politics, so they disassociated faith from reason. But they unwittingly went too far—and we eventually lost the sense of a God who is "constantly, annoyingly present in the world."[10]

Yet in an age of profound, perplexing, and even frightening change, millions of people are rediscovering from the deepest human wisdom a simple spiritual reality: we're grounded.

A Spiritual Revolution

Almost one in four Americans no longer identifies with any particular religious tradition, a number that rises to one in three if you count only American adults under thirty. In Canada, the national number is slightly more than one in four; across Europe, the percentage of religiously unaffiliated people is higher. In societies that were once strongly shaped by Protestantism and Catholicism, increasing numbers of people have opted out of conventional religion at historic rates. In terms of raw numbers, between 660,000 and 700,000 Americans per year in the last decade have left religion, making "no religion" the second largest "religious" group in the United States—and the only group posting numeric gains in all fifty states.[11] In an unexpected turn of events, the "nones" are being joined by the "dones," those believers who were once faithful participants but who now have had enough of institutional religion.[12]

Belief in God has softened since the mid-twentieth century, as most Western populations register overall declines in theological certainty and theism. Attendance at religious services has reached near record lows across the developed world, and erosion of other measures of religious adherence is obvious as well.[13] Sociologists of religion Michael Hout, Claude Fischer, and Mark Chaves sum up the American situation as follows: "The historic distancing of Americans from organized religion continues to evolve. More Americans than ever profess having no religious preference. Their quarrel appears to be with organized religion."[14] All of these changes have caused much wailing and gnashing of teeth in conventional denominations, as the clergy and the faithful struggle to come to terms with what has happened and wonder what the postreligious future holds for them.

Yet despite the move away from organized religion, something else is happening. Belief in God, although reported at lower cultural levels than in previous decades, still remains surprisingly widespread. In the United States and Canada, roughly six in ten people say they believe in God with some degree of certainty; in Europe, the number is five in ten. If you include the number of people who believe in a universal Spirit, higher power, or life force, the percentage goes up by about twenty points. Public Religion Research Institute has developed a "spiritual experiences index," indicating that 65 percent of Americans score in the moderate to "very high" range of spiritual connection, sense of wonder, inner peace and harmony, and oneness with nature—data that lends credence to the argument that God-in-heaven is giving way to the Spirit-with-us. Even atheists like Sam Harris admit that mindfulness, enlightenment, and spiritual awakening are possible and desirable for a happy and ethical life separated from the idea of conventional theism.[15] Indeed, with intense cultural interest in spiritual practice and the surprising resilience of God, Hout, Fischer, and Chaves argue that "disbelief" is *not* the primary factor prompting religious defections.

The implication seems stunningly clear. *People believe, but they believe differently than they once did.* The theological ground is moving; a spiritual revolution is afoot. And there is a gap between that revolution and the institutions of religious faith.

Why is this happening? The answer may be simpler than some suggest. At the same moment when massive global institutions seem to rule the world, there is an equally strong countermovement among regular people to claim personal agency in our own lives. We grow food in backyards. We brew beer. We weave cloth and knit blankets. We shop local. We create our own playlists. We tailor delivery of news and entertainment. In every arena, we customize and personalize our lives, creating material environments to make meaning, express a sense of uniqueness, and engage causes that matter to us and the world.

It makes perfect sense that we are making our spiritual lives as well, crafting a new theology. And that God is far more personal and close at hand than once imagined.

But most religious institutions have not been able to grasp this. For more than a century, Western society emphasized the importance of large institutions for the good of community. We believed that centralized, top-down organizations were the best way to manage business, politics, and social problems. And this included religion. Christians built massive national and international structures, with God-in-heaven as CEO sending down directives to do good. And it was very successful, for a while.

Until, of course, people lost trust—or simply lost interest—in distant institutions and distant Gods. Whenever a gulf opens between the way people experience God and how institutions respond (or fail to respond) to such concerns, historical conditions ripen for spiritual revolution, reformation, and awakening.

Conversations like the one with my airplane companion illustrate the dynamic perfectly. Leaving the institutional church behind, she has joined the ranks of the "nones." However, she also understands that God is with her, in her work and her relationships, through art, and in communion with nature. Her testimony is remarkably like that of millions of others across Western societies.[16] Yet these stories are rarely taken as a whole, giving voice to an important cultural critique, meaningful spiritual longing, or serious theological perspective. Instead, they are often ridiculed, called tedious or boring, most often derided as "radical individualism," "cafeteria religion," "navel-gazing spirituality," "Oprah church," or, in more sophisticated philosophical terms, "moral therapeutic deism." Entire books have been written and at least a couple of careers made by pointing out how dangerous such views are to the fabric of community, especially to religious and civic institutions. Yet for all their attempts at journalism or academic objectivity, when these analyses are professionally deployed to describe experiences like those of my seatmate, they too often smack of intellectual superiority and moral defensiveness, carrying a whiff of judgment if not outright insult.

And I guess I am tired of being insulted.

For my entire life, I have been a practicing Christian. I even once wrote a book that opened with the line, "I am a church-goer."[17] I still go to church. To be honest, however, my attendance is much more sporadic than it once was. Although I have advanced degrees in religion, I am neither a minister nor a teacher at a divinity school. I have written about churches and the future of churches for more than a decade. I am, despite all this, what is called a "layperson." Although I write about religion, like most laypeople I do not spend the majority of my time in a professional religious setting. When not asked to preach (something I like to do as a spiritual practice) on a given Sunday, I sit in the pews along with everybody else—the intensely devout, the sleepy, the fidgety, the doubters, the bored, the hyperorthodox, the nominal, the distracted, the joyful, the irked, the true believers, the dullards, and now the Tweeters and texters. The pews are a much more diverse place than most outsiders imagine, but it seems clear enough: the ties that once bound are loosening, and the ranks are thinning.

Critics say this is happening because we are uncommitted, disloyal, or too lazy to get up on whatever Sabbath we celebrate. We do not understand community, or we like sports better than church. We are consumers more interested in getting our own needs met than in meeting the needs of the world. We are too busy. We are self-centered, lacking a moral passion for charity or social justice.

I suppose that any of this may be true for some people. But it is not true for me. Much to my surprise, church has become a spiritual, even a theological struggle for me. I have found it increasingly difficult to sing hymns that celebrate a hierarchical heavenly realm, to recite creeds that feel disconnected from life, to pray liturgies that emphasize salvation through blood, to listen to sermons that preach an exclusive way to God, to participate in sacraments that exclude others, and to find myself confined to a hard pew in a building with no windows to the world outside. This has not happened because I am angry at the church or God. Rather, it has happened because I was moving around in the world and began to realize how beautifully God was everywhere: in nature and in my neighborhood, in considering the stars and by seeking my roots. It took me five decades to figure it out, but I finally understood. The church is not the only sacred space; the world is profoundly sacred as well. And thus I fell into a gap—the theological ravine between a church still proclaiming conventional theism with its three-tiered universe and the spiritual revolution of God-with-us.

People like me? We are not lazy, self-centered, or individualistic church shoppers. We are heartbroken. Heartbroken by the fact that the faith traditions that raised us and that we love seem to be sleeping through the revolution.

Many people have left organized religion because they experience too great a distance between the old structures and their experience of God. Yet there are surprising moments when the revolution actually makes it into church—a courageous sermon that turns things upside down, an old hymn tune with earthy new words, a poem that rivals the beauty of scripture, a call to plant a garden or march for justice. Even within some houses of worship, people are getting it. Once thick ecclesiastical walls have proved a surprisingly porous boundary between the church and the world, and the questions that used to roil the cultural edge are being heard inside many congregations too. The questions are now inside the church as well as outside. And people are far less afraid to ask them than they once were.

In some faith communities, people are coming up with new answers and new possibilities for their own lives, in ways more empowering, satisfying, and meaningful than the established ways of engaging faith. And in all the faith communities where this is happening, the spiritual thread is similar: God has moved off the mountain, and everyone is trying to figure out what that means for their lives and the life of the planet. What seems like a mess of data and conflicting choices may well be a multitude of people retracing one another's spiritual steps, all writing a new theology by happenstance.

If one pays attention, it is possible to trace a pattern of theology on this spiritual ground. "Theology" is a funny word, maybe offputting to some. It means, quite simply, "the study of the nature of God." God and the drive to somehow understand the nature of God continue to fascinate. Where and how do people encounter God in a postreligious age? What kind of theology are people themselves making? Once, people went to a church or synagogue to find God. There, one could have a certain confidence that a heavenly Father cared for his people and would bless or save those who followed the rules. Not so much now. The conventional understandings of God have become increasingly irrelevant throughout Western culture, societies once shaped by the most magnificent visions of the transcendent God. Those views are being challenged by an emerging embrace of God-with-us, a from-the-ground-up theology evident in attitudes toward nature and culture and in our hopes, dreams, and actions.

The conventional God existed outside space and time, a being beyond imagining, who lived in heaven, unaffected by the boundaries of human life. Thus, Western religion developed a language of what theologians call the *omnis*. God was omnipotent, omnipresent, omniscient: all-powerful, in all places, and all-knowing. But the grounded God is a God in relationship with space and time as the love that connects and creates all things, known in and with the world. The *omnis* fail to describe this. Instead, we might think of God as *inter,* the spiritual thread between space and time; *intra,* within space and time; and *infra,* that which holds space and time. This God is not above or beyond, but integral to the whole of creation, entwined with the sacred ecology of the universe.

The spiritual revolution is about two things: God and the world. It is about God, but it does not wind up being otherworldly. It is about the world, but it does not result in secularism. This is a middle-ground revolution, in which millions of people are navigating the space between conventional theism and a secularized world. They are making a path that enfolds the mundane and the sacred, finding a God who is a "gracious mystery, ever greater, ever nearer" through a new awareness of the earth and in the lives of their neighbors.[18]

Because this book is about the world, it cites news, trends, data, literature, and pop culture to understand changes in faith and practice. Because it is about God, it also cites great spiritual texts, ancient traditions, and wise teachers to explore the meaning of a life of faith. Sometimes the voice is that of a sociologist or journalist. In other cases, however, the voice is more like that of a preacher or theologian. *Grounded* observes and reports a radical change in the way many people understand God and how they practice faith; at the same time, it provides greater clarity about these changes, so that people walking this path may do so with more confidence and certainty. It both explains and encourages.

The connecting point between the two perspectives is spiritual memoir, drawing from experiences in my own life and the lives of those close to me. I know about these changes because, like so many others, I am living them. This is a report of a sacred revolution as it is occurring and a sustained assertion that this revolution is not nearly as amorphous or disordered as it otherwise might seem. Rather, there is a pattern of God all around us—a deeply spiritual theology that relates to contemporary concerns, provides meaning and hope for the future, and possesses surprisingly rich ties to wisdom from the past.

And this revolution rests upon a simple insight: God is the ground, the grounding, that which grounds us. We experience this when we understand that soil is holy, water gives life, the sky opens the imagination, our roots matter, home is a divine place, and our lives are linked with our neighbors' and with those around the globe. This world, not heaven, is the sacred stage of our times.

Part One

NATURAL HABITAT

We need the sun, the moon, the stars,
the rivers, and the mountains and birds,
the fish in the sea, to evoke a world of
mystery, to evoke the sacred.

—*Thomas Berry*

I woke around five in the morning and, with unnatural enthusiasm, nearly jumped out of the hotel bed. Back home on the East Coast, it was eight o'clock. But here in Santa Barbara, California, it was still before dawn. I pulled on capris and a sweatshirt and, with determined stride, walked across Cabrillo Boulevard to the beach to greet the morning light.

It had been overcast for days, but I glanced up and saw stars above. No fog this morning, perhaps just ocean mist. At first I strolled along the bike path. But then I crossed over the low dune of sand and ice plant to the water's edge. I kicked off my shoes and walked in the wet sand, the gentle surf occasionally washing over my feet. As the sun came over the mountains, the sky slowly lightened. The color was unlike any I had ever seen. The whole scene appeared like an aging photograph: the highest sky was a deep gray-indigo, the sun at the horizon glowed golden with only soft hints of rose, the mountains were still dark in shade, brown-hued sea birds reeled overhead, and the whole thing was reflected in the waters of low tide, forming a sandy mirror image.

I did not feel, however, that I was looking at a pretty picture or, like a tourist, observing a scene. Instead, at the place where the earth, water, sky, and creatures met, everything was of a piece. There was no clear distinction between individual things; instead, the hazy light endued a sense of wonder that connected the whole. I was part of it. Inwardly, I heard the words, "The world is charged with the grandeur of God," from the poem by Gerald Manley Hopkins:

> Oh, morning, at the brown brink eastward, springs—
> Because the Holy Ghost over the bent
> World broods with warm breast and with ah! bright wings.

Without thinking, I fell to my knees and uttered, "Thank you."

Then, with no intention of doing so, I leaned forward and kissed the beach, wanting every part of my body to touch the wet earth. Tears streamed down my face and mingled with the sea at the continent's edge. If people had seen me, they might have thought me a fervent Muslim prostrating in prayer, a sun worshipper at morning devotion, or a dedicated evolutionist thanking her ancestors for coming out the waters. But I was just a person taking a walk at first light, someone who, overwhelmed with the beauty of the earth, the water, and the sky, was, quite literally, pulled to the ground by gratitude.

God is here.

Dirt

We must abandon the external height images in which
the theistic God has historically been perceived and
replace them with internal depth images of a deity
who is not apart from us, but who is the very core and
ground of all that is.

—*Paul Tillich*

Rowan eats dirt. And he digs holes. He would probably tun-
nel back to his native Ireland if we let him. When he is not
eating dirt, he lies on it. Full belly on the ground, legs
stretched out in front and to the back with every inch of his body
pressing into the soil. Although he appears to be relaxed, he is on
alert—fully aware of every sound, every movement around him.
The dirt seems to make him more attentive, ready to chase the first
squirrel that dares trespass into the yard. He is a Glen of Imaal Terrier, a solid dog with short legs; scruffy and tough, he is what is
known as an "earth dog." Indeed, the word "terrier" is derived from
the Latin word *terra,* meaning "earth." As if to underscore the point,

Rowan was born in mid-April, just two days before Earth Day. For him, Earth itself is his natal saint, the dirt his dwelling place.

He is the second terrier I have owned, and I cannot help but wonder why I like earth dogs so much. Perhaps it is some sort of recompense for my own distance from the land. I was a city kid, born of two city people, from several generations of city dwellers. I never really liked dirt. It was, well, so dirty. Unfamiliar, really. Full of bugs and worms. The world of my childhood was paved over, save some small grass patches and a garden or two. When I was a little girl, I meticulously avoided all sorts of soil, howling in horror if I muddied a dress. Until my mother planted some vegetables in a tiny square of dirt in our side yard—between two cement slabs—I thought that tomatoes grew in cellophane packages at the A&P. It never occurred to me that what we ate came from dirt. After I learned this fact, I refused to eat vegetables for about a year.

Like other city people in mid-twentieth-century America, we considered ourselves superior to country people. The country was a place one came *from* to make a success of life. Country people were poor and uneducated, with rough hands and dark half-circles under their fingernails. My stepgrandmother came from the country to the city. Most of her relatives stayed behind. "They are farmers," she explained. I was not sure that was a good thing. She seemed glad to have moved, to have a nicer house in a good neighborhood, and to be married to a businessman. But she once told me, "I miss the sweet smell of the dirt." I did not know what she was talking about.

Some Sundays, we drove out to the country just for a ride, the way people used to take Sunday drives in those days. Dirt did not smell sweet. It smelled of something else—cow poop. Not very appealing. And then there were my misadventures on Girl Scout hikes and campouts. I was a terrible klutz with nature. I constantly stumbled on rocks and slipped in mud, thus proving, to my own mind at least, that the earth was a threatening and inhospitable place. I found critters in my sleeping bag after a cold night on hard ground. I cried so much that, the next night, one of the troop leaders took me to a local motel until my mother came to rescue me from the hell of outdoors.

Because of all this, I was grateful for church, a safe haven from the untamed world of nature. God apparently preferred the indoors too. His sacred abode was the Methodist church in our neighborhood: four white walls, wooden pews, and colored glass windows. There, a benevolent deity sheltered his followers from every storm, and from the wicked wilderness as well. It never occurred to me that someone might seek God in the woods or on a mountain or at a beach, because God was so readily available in the building up the road. Church, unlike nature, was safe. When it came to it, I preferred singing hymns to digging in the dirt.

In 1969, in the wake of the chaos caused by race riots, my parents left the city for the country. This rural migration seemed a strange reversal of things, as we left everything familiar for a new house built in the woods. Who *left* the city? At first, moving to the country proved much of my childhood prejudice against dirt true—especially when a wall of mud slid down a neighboring hill where a house was under construction and wound up in our basement and swimming pool. Or when I was forced to share a gym locker with a girl who came to school having just helped feed her family's goat herd. Her clothes—and mine—smelled of goat.

But something else happened too. There were acres and acres of undeveloped land around our neighborhood. Day after day, season after season, my brother, sister, and I explored the forests and farms that made up our new world. There were ponds and streams, dense stands of old trees, small deserted graveyards, and ruins of abandoned houses. There was a huge reservoir surrounded by woodlands. Beyond the trees were farms, where we learned the pleasures of biking to the edge of a cornfield and playing hide-and-seek amid the summer stalks.

We quit going to church. It was just too far from our new house to return to the family congregation. Despite our former faithful attendance, we found we did not miss it. Although I had always believed God lived in that building, I unexpectedly discovered that God was also present in the woods as I followed streams through the forest. Sitting by the lake, skating on a frozen pond, riding my bike on dirt roads—it was as if I could hear God whispering to me. At the Methodist church, I learned how to follow the rules, how to be an obedient Christian girl. But the country—the place of dirt that I had previously feared—became a school of wonder. Those woods and farms were a sanctuary of the sacred, a place where the Bible actually spoke. There were sheep and goats in pastures, fields ripe to harvest, and vines and trees bearing fruit.

Freed from memorizing Bible verses in the church basement, I sank into the world charged with the Word of God. There I not only heard about God, but I met God while watching tadpoles in the spring and listening to the wind-rustled golden trees in the autumn. And I would sit on the ground, by the stream or under a leafy canopy, feeling the dirt's moist chill, where I sensed the life of soil. I learned to love being outside. I left my brother and sister behind, wandering solitary through the countryside, an adolescent girl accidentally embodying the spirit of Thoreau, finding heaven under my feet as much as over my head.

One day when I was twelve or so, I walked in the back door after such an adventure. My shoes were muddied, my pants dirty.

"Look at you! Take those clothes off right away and put them in the washer!" my mother cried. "I thought you hated dirt."

I slipped into the laundry room, talking to myself. "I thought I hated it too."

"Where Is God?" and the Dirt

At first hearing, it is very difficult for many contemporary people to imagine God having anything to do with dirt. We are the off-spring of an earlier revolution—the Industrial Revolution. A few hundred years ago, our ancestors decreed that the earth and all therein were "resources" to be used for profit based on technical advances in labor, production, and science. This revolution did many things—some good, some bad—but it fundamentally trans-formed how we understood the dirt. The soil became an object to be managed (in the case of productive farms) or removed (in the cases of mining and urban development). Over the decades, we moved to cities away from the land, severing both spiritual and physical connections humans had known through most of his-tory. People became estranged from the land; the dirt became an "it."[1]

Generations ago, though, no one would have wondered about God and dirt, for divinity and soil were easy companions. In a pre-industrial world, Creator and creation were part of the same theo-logical ecosystem: the ground was created and sustained by a gracious God who walked about in a garden and whose son, Jesus, spun agricultural tales for his hearers' spiritual benefit. For the bet-ter part of the last two centuries, however, most of us have forgot-ten the deep earthy perspective of sacred texts. And most of us have had to relearn the relationship between God and dirt. Except farm-ers. They remember.

A mile from my house is a seasonal farmers' market, the place where I buy most of our family's food during the summer. One

Wednesday, an unusual announcement stood at the entrance of the parking lot:

BOOK SIGNING TODAY!
Forrest Pritchard, author of *Gaining Ground*

I had seen the book in the window of a local gift shop a few weeks earlier and almost bought it then. At a table under a tent sat a fortyish man with a pile of new paperbacks at his elbow, pens at the ready. People were hurrying past, their reusable bags stuffed with produce.

"Slow day?" I asked.

"Yes." He sighed.

"I'm an author too," I replied. "Writing books is about as tough as farming, I figure. At least book signings are."

He laughed.

"What's your book about?" I asked.

Gaining Ground, he explained, was a memoir about becoming a farmer. Although he was raised in a seventh-generation farming family, his parents had pretty well given up farming the ancestral land. When he graduated from college, they tried to get him to earn a master's degree and take a city job, but he felt a different call. He returned to the farm. Over the decades, the land had become increasingly unproductive, making it difficult to earn a living from farming. The story recounted a journey in which he gave up using the conventional farming practices that had "broken" the land and instituted those that restored the pastures to an organic and sustainable state, where he now raises grass-fed livestock.

"I'm working on a book right now about food and faith," I told him. "Does religion play any role in your story?"

"Not really. Not church, if that's what you mean. I'm not a religious person," he offered. "I was raised an Episcopalian, but I don't practice anymore."

"So you'd consider yourself secular?"

"Well, no," he replied, a sly smile on his face. "You see there's no such thing as a secular farmer. The seasons are spiritual. The soil is, well, spiritual. Farmers are a spiritual lot."

Then he told me a story, one also recorded in *Gaining Ground,* of a cold day in February when he found himself kneeling on the ground:

> A small swath of earth was now revealed. The soil . . . was soft and dark. I slid my fingers into the dirt, cupping a handful of earth to my nose. The aroma of the broken ground was profoundly rich, at once mysterious and inviting. In the depths of winter—with the pastures grazed low, the sycamores stark and leafless, the creek banks rimmed with ice, and the sky a gray blanket spread from mountaintop to mountaintop—here the earth abided. The soft warmth spoke to me, saying, *I'm waiting now, but I will be ready. We are mutual participants, you and I, intertwined.*
>
> The language was as clear as if spoken aloud. It was no accident that I found myself on my knees, held there, transfixed. My ancestors knew this communication. It tapped into who they were, and who I was. We flowed together.[2]

"The earth speaks to me," he said as his cadence slowed. "The soil, spirit, and us, it is all of a piece. We can know that, or we can ignore it. But it is real."

He did not use the word "God," but he was talking about religion—although not institutional religion, of course. Rather, he was explaining what is perhaps the source of the most primal of all human impulses toward God—fertile land. This is seen in many different contexts, from tribal religions to the practices of ancient Druids, structured Egyptian prayers and priesthoods to rites of human sacrifice, Green Man to pagan priestesses, rain dances and celebrations of wheat and corn to Near Eastern creation myths, including one still well-known story in which God makes life from dirt. For millennia, land was the beginning of faith: gratitude for it, struggling with it, reflecting upon it, recognizing its power, fearing its loss, or seeking its increase. Without the long human relationship with the soil, there would be no great cycles of feasts and fasts, no appreciation of ritual foods, no practices of tithes and thanksgivings. Indeed, the God we know—as well as the God we hardly remember—is the Spirit of the Soil.

If we had had this same conversation twenty-five years ago, I am not sure I would have understood Pritchard's point. I would have thought him some sort of New Age-y spiritual type, certainly a pantheist. Pantheists believe that God is everything, and everything is God. Western people, especially those who grew up in Christian or Jewish families, do not generally embrace pantheism. There was, even in Pritchard's lyrical description, a subtle theological distinction between soil and farmer. There were recognizable actors in the scene: living soil and a grateful cultivator. A third participant was invisible, the spirit of the land that speaks, the spirit that allows the farmer to hear, the spirit that pulled him to the ground. "We flowed together," he said. The spirit is *with* and *in* the soil and the farmer, a binding power beyond and yet still a part, where two become one. Indeed, this is the mystical marriage of land and human, joined in holy union to bring forth fruit, entwined by God's love.

Theologians call this sort of intimate *with*-ness "pan*en*theism," a word that sounds like "pantheism" but is changed by the introduction of *en* in the middle. Panentheism is the idea that God is with or in all things. A nuance to be sure, but an important one. Panentheism recognizes the distinctions between things, at the same time that it affirms the indwelling force of spirit (typically called God) that draws all things into relationship with all other things. To put it simply, a panentheist says, "God is not a tree; a tree is not God. But God is with the tree; and the tree is with God" (prepositions matter). I do not know if Forrest Pritchard has ever heard the word "panentheism," but I do know that on a particular summer morning, he shared with me, a fellow writer at the farmers' market, an experience of it.

Although a story like Pritchard's would have been relatively common at a time long ago in human history, following the Industrial Revolution this kind of spiritual intimacy between land, creature, and Creator made less sense. Not only did that revolution move us away from the soil; it also turned the land into an object to be managed instead of a relationship to be experienced. When something becomes an object, it is much easier to use—or abuse—for one's own purposes. Western religion, often afraid to lose the Creator-creation distinction, quickly baptized theologies that distanced God from the dirt and emphasized human lordship over the land. The soil-y God was left to mystics, monks, women, and mostly the poor—people on the margins of the religious community whose orthodoxy has always been suspect and whose institutional power was negligible. And farmers, evidently.

With more people paying attention to the environment, the state of the soil has emerged as a widespread interest, especially among those involved in local food movements, issues of food and health, and the relationship between food and justice. For many contemporary people, these social and political concerns have directed them to the ground, since the health of the food depends on the vitality of the soil. New connections are being fashioned between farmers and consumers about the importance of the land to our lives. A good deal of this awareness arises from science, but part of it seems to be a spiritual longing to rediscover the grounded God of our agricultural ancestors.

Some contemporary thinkers, especially those shaped by ecological or feminist concerns, have wondered what this earthy reorientation means for faith. Theologian Sallie McFague sounds a note that harmonizes with Forrest Pritchard's experience when she writes: "God's love is the power that moves the galaxies and that breathes in our bodies. One way to imagine this relationship between God and the world is with the metaphor of the world as God's body." She continues:

> The world, the universe, is the "body of God": all matter, all flesh, all myriad beings, things, and processes that constitute physical reality are in and of God. God is not just spirit, but also body. Hence, God can be thought of in organic terms, as the vast interrelated network of beings that compose our universe. The "glory" of God, then, is not just heavenly, but earthly.[3]

This, she concludes, is the "radical intimacy" of God and the world. Pritchard and McFague, a farmer from Virginia and a scholar from British Columbia, are saying pretty much the same thing.

We're Dirt

Since human history began, people have wondered how the world came to be—and how we came to be on it. Our ancestors told stories about creation, the ground under our feet, and the animals, birds, and humans that make their home upon the earth. These stories cross all cultural boundaries, and they share similar characteristics and themes. One of the dominant motifs is the relationship between soil and our souls. Whether it is the Maori tale of shaping a woman from the scarlet soil, the Navajo story of man and woman journeying through the worlds to find a home on the land, or a dedicated humanist's case that life crawled out of the sea to the shore, through the centuries we human beings have tried to make spiritual sense of the obvious link between the ground and our very existence.

Jews, Christians, and Muslims share a creation story from the Bible, found in the early chapters of the book of Genesis. Like many such stories, it begins with sky and earth intertwined in darkness. God first brings forth light, then separates what is above from what is below, thus making oceans, land, and sky. Although some people insist that Genesis 1 is a literal scientific account, it is best understood as what Old Testament scholar Walter Brueggemann calls a "liturgical poem," a form for use in worship that invites a community "to confess and celebrate the world as God has intended it."[4] In the opening pages of the Bible, a cosmic vision of creation unfolds with the making of plants and forests, the stars and suns and moons beyond, all the fishes and birds and animals, and finally human beings. At each juncture, God proclaims blessing on what has been made, declaring it good, and with the creation of humankind the whole of the universe is pronounced "very good." At the end of the poem, God sends human beings out to till and keep the soil and to work on behalf of the earth, delighting in all its gifts.[5]

From its opening majesty, the narrative moves to Genesis 2, a quirky and even charming tale of the specific creation of men and women. The Bible's second creation story more closely resembles other ancient tribal myths than does Genesis 1 with its structured poetry. In Genesis 2, God is not at a mysterious distance. Rather, the story takes place in a garden, an ancient metaphor for the earth. Here God is an unhappy farmer, for the world looks rather like Oklahoma during the Dust Bowl. The earth, covered with red dust (Hebrew *adamah*), is not a generative and hospitable place, because there is "no one to till the ground." So God causes springs to come up from the earth itself, makes a clay, and forms a man (*adam*) from the ground. God breathes into him, and gives life to this "soil creature." God places Adam in the garden, to grow it and to care for the rivers and plants and animals, and eventually draws Eve (*havah,* meaning "to become," "to breathe," or "life") from Adam's body to be his partner. Thus, Adam and Eve, not a literal first couple, but rather Soil and Life (their "names" from the Hebrew words) marry, and their union produces the human race.

Of that creation, theologian Norman Wirzba writes:

> God fashions the first human being by taking the dust of the ground into his hands, holding it so close that it can share in the divine breath, and inspiring it with the freshness of life. It is only as the ground is suffused with God's intimate, breathing presence that human life— along with the life of trees and animals and birds—is possible at all. God draws near to the earth and then animates it *from within.*[6]

We are animated dirt. Soil and life joined. From living ground we were made; to living ground we will return.

Unlike other ancient Near Eastern creation stories, where humans are often gifted with exalted origins and elaborate tasks to please the gods, Adam and Eve are made from humus, placed in

God's garden, and directed to care for the soil from which they came. In Genesis, God instructs Adam and Eve to "till and keep" (2:15), that is, "serve and preserve," the soil. Thus, humankind's divine vocation is to be earth's custodians, the overseers of the soil. The early biblical heroes are all shepherds, farmers, and tribal judges, unlike the kings or warriors who figured prominently in the religions of Israel's neighbors, Sumeria and Mesopotamia.[7]

The origins of what would become widespread agricultural practices and the world's great religions developed simultaneously about seven thousand years ago. As ancient humans domesticated animals, terraced fields, and built water systems, they ruminated on the ground and God, drawing connections between creation and cultivation, between soil and the Spirit. Their stories formed the basis of many religious texts, including the Hebrew Bible, a collection of wisdom based in an agrarian way of life and an agricultural spirituality. "Beginning with the first chapter of Genesis," explains Old Testament scholar Ellen Davis, "there is no extensive exploration of the relationship between God and humanity that does not factor the land and its fertility into that relationship."[8] The whole story of the Hebrew Bible is that of land, its abundance, and its fruitfulness, and how humans are disconnected from the land by sin or connected to it through acts of faith and justice.

Land may be understood in scientific terms, that is, as the source, the material basis, of the food supply (no dirt, no food, no us); or it may be viewed through the eyes of spiritual awareness, as part of a divine ecosystem. From a theological perspective, when we care for the earth, we are practicing obedience and holiness; disregarding the ground is sinful and evil. When one reads ancient texts, like the Hebrew scriptures, with this understanding in mind, it is difficult to separate out passages about the literal earth from the spiritual allegories and metaphors about the earth, much less separate human beings from humus or humus from the hands of a Creator. Ground and God and us are nearly of a piece, which seems a purposeful theological construction on the part of ancient poets, prophets, and philosophers.

Losing Eden?

Even as more and more people are beginning to see God in the ground and finding a revitalized spirituality there, we are also discovering how fragile and endangered the earth is. The first time I ever heard someone explain that the soil was in distress was in college. A curmudgeonly professor was lecturing in European history class. The subject was Russia and Communist expansion, and the day's topic was the Ukraine, the breadbasket of Europe. I was duly taking notes when he went off on a tangent about the soil, how important it was, why the Ukraine was so significant, and how similar it was to North America's Great Plains. The students, mostly from suburban Los Angeles, looked bored.

Then his tone became urgent. "You know those farmlands and eucalyptus groves as you come over the pass in Thousand Oaks, the miles of fields and pastures in Simi Valley?"

A few students paused, now paying attention, registering mental recognition of the scene.

"In another decade or two," he continued, "that will be houses and condominiums and shopping centers and schools. All the best land will be covered by subdivisions. The eucalyptus will be gone, and the monarch butterflies will lose their migration route. And the farmers and growers will have to go somewhere else, mostly uphill or farther out to the desert to more marginal land. Erosion from storms will be worse. Once the soil is gone, it is gone. You can't get it back."

Although I had observed wounded landscapes, it did not occur to me that dirt was threatened on a larger scale. Soil was like air or water, a boundless gift of creation, always present. As a Christian, I was grateful for the land, and I understood that it had been given to us to rule over like kings (our pastor told us this was in the book of Genesis). No matter where my family moved or how far I traveled, the ground was a fact of existence. It was where we planted ourselves, and although we often ignored the soil beneath our feet, there were always people to tend it. Over the years, it has been a dirt patch in a Baltimore backyard; acres of land in the Maryland woods; the mealy, worm-filled country vegetable garden of our next-door neighbors; Arizona's desert sands, where only cactus or palo verde trees can grow; the rich soils of coastal California covering great rifts below; the hard clay of the Mississippi, with its last stand of old forest in Memphis; and the vast suburbs of northern Virginia comprising Colonial glebes and old plantations. The soil varied, the ground friendly or occasionally infuriating, but I was not aware that it was in crisis, for soil seemed eternal.

Agronomist Wes Jackson calls the idea that soil is limitless and can be used in any way human beings please "the devastating assumption of the modern world." Jackson insists that "soil is as much a nonrenewable resource as oil" and explains that it took hundreds of thousands—if not millions—of years of geologic and climatic events (mountain uplift, earthquakes, and an Ice Age) to produce the rich soils of Europe and North America. "Once destroyed," Jackson warns, rather like my professor in the late 1970s, "for all practical purposes in human time, it is destroyed forever."[9] The earth's math is simple: no soil, no food, no us.

Yet soil is being lost at an alarming rate all over the planet. During the last century and a half, the planet has lost half its topsoil. According to a Cornell University study, American soil is disappearing ten times faster than the rate at which it can be replenished; China and India are experiencing erosion rates thirty to forty times faster. In the last forty years alone, about one-third of the world's formerly productive soil has become unusable, and the planet continues to lose approximately twenty-five million acres a year to erosion.[10] This is an environmental crisis to be sure, but it is a moral and ethical one as well.

Something odd is happening, however, as this disaster is unfolding. At the same time that the earth is losing its soil, more people than ever are making their way back to the ground. It is as if we are returning to the roots of the crisis, discovering the soil when it needs us most. In the early 2000s, I spent most of my time researching vibrant churches. In the course of that work, I kept running across congregations with gardens—rural churches growing crops for local food banks or homeless shelters or just to raise money to defray the pastor's salary, suburban churches with lush plots where parishioners swapped seedlings along with neighborhood gossip, urban churches that turned tiny front yards into great community gardens. One Episcopal study found that that are 250 churches or other groups in their denomination alone now operating farms on their land.[11] Across a denominational spectrum, congregations are raising food for charity, to supplement church budgets, to do justice, or just for the fun of it—often turning food deserts into lively centers of local food movements.[12]

The Garden Church of San Pedro, California, is pushing beyond growing food. The new congregation has a vision of church as a "living sanctuary" based in the earth itself. As its mission statement says: "The Garden Church is reimagining church as an interconnected organism, worshipping, loving and serving together as we transform a plot of land into a vibrant urban garden" where people encounter "the Divine in community, scripture, nature, and the life of useful service." The congregation has purchased an abused piece of land in a poor neighborhood and is working to renew the soil and plant a garden. The garden will also be the church—there are no plans for a conventional building. Instead, vegetable beds will surround an outdoor Communion table; a greenhouse will serve as worship space during the rainy season. Church leaders are called "cultivators," and participants meet in both gardening and theology groups, learning soil and scripture as a pair. The Reverend Anna Woofenden says that the church will be "a community where the church is in the garden, and the garden is the work of the church."[13]

Congregational gardens, however, are just a small part of a changing attitude toward food and the land. In my suburban neighborhood, only ten miles from downtown Washington, D.C., there are gardens in front yards and behind fences, and neighbors trade stories about growing conditions as well as vegetables from a good harvest. Folks talk of getting chickens and whether that would increase the local fox problem. A widely anticipated event is the yearly seedling sale at the Unitarian church, because everyone knows that its soil has been well cared for and grows particularly hardy local plants.

The National Garden Association reports that one in three households are now growing food, a rise of 17 percent from 2008 to 2013. The largest increase has been in urban gardening (up 29 percent) and among young adults, with more than thirteen million people under thirty taking to the soil. The passion for gardening spreads across all education and income levels, and it includes people who live in rural, suburban, and urban areas.[14]

And it is not just hobbyists. Cities are moving ahead in the work of renewing land and neighborhoods through local farming. Chicago has initiated a major urban farming program, complete with agricultural training, aimed at reclaiming devastated city neighborhoods and addressing the problem of food deserts. Citizens around Waterloo, Ontario, have created a regional food charter to develop a local food system, strengthen community development, provide access to healthy food, address issues of climate change, and promote integrated farming and food policies.[15] Detroit is turning blighted and abandoned blocks into urban farms, providing both healthy local food and jobs.[16]

Launching a garden or an urban farm is not easy. About five years ago, not knowing that we were at the edge of a trend, my family tried to establish a backyard garden. Novice that I was, I thought this was a matter of digging some holes, planting seeds, and watering the plot once in a while. The first year, everything died. We discovered we have bad soil, front and back. Full of roots, our ground is hard and lifeless. Years ago, it was at the end of a lane where teenagers used to park and drink. We frequently dig up broken beer bottles and odd bits of glass and trash. So the second year we worked the soil, trying to coax it back to life. The garden did better, establishing itself well, until a summer drought and a tomato fungus did it in. The third and fourth years, I turned to growing herbs in containers and met with more success. Last year, we built raised beds, filling them with organic soil and all sorts of naturally composted additions. The garden finally produced abundant tomatoes, zucchini, cucumbers, and beans. Now I love to sit by the beds, poking around in the moist dirt looking for worms. I have learned to care for it, this small patch of land that we are working to restore. The real work of gardening is in the dirt.

Both my history professor and Wes Jackson correctly claim that the soil is not limitless. Like oil, soil comes from a long process that includes the earth's carbon cycle. Most soils contain carbon, an essential element of life. Built into the planet is a cycle of creation, energy, and transformation of carbon that took many millions of years to form the ground as we know it.[17] But the carbon cycle that makes the dirt is now dangerously out of balance. There is now too much carbon in the air and not enough in the soil, wreaking havoc on once regular weather systems. The shift in rain is causing soil to either wash away or dry up, making it unable to sustain the trees and plants that naturally balance the carbon dioxide between earth and air. And this is what the history professor and Wes Jackson referred to when speaking of limited soil: the long process that created the ground beneath us. We don't have millions of years to get it back.

Lucky for us there is also a shorter cycle of soil renewal: photosynthesis. This is the cycle by which our plants grow and through which sunlight produces plant sugars, which in turn feed colonies of microorganisms in the plant's roots; those billions of bacteria, fungi, and protozoa burrow about, forage, eat, and die, creating humus, the mealy layer of topsoil one sees in the best gardens. Through surprisingly simple practices, such as composting, land management, organic and natural farming methods, introducing earthworms, and sowing forage grasses for livestock, we can hasten the production of soil in this short-term cycle. By increasing carbon compounds in the ground, the soil is made richer, able to absorb and hold more moisture, and is less apt to erode. Some scientists believe that we can certainly slow, and in some cases perhaps reverse, soil erosion in these ways. If we attend to this more immediate carbon cycle, we cannot get back what we have lost, but we can create more usable, healthy, and protective topsoil. In effect, we can gain ground. And in gaining ground, we might also be able to mitigate some effects of global warming.[18]

It can be overwhelming to think of the crisis of the land, but we can do something about this. By tending the soil, we imitate the creative process in Genesis. We can "breathe" new life into the ground. This reconnects us with both soil and life, opening us up to new ways of experiencing God with us in the world.

Soil itself is alive. Although plagued with poor health, disregarded through bad practices, and threatened even with death, might the possibility of resurrection be right under our feet? As more Americans work community and home gardens, we are learning that the ground itself is a microuniverse upon which all carbon-based life forms—like us—depend. With the increase in the number of people learning to grow their own food, surely there is a corresponding shift in our understanding of soil and the life of the earth. In a surprising way, we can all create Eden, a world teeming with life.

As Fred Bahnson, founder of a community garden in North Carolina, says of the land he and his friends restored: "The soil here was deeper than in the rest of the garden, the color and consistency of chocolate sponge cake. . . . There is an entire ecosystem in a handful of soil: bacteria, fungi, protozoa, nematodes, earthworms. Through their breeding and dying such creatures vivify the world." Here is one of the most profound of all religious themes: death and resurrection. Bahnson, trained as a Methodist minister, spent a year traveling to faith-based farms around the United States, from abbeys to communes to a Jewish retreat center. His pilgrimage taught him about farming and soil, but even more about God and the garden. "Soil is a portal to another world," he insists, the world as God intends it to be.[19]

Although farmers have always known that our life and destiny are tied to the health of the soil, much of that wisdom had been lost as technology-driven, single-crop, large-scale farming replaced more intimate connections with the land. Indeed, in recent centuries, farming emerged as a mechanical process of food production rather than a mutual relationship with the earth. Attending to soil is the heart of an emerging awareness referred to as "neo-agrarianism," or soil farming. Indeed, the U.S. Department of Agriculture has created extensive education and programming on soils, tracking national soil health and teaching dynamic soil management to new generations of farmers attuned to "the movement of farming nature's way."[20]

For millennia, the ancients looked to the heavens, to the light of millions of stars above, to find God. Although the stars still move us to wonder, contemporary people are learning that the soil beneath our feet is as mysterious, complex, and awe-inspiring as gazing into the night sky. "I was stunned by what I learned about life in the soil," says journalist Kristin Ohlson, "that when we stand on the surface of the earth, we're atop a vast underground kingdom of microorganisms without which life as we know it wouldn't exist. Trillions of microorganisms, even in my own smallish backyard, like a great dark sea swarming with tiny creatures."[21]

Bahnson calls the soil a sacrament. Even the most secular writers understand that the ground calls forth an ethical, moral, and spiritual response. We are powerfully connected to the ground, and the soil is intimately related to how we understand and celebrate God. The late Irish Catholic priest and philosopher John O'Donohue called the land "the firstborn of creation" and the "condition of the possibility of everything." The earth itself, he insisted, holds the memory of the beginning of all things, the memory of God.[22] When Sallie McFague offers the metaphor of "body" to describe the relationship between God and the world, she is reminding us of both scientific truth and a sacred mystery. "What if," she asks, "we saw the earth as part of the body of God, not as separate from God (who dwells elsewhere), but as the visible reality of the invisible God?"[23]

What if, indeed? I suspect that if we did, we would be both more responsible toward the soil and more aware of God-with-us.

An atheist friend of mine is fond of saying, "I just don't believe that God is an old man sitting on the throne in heaven." Me neither. Nor do the millions of people who still trust in God, yet reject this particular conception of God.[24] McFague calls it the "transcendent sky-God tradition."[25] Instead of seeing God as distinct and distant from the world, we are acquiring a new awareness that the universe itself is God's body, a complex and diverse interdependent organism, animated by God's breath, the spirit of creation. We are with God and God is with us because—and some people may find this shocking—we are in God and God is in us. Maybe the far-off heavenly Father is finally retiring, replaced by a far more down-to-earth presence, a presence named in Hebrew and Christian scriptures as both love and spirit. I once heard poet Wendell Berry remark, "The idea of heaven doesn't take religion very far," because the distance makes for too great an abstraction. "Love," as the very being of God, he continued, "has to wear a face." And that "face" is "our neighborhood, our neighbors and other creatures, the earth and its inhabitants."[26]

Despite this powerful vision of earth and the beauty of the ground, religion has not often been a friend of the soil.

Soil, Sin, and Salvation

For liturgical Christians, Easter Vigil is the most important service of the year. Held in the last hours before Easter morning, it begins in the dark as the community of faith waits for the rebirth, the empty tomb that witnesses to the resurrected life of Jesus. During the service, new Christians—both infants and adults—are baptized and welcomed into the church by candlelight.

Baptism is always beautiful, but most especially at Easter Vigil. The priest pours water from a pitcher into a font amid prayers of blessing. Infants are presented in christening gowns, children strain to reach the baptismal font, and adults have their foreheads splashed with holy water. Washed in the water of the Spirit, made clean forever. Welcomed into God's household. In traditional churches, baptism is an affair rather different from some I experienced as a teenager. Then, I was an evangelical Christian, and our baptisms were not so pristine. A group of us would go outside, ushering a new convert to a nearby stream or pond. The water could be murky, seemingly impure rather than sanctified, but it did not matter. The pastor or youth leader would dunk the newcomer anyway, a drenching testimony of sin washed away and new birth in Jesus. Secretly, I was grateful that my parents had baptized me as a baby in the Methodist Church, for I wondered how one could be washed of sin when the water itself was not safe to drink.

On this particular Easter Eve, in the darkened church, I trusted the water. And I did not expect anything surprising regarding this ancient act. The priest intoned the traditional words, "Sanctify this water, we pray you, by the power of your Holy Spirit, that those who here are cleansed from sin. . . ." I had heard the prayer a thousand times, but this night it sounded odd. For the first time I realized that at the center of the liturgy was a confusing, confounding spiritual metaphor: that salvation meant washing away dirt.

It is one of the basic concepts of Christianity: baptism removes our sins. My surprise? I had spent the previous forty days of Lent studying soil, rediscovering what it means to be grounded in the world, and reading creation stories and articles about the topsoil crisis. And I had readied the garden, worked the soil in my backyard, coaxing dirt to life. Dirt was not dirty—it was beautiful. God made it; I was tending it. Caring for soil is hard work. The last thing I wanted to imagine was it being washed away. I was fighting for the dirt. I wanted more dirt, better dirt, richer dirt. I was adding stuff to it to make it darker, mealier. I wanted dirtier dirt. Yet the liturgy was describing a kind of spiritual soil erosion. The metaphors of church struck with an angular force against the metaphors of the garden.

Over the centuries, sin—especially regarding human sexuality—has been equated with dirt. When a woman is sexually active, she is considered soiled. When we speak of something vile, we refer to it as filth. We speak of pornography as smut. We refer to ethical choices as muddied, love of creation or earthly things as worldly. Indeed, the terrain of sin is described by a vocabulary of soil. And many religious traditions get rid of it by ritual cleansing, baptisms, and other rites of washing it away.

In many dictionaries, the definition of "soil" as a noun is typically scientific: "soil: the portion of the earth's surface consisting of disintegrated rocks and humus; a particular kind of earth; the ground as producing vegetation or cultivated for crops." But the second definition, as a verb, turns sinister: "to soil: to make unclean, dirty or filthy; to smirch, smudge, or stain; to sully or tarnish, as with disgrace; defile morally." Its synonyms are "blacken," "taint," "debase," "pollute." The term "dirt" is perhaps even worse than "soil." "Dirt" comes from Middle English, but goes back originally to a Norse word, *drit,* meaning "mud, dung, or excrement"; the related *dritty* means "smutty or morally unclean." With this etymology in mind, it is easy to understand the theological leap from dirt and soil to sin and evil.

All this may seem like a tempest in a linguistic teapot except for the fact that human beings have treated the land terribly. For thousands of years, where people have gone, environmental destruction has followed. One need only look to the formerly fertile lands of the Middle East, the great swaths of African desert, or the declining prairies of North America to see that we have not cared for the soils that fed us. In 1938, the U.S. Soil Conservation Service sent its chief researcher, Dr. W. C. Lowdermilk, to study the history of soil erosion around the world. Concentrating on the beginnings of human agriculture about seven thousand years ago in Mesopotamia and Egypt, Lowdermilk reported on great cities and civilizations laid waste by soil erosion, loss of topsoil, poor grazing and plowing practices, destruction of forests, and the silting of streams and rivers. Describing his team's disappointment at crossing the Jordan River, Lowdermilk said that they had hoped for a "land of milk and honey," but found instead "denuded highlands" and "abandoned village sites":

> We found the soils of red earth washed off the slopes to bedrock over more than half the upland area. These soils had lodged in the valleys where they are still being cultivated and are still being eroded by great gullies that cut through the alluvium with every heavy rain. Evidence of rocks washed off the hills were found in piles of stone where tillers of soil had heaped them together to make cultivation about them easier. From the air we read with startling vividness the graphic story as written on the land. Soils had been washed off to bedrock in the vicinity of Hebron and only dregs of the land were left behind in narrow valley floors, still cultivated to meager crops.[27]

Europeans continued many of the same poor practices, exporting them around the world through colonization—colonization that was often driven by the attempt to find new farmland to replace what had been ruined or destroyed back home. Lowdermilk referred to the history of farming as "suicidal agriculture" and in a government report wondered, "If Moses had foreseen what suicidal agriculture would do to the land of the holy earth, [he] might have been inspired to deliver another Commandment . . . 'Thou shalt inherit the Holy Earth as a faithful steward, conserving its resources and productivity from generation to generation.'"

We humans have not learned well, however, for more recent examples abound—like the Dust Bowl. Most Americans know the history of a desolate landscape destroyed by drought and deep plowing, resulting in massive dust storms across a once fertile prairie. But few understand that Dust Bowl conditions are returning after recent years of severe drought. "It is just as dry now as it was then, maybe even drier," 101-year-old Oklahoma farmer Millard Fowler says. "There are going to be a lot of people out here going broke."[28]

Other episodes of soil loss are not as well known, such as one in Georgia. Once Georgia's hills were not red. They were covered with rich topsoil and millions of acres of farmland. Because of poor farming practices, however, by the early twentieth century the state's Piedmont area had lost seven inches or more of fertile soil. In some cases, the entire top layer of earth was washed away in rains and floods. The hills were stripped bare, previously unknown gullies and valleys opened up, and streams and rivers filled with silt. It was an agricultural disaster, as the state lost millions of acres of farmland.

Of course, for many centuries, farmers knew nothing of soil science or land management, simply choosing to use the ground as they would, seeing the soil as something that needed to be broken, tamed, or moved in order to make the land work. I cannot help but wonder if descriptions of sin in terms borrowed from language about the land has aided and abetted its misuse. Rather than seeing it as "holy earth," we have seen dirt and soil as theological problems that must be overcome, to be regulated by religious rules or washed away in water and blood, making our souls as white as snow. The biblical language foreclosing a notion like "holy earth" was the vocabulary of ritual purity. Where do we think the old aphorism "Cleanliness is next to godliness" comes from? Holy things are clean, while what is unholy is unclean.

Of course, most religions are not speaking of actual dirt as the problem of human moral failing; rather, clean and unclean are states of being nearer or farther from God. But if "unclean" and "being soiled" become the dominant metaphors for sin, it is just a small step to the demonization of real dirt. And removing, controlling, or subduing the earth is necessary to both spiritual salvation and human survival. If being dirty means we are an unclean people on an unclean land, dirt stands in the way of both holiness and dinner. Theologically, it can be difficult to experience soil as anything but a problem.

Within monotheistic religion, however, there is alternative reading of soil. Biblical creation stories abound with praise for the soil: God creates the ground and calls it good. Then the land brings forth life, and God calls it good. Humankind is made from the dust, and God sees that as very good. But that is not all. The soil is the first victim of human evil; as a result of Adam and Eve's disobedience and Abel's murder, the land is wounded, crying, and bloodied. Noah, considered righteous by God, was praised as a cultivator of the ground, "a man of the soil," a new Adam. Moses walked on holy ground and received the law on a mountain. For the people of Israel, land is a blessing and bounty as a result of their faithfulness, and fruitful soil is the gift of God to an obedient people. King David, the greatest biblical king, was first a shepherd, and the poems attributed to him are full of the lyrical praise of nature, as the earth itself is the stage on which God's glory is played out. Heaven is not a place among the stars; rather, it is a land of milk and honey, where "the mountains shall drip sweet wine" and God's people "shall make gardens and eat their fruit" (Amos 9:13–14). In Islamic tradition the Prophet Muhammad prostrated himself on the ground, and so many carry a *turbah,* a small earthen tablet, on which to place their foreheads when they pray.

Soil is not the problem. Rather, the infertility of the soil is the problem. The sin is not that human beings are unclean. The sin is that we have failed the soil; we have not attended to it, or we have abused it. We humans willfully disregarded our vocation to protect and keep the earth, choosing instead to do violence upon it. Thus, soil may be either blessed or cursed by our activity. Soil is good but may become bad, something sacred and fertile ruined into what is profaned and hardened. Our problem is that we hardly understand our own involvement in the degradation of the ground. And we have become jaded and unaware of the spiritual power of dirt.

Jesus talks about this in one of his stories. A farmer sowed his seeds, some of which fell on bad soil, with rocks or little water or thorns, and died. But "other seed fell into good soil and brought forth grain, growing up and increasing and yielding thirty and sixty and a hundredfold" (Mark 4:8). Jesus explains that the seed is God's love and the soil is us. The moral of the story? We are not soil-y enough! Spiritually, we would be better off more soiled rather than less. Being soiled is actually the point. A friend of mine who is a pastor and gardener insists, "God loves dirt more than plants, soil more than what it yields. God is a dirt farmer, not a vegetable gardener."[29] Soil is not sin. Soil is sacred, holy, and good. When we care for it, we are doing God's work. Soil is life. And it is time for us to reclaim the dirt.

Holy Dirt

On a cool and unusually cloudy day in New Mexico, I drove out of Albuquerque some seventy miles north to the tiny town of Chimayo, known primarily for two things: chilies and a church. Although this may seem an odd combination, it really is not. The chilies and the church both depend on the area's unusually fertile soil, a gift of the sands and springs of the Sangre de Cristo Mountains and the Santa Cruz River. The ancient Tewa tribe, for whom Chimayo was the location of creation, found the rich red clay of the area the ideal location for growing chili peppers, the best in the entire region.

But the church? In a small building attached to the side of a Catholic chapel, there is a pit of red sand, a well of "sacred dirt" that Native Americans believe continuously refreshes itself, like a spring. Although no longer visible, originally there was a spring next to the sand well. Those seeking healing would mix soil with water to make a red clay, which was then applied as a cure. Over the centuries, many people have reported being healed here, so many that it is called the "Lourdes of North America." Its popularity has continued to soar as a pilgrimage site. About three hundred thousand people come to Chimayo to kneel and pray at the dirt each year. During Holy Week, thousands of penitents come, as at Catholic shrines in Mexico or the Philippines, to flagellate themselves or otherwise imitate the suffering Christ in a quest for spiritual or physical healing.

I visited on a Tuesday in the autumn, not the busiest day or season in Chimayo. There was a small group gathered for Mass in the church, but I skipped the prayers and went directly to the side chapel. I ducked as I walked through the low door of the old building, which was full of discarded crutches, used hospital identification bracelets, tokens of thanks and supplication, and the photos of the healed or those longing to be healed. *Santos,* the statues of many saints, lined the hall to the even smaller second door, the entrance to the *potico*—the room with the sand well. Many days, a long line of hopeful visitors stretches out the door. But I was alone, accompanied only by the words of the priest intoning the ancient Mass, barely audible through the church wall.

As a Protestant, I was not entirely sure what to do. But I knelt down reverently next to the hole, as seemed appropriate. I scooped up a small bit of sand in my fingers and unthinkingly rubbed the dirt on my forehead, as if marking myself with holy water. Tiny grains fell into my eyes, making me blink. Then, like other pilgrims, I used the shovel to put a bit of sand in a plastic bag to take home. As I sealed my bag, I thought of Jesus healing a man born blind:

> When he had said this, he spat on the ground and made mud with the saliva and spread the mud on the man's eyes, saying to him, "Go, wash in the pool of Siloam" (which means Sent). Then he went and washed and came back able to see. (John 9:6–7)

This was biblical stuff, I thought. The pain in my arthritic shoulder, however, did not subside.

I remembered another such place that I visited about twenty years ago, one not nearly as old as Chimayo. In the woods of central Minnesota, there is a small building called the House of Prayer. There, in the center of the round chapel is a hole in the floor, a patch of bare earth, purposefully constructed to connect retreat goers with a grounded spirituality. The priest at the center told me that Hopi Indians called such earth wells *sipaqu,* the point of emergence, and built their kivas, their sacred rooms, around such holes.

For many of North America's native peoples, the round well of sand symbolically represented the blood of Mother Earth, the beginning of life, the ground at its most fertile. The miracle of creation, of female blood at birth, was often ascribed healing power. At Chimayo, the primal stories of Mother Earth were overlaid with the stories of Jesus and his blood given for the life of the world. This was not the blood of a sacrificial victim, rather it was the blood of procreation. The tiny pit of miraculous sand was not the work of some spiritual charlatan, a Catholic Elmer Gantry. Rather, this spot was one of ancient birthing, of healing, of the red blood of the earth.

I walked away from the Chimayo shrine puzzled and more than a bit theologically confounded. I wandered into a gallery across the street where Señor Medina sells paintings and chili peppers.

"Hola!" he said as I entered. "Come here."

He pointed to a large table of ground dried chilies, dozens of varieties, in plastic bags for sale on his porch.

"Are you feeling pain?" he asked.

I am in my mid-fifties. I rubbed my aching shoulder. And, after all, I am visiting a Catholic healing shrine!

"I can help with that."

"What?" I asked.

"Here," he directed. "Put this pistachio in your mouth, but don't eat it."

I was skeptical, but I followed his instruction. Then he handed me a tiny chaser—about a quarter of a teaspoon—of ground chili pepper from his farm.

"Chew this and the nut together," he directed.

I did and—whew!—it was hot. And absolutely amazing. The best chili pepper I have ever eaten. I laughed, with tiny tears running down my cheeks. The active ingredient in chili peppers, also known as capsaicin, has curative properties for pain and inflammation. Señor Medina was not inviting me to a mystical experience. He was offering to relieve my pain with chili peppers, the major crop of Chimayo's farms, grown in the same soil as that in the round hole in the *potico*. With thanks, I bought a bag of #1 ground chilies from him and tucked it into my purse with the bag of sacred sand from the church.

The earth heals. I carried proof of such miracles in the two zip-top plastic sandwich bags in my purse. As I drove away, I felt the warm afterglow of Chimayo, but not from some mystical experience. Mostly it was from the spice I still tasted in my mouth.

Earth Is for Real

Walking through a bookstore, the end cap of religion books drew my eye. The movie *Heaven Is for Real* had just been released. The film, based on the book by the same name, is about a boy's near-death experience. As part of its promotion, the store featured a dozen books about miracles, near-death experiences, and going to heaven. Most of them claimed to offer evidence—either scientific or spiritual—for the afterlife, the paradise "up" or "out there" where the dead dwell with God.

I stared at the books. We are confused about "heaven," talking about it as both a place and a state. Heaven, as a state in the afterlife—well, who really knows about that? What happens after we die has always seemed to me a great mystery, something that is only hinted at and that must be approached with profound humility.

But "heaven" as a place is not much of a mystery. Traditionally it is the divine real estate at the top level of the old three-tiered universe, but that structure is giving way to a different sacred arrangement. We are here, on this planet, walking around on the same ground, depending on the soil for life. And God is with us. Earth is not an illusion, a tragic dream, or a spiritual metaphor. Earth is definitely for real. Finding God in the dirt allows us to experience faith in new ways. What farmers have known for centuries, many are just now beginning to understand, whether through gardening or experiencing the holiness in dirt.

*Early one morning, I walked around my garden barefoot. Reach-*ing down, I scooped up a handful of soil and examined it closely, appreciating the loam. The ground was damp with morning dew under my toes. The tomato plants stood tall, the zucchini spread out everywhere and contended with the cucumbers for taking up the most space. There were bees and hummingbirds and tiny gold-finches flying among the fruit and flowers. I pressed the soil against my cheek and recalled some words from poet Mary Oliver:

> *The god of dirt*
> *came up to me many times and said*
> *so many wise and delectable things, I lay*
> *on the grass listening*
> *to his dog voice,*
> *crow voice,*
> *frog voice; now,*
> *he said, and now,*
> *and never once mentioned forever.*[30]

I glanced again at the clod in my hand. Had I ever believed that God was in a far-off place called heaven? For that matter, was I ever spiritually satisfied worshipping God inside a building with four walls and no connection to the world outside? Over the decades, faith has taken me increasingly toward the soil, not away from it. To this garden, to the earth. And God is here. God the Earth-maker, God the Gardener. God the Ground of Being.

"We are not tourists here," writes philosopher Mary Midgly. "We are at home in this world, because we were made for it."[31]

Water

Water is the blood of the earth, and flows through its
muscles and veins. . . . It is accumulated in heaven and
earth, and stored up in various things of the world. It
comes forth in metal and stone, and is concentrated
in living creatures. Therefore it is said that water is
something spiritual.

—*Chuang-tzu*

Sometime before 1658, John Morris, my first immigrant ancestor, sailed up the Chesapeake Bay and then into one of its
major tributaries, the Potomac River, to make a new home in
Maryland. Like many other English settlers of his time, he was
probably convinced to make the trip by a popular account by Captain John Smith that described this lush world, with its unique inter-
section of land and water, as a place where oysters "lay as thick as
stones" and its rivers contained more sturgeon "than could be de-
voured by dog or man," with "grampus, porpoise, seals, stingrays,
brits, mullets, white salmon [rockfish], trouts, soles, [and] perch of

three sorts." Smith proclaimed to eager English readers: "Within is a country that may have the prerogative over the most pleasant places known, for large and pleasant navigable rivers, heaven and earth never agreed better to frame a place for man's habitation."[1] To John Morris, Maryland surely sounded like paradise.

Three hundred years later, I was born about fifty miles from where he landed, to a family who stayed close to where their ancestors arrived many generations ago. Unlike most of my relatives, however, I moved. A lot. I have lived in many places, ten different states, including the far western states of Arizona and California. In 2000, my husband and I moved to a house just south of the Colonial town of Alexandria, Virginia, about a mile from the Potomac River, across the river from where my ancestors first settled. After years of wandering, I returned home.

But I never paid much attention to the river. It seemed mostly a barrier to Washington, a trial to cross during rush hour on one of too few bridges, and a sludgy, flooding mess during heavy rainstorms. The Potomac was something I drove by or flew over on my way to work. The river was nothing like what had once been described by Captain Smith—hardly a paradisial waterway to a land of pleasant habitation.

One day, after I had returned from a vacation, I complained to a friend: "I have writer's block. I have nothing pretty to look at, no inspiring vista to gaze on when writing."

She said, "You don't live far from the river, do you?"

"That's not interesting," I replied. "The Potomac is so polluted. Ugly, really."

For a moment, I bit my tongue and quietly reconsidered the remark. There had been many evenings when I had flown home over the river and witnessed surprising beauty from the sky. The waters were often hued orange and red and purple, mirroring dramatic sunsets, and the river's multitude of creeks and streams reached into the land like a watery web. Tides and marshes formed a fluid vista below, almost as a reminder to the powerful and political flying overhead that the river will remain long after they are forgotten.

"You should write there some mornings," my friend interrupted. "Take a journal and work at a bench along the river. It might change your perspective."

I took her advice.

September 18, 2013, 10 A.M.

This morning, I'm sitting at the park where a creek empties into the Potomac and marks the south boundary of Alexandria. The main view is that of the Woodrow Wilson Bridge, spanning the river and carrying a ceaseless flow of traffic to and from Maryland and Virginia. I've never sat here before. I always drive past in my car or fly over it to National Airport.

How different it looks from here. Less urban. Yes, there are cars and planes and multistory structures. But there are also trees and rocks and rippling waters. Blue sky. And birds. Lots of birds: geese, ducks, heron, and osprey. Their calls and quacks compete with the sound of automobiles and jet engines. Creation, as crippled as she is, still has power here at river's edge. Things look different from the ground.

Day after day, page after page, the Potomac quietly captured my heart. I have learned to pay attention to the river.

Eventually, I moved downstream, exploring the riverbank on foot. Many mornings, I walk about two miles on a path along the river not far from my house. It is not John Smith's river anymore— the trees are smaller, the water dirtier, the fish far fewer. But there is still something about this river, one of the major sources of the Chesapeake Bay. You feel its power, and you feel it fighting for its life. Its currents carry the memory of place, of the native peoples, of the many stories that unfolded on its shores. There are turtles and frogs. A few beaver have returned, as have the eagles. There are cattails, wild irises, and honeysuckle. Trash floats by too, especially plastic bags and water bottles, but there are human beings who are wildly protective of this river and who pick up after their more careless kin.

Walking along the Potomac has taught me many things. I learned that the place where water touches land is called the riparian zone and is one of the most significant ecosystems on the planet. From the Latin word *ripa,* meaning "riverbank," the riparian zone acts as a natural filter, cleaning water as it moves into the larger watershed, and protects surrounding soil from erosion by slowing the course of the river. In the process, the riparian zone actually creates new soil and provides vibrant wildlife habitats. The river's edge may be a thin sliver of land, a large marsh, a mangrove wood, or a cottonwood forest. No matter the particular form or location of the riparian zone, however, the place where water and land touch is necessary for life on earth. What happens on the banks of the creeks, streams, and rivers is vital to the health of the entire watershed. And the watersheds, in turn, are vital to the health of the whole planet. Both the river itself and the marshy world at its edge are what one NASA scientist calls "the sine qua non of life."[2]

On a walk one late winter day, I changed my path. The new route took me through a stretch of trees at water's edge, over a small pedestrian bridge, and up a hill. Two things struck me that morning: first, how many trees had fallen in the river; and second, how the mud flats under the bridge appeared lifeless and polluted. A riparian world in crisis, hardly teeming with life. Everything was brown and gray, like a sepia print.

An unexpected movement caught my attention. A tiny turtle, a really small one, was meandering through the muck. Sometimes the turtle moved above the surface, sometimes just below. I remained transfixed, watching this determined fellow, the only detectable sign of life in the whole of the muddy marsh. The next morning, the turtle returned. And again the next. Then there was another one, larger this time—the mother turtle perhaps? Each day, I stood on the bridge waiting, watching for the turtles. Somehow they gave me hope for the water.

The native peoples who originally inhabited the Potomac's woods believed the turtle represented the earth and connection with the environment. Indeed, the natives called America "Turtle Island," the place of wisdom and peace. In some religions, turtles are considered divine—symbolizing that the way to heaven is a deliberate journey through the earth and along its waters.

And I started to understand that the river itself is sacred, the watery way of salvation.

"Where Is God?" and Water

There is an odd remark at the beginning of the Gospel of John. A man named Nicodemus asks Jesus how a person might enter the kingdom of God. Jesus answers, "Very truly, I tell you, no one can enter the kingdom of God without being born of water and Spirit" (3:5). Some Christians have interpreted "water" in this story as baptism, certainly a legitimate reading of Jesus's response. In the history of preaching on this verse, however, it is a rare sermon or commentary that emphasizes the water as literal rather than as symbol. Most interpreters jump quickly to the Spirit, relegating water to theological runner-up. Jesus did not do that. He twinned water with Spirit (often depicted as "wind" or "breath"), seemingly placing the two on equal footing. I have often wondered: Is Jesus speaking of God as water? As a Gospel writer, John uses many metaphors for God—Word, light, vine, door, bread, shepherd, love. Just a few pages later, Jesus declares, "God is spirit" (4:24). Why not water? Water need not be important only as an element in ecclesiastical ritual. Water might just be water. And perhaps God is water as well as spirit. It is easy to imagine John's Jesus saying, "We enter into the sacred presence through water and wind."

Water covers 71 percent of the earth's surface and is vital for life on this planet. Our bodies are nearly 70 percent water as well (depending on our size), and we cannot survive without it. Evolutionary biology reminds us that life on earth originated in the waters, that the first ground-dwelling creatures crawled out of the surf onto the land. Plants, and therefore all our food, depend on both the water cycle and an appropriate supply of water. Water is the continuing source of life for this planet. This tiny blue marble, as the first astronauts called it from space, so fragile from afar, is a planet of azure-endued life. "How inappropriate to call this planet 'Earth,'" noted science fiction writer Arthur C. Clarke, "when it is clearly 'Ocean.'" If the earth is God's body, as Sallie McFague noted, then water is its lifeblood.

Despite the fact that there is so much water on the planet, very little of it can be used directly by us. About 96 percent of the earth's water is saline, in the oceans and seas. Although the salty oceans are the source of evaporation in the water cycle and their water supports marine life and necessary ocean plankton, we can neither drink it nor farm with it. A little less than 2 percent of the earth's water is ice. And that leaves about 2 percent as freshwater, the usable sort of water for us humans, but most of it is trapped underground. Only a very tiny fraction of the world's water, less than

0.3 percent, is readily available freshwater—our rivers, lakes, and streams—which we drink, wash in, and use to raise our food.

Water is plentiful and necessary, but rare in usable forms. Yet we often take water for granted, especially those of us who live in developed countries, where clean and safe water flows through taps and hoses. In his book *Blue Mind,* author Wallace Nichols quotes a story from David Foster Wallace about three fish:

> There are these two young fish swimming along, and they happen to meet an older fish swimming the other way, who nods at them and says, "Morning, boys. How's the water?" And the two young fish swim on for a bit, and then eventually one of them looks over at the other and goes, "What the hell is water?"[3]

Before I started walking the Potomac, I did not know much about water despite the fact that I had previously lived in drought-prone states like Arizona and California, where water is precious and a daily topic of conversation. For much of my life, I have been like one of the young fish: water was generally invisible to me. I assumed its existence, failing to grasp the miracle and complexity of it, especially the freshwater on which our lives depend. That raises a question: If the water is invisible to the fish, is God, as the One in whom we swim, also invisible? As we pay attention to rivers and seas, we might also discover God's fluid presence with the water.

The Spiritual Quest for Water

Throughout human history, the quest for God has often been connected with a quest for freshwater. Just off the road in the Scottish village of Invermoriston is an ancient well fed by a spring that has existed since pre-Christian times. According to local legend, the spring was once toxic and people feared the water, believing it was possessed by evil spirits. When people drank from it, they sickened and developed ulcers. The bad water killed many. Around the year 565, Columba, the missionary abbot from the Isle of Iona, arrived in the village and prayed over the spring. The evil spirits fled, the spring ran clear, and the water became fit to drink and acquired healing powers. Columba's ancient biographer wrote: "Since that day the demons have kept away from the well. Instead, far from harming anyone, after the saint had blessed it and washed in it, many elements among the local people were cured by that well." The missionary's fame spread through the Scottish highlands, where he performed many miracles with water—not least when he encountered a great sea monster and chased it into the deep waters of Loch Ness.[4]

Columba's story is only one of many such tales recounted in Christian legends and church history. Many stories of biblical figures, prophets, saints, and healers involve water. Shrines, temples, and cathedrals were built over springs and ancient healing wells, including famous Christian sites like Chartres Cathedral and the shrine at Lourdes in France. At the entrance to the church founded by Columba on the Isle of Iona stands a holy well, a place of baptism and cleansing for converts and pilgrims. Celtic Christianity is replete with legends of heroes and shamans who journeyed over water, of sea monsters, river goddesses, well-dwelling wizards, musical waterfalls, and healing dews. Indeed, every saint in Irish and Scottish lore performed miracles having to do with water, including Patrick, who, like Columba, drove malevolent spirits from springs and wells and then used the blessed water to baptize converts.

And the quest for sacred water is not limited to Christianity.

From the Ganges to Lourdes, from the Jordan to Japan's sacred waterfalls, and around the globe, faithful pilgrims make their way to places where they believe holy water will cleanse or cure them. The Hebrew creation story in Genesis begins with water; it is the only thing that exists with God before the rest of world is made. Jewish spiritual texts are replete with water stories, whether of the great drought of Joseph's time, Moses parting the Red Sea, or the Jews' ancestors crossing the Jordan River into the promised land. Indeed, water is such a powerful force in the Hebrew scriptures that the same word, *ayin,* signifies both "spring" and "eye," especially the eye of God. Ancient biblical tradition suggests that waters— wells, springs, oases—are also places of renewal, hospitality, and spiritual vision, where human beings see God and receive God's blessing. Muslims depict God as the One who sat upon the waters and also believe that water existed before creation began. In the story of Hagar, when Ishmael's banished mother desperately seeks water in the desert, an angel appears to her, miraculously revealing a spring that saves her and her young son from certain death. For Muslims, water is thus associated with creation, motherhood, and God's provision, and the faithful imitate Hagar's frantic search as part of their pilgrimage to Mecca.

Hindus revere all water as sacred, but especially rivers. Most Hindu holy sites are located near water; the most important pilgrimages are to the Ganges River, where one is made pure, sins are forgiven, ancestors are honored, and the dying are ushered to heaven. Buddhists offer water at shrines to achieve serenity, clarity, and purity, virtues on the path to enlightenment. In some Buddhist traditions, water represents prayers and a bowl of water is a ritual element at funerals. Taoism uses water as its primary metaphor, emphasizing it as the female source of all life, but it also sees water as the image for an entire way of life, leading to its nickname, the

"Watercourse Way." In the native traditions of many cultures, water represents fertility and renewal, the feminine aspect of divinity, and often symbolizing birth and spiritual rebirth. Ancient pagan religions used baths and bathing for ritual cleansing and healing, to seek spiritual wisdom, and to make offerings to the gods.[5]

Water is so ubiquitous in spiritual traditions that Ian Bradley, a professor at St. Andrews University in Scotland, discerned eighteen different metaphors for it common to most world religions—including water as an image for heaven or paradise, the location of human encounters with God, and the source of life. It functions as a metaphor for death and the journey to the next world, union with the divine, wisdom, and the sacred feminine. It may signal hospitality and generosity, it possesses holiness or blessing, and it is used in the practice of healing.[6]

In the Christian Bible, water plays a central role. Beginning with the Old Testament's first book, Genesis, water is present with the Spirit before creation; in the last book of the New Testament, Revelation, life-giving water flows from the being of God's own self. Throughout the Old Testament, watery images serve both as signs of God's power (for example, the flood, which Noah and his family survive on the ark, and the closing of the Red Sea, which drowns Pharaoh's army) and the promise of God's restorative justice (when the desert shall run with streams and fountains spring forth). Indeed, the power of water as a fertility symbol and the spiritual feminine is evident also in these ancient stories. Three of Israel's patriarchs—Isaac, Jacob, and Moses—meet their wives at a well, signaling to keen readers that their unions will be fertile. A later biblical story makes the same connection in an overtly sexual way; when King David spies Bathsheba bathing, he takes his beautiful married neighbor to be his mistress, a relationship that results in the birth of Solomon, Israel's wisest ruler. From water comes life.

The New Testament, written in the first century CE, is set in what is now Israel, ancient home to the Hebrew people, but then it was occupied by the Roman Empire. This is the place God had promised them would be a land of milk and honey. In ancient geography, Israel was part of the Fertile Crescent, home to the watersheds of some of the greatest and most storied rivers of human history. It was in these watersheds that humans first invented and practiced irrigation, making possible the development of agriculture and the growth of cities. But they were also susceptible to drought, and the idea of water management was almost unknown.

The Jordan River was the major source of water in Israel (and remains so until this day); it was the place where John the Baptist baptized hundreds of people, including his cousin Jesus. The Sea of Galilee, a freshwater lake fed by the Jordan, was where Jesus preached his most important sermon and performed his most dramatic miracles. But of equal importance for human habitation in Israel is the underground water supply, the springs hidden from view: the freshwater of aquifers accessible for much of history only by deep wells.[7]

At the very beginning of his teaching ministry, Jesus meets a woman at one of those wells, called Jacob's Well, and strikes up a conversation with her:

> "Give me a drink." (His disciples had gone to the city to buy food.) The Samaritan woman said to him, "How is it that you, a Jew, ask a drink of me, a woman of Samaria?" (Jews do not share things in common with Samaritans.) Jesus answered her, "If you knew the gift of God, and who it is that is saying to you, 'Give me a drink,' you would have asked him, and he would have given you living water." The woman said to him, "Sir,

you have no bucket, and the well is deep. Where do you get that living water? Are you greater than our ancestor Jacob, who gave us the well, and with his sons and his flocks drank from it?" Jesus said to her, "Everyone who drinks of this water will be thirsty again, but those who drink of the water that I will give them will never be thirsty. The water that I will give will become in them a spring of water gushing up to eternal life." The woman said to him, "Sir, give me this water, so that I may never be thirsty or have to keep coming here to draw water." (John 4:7–15)

I have heard many sermons on this passage; indeed, I have preached a few. Typically Christians cite this passage to prove a unique claim of Jesus—that Jesus is "living water," a moniker that identifies Jesus as divine. In the story, Jesus does more than Jacob, the Hebrew patriarch who provided the drinking well, a spot most likely deemed sacred by local villagers. Instead, Jesus implies that he is water, not just a well. As he and the woman talk throughout the rest of John's chapter, Jesus layers on spiritual metaphors for water: liberation, yearning for salvation, hospitality, healing, and as a source of life. With each poetic turn, his invitation to these waters becomes more compelling. Wisdom, like a spring, bubbles up through his insights. He gives water, and he is water. Just as John had indicated earlier, the kingdom comes through water and spirit.

The encounter is an interesting parallel to the story of Eve. In Genesis, the devil tempts the woman to eat forbidden fruit to gain divine knowledge. At the well, Jesus invites this Samaritan woman to drink God's water to gain spiritual wisdom. The entire story is a reversal of the one recounting the origin of sin; here, Jesus and the woman reenact Eden with a different result. The woman's eyes are opened; she understands. Yet, instead of being run out of the garden by an angry god, she runs and tells her friends that she has met the One who is Living Water. She is not cursed. Rather, the woman is blessed and offers blessing. Water is present at creation, and it is here also, at the world's re-creation through Jesus.

This story, with its multiple meanings, frames the Christian imagination regarding water. Oddly enough, in the spiritual history of water, it is not really unique. (Its most unique feature is how ordinary it is; unlike many other ancient water stories, there are no supernatural elements present, no demons, no monsters. There is only Jesus's insight to the woman's spiritual needs.) The story of Jesus and the woman at the well echoes shared human experience, perhaps even a universal one. God provides—or the gods provide—water and the water is (in some way or another) divine. Although later Christian theology will carefully draw a distinction between water-as-symbol and water-as-God, one must admit that even for the staunchest monotheist the metaphorical territory here is pretty thin. Water is life; life is water. Living water is God; God is living water.

In the not too distant future, however, living water might be mere theological memory—a spiritual element increasingly lost to rising generations. If nothing else, our descendants will surely interpret the spirituality of water in starkly different ways than we do now. Water is under siege all over the planet, watersheds are collapsing, streams and rivers dying, even once safe water systems face toxic threats. The story of Jesus and the woman at the well—the search for both safe water to drink and the water of salvation—may be more urgent than ever. Much depends on how we navigate these rivers of change.

Healing Wells

Given the universality of water in stories of creation and healing, it appears that human beings have always understood that water is vital for happiness and well-being. In recent years, however, the connection between water and happiness has been explored by a host of mainstream scientists, especially neuroscientists. Researchers around the globe have demonstrated that being in natural environments with water makes human beings more relaxed, happier, and more satisfied with life. For example, a Canadian study discovered that taking a fifteen-minute walk along the Ottawa River boosted energy and positive emotions for the participants.[8] A United Kingdom social psychologist found that photographs of waterscapes prompted feelings of relaxation and a desire by subjects to want to live near the particular scene. And it is not only pictures of water—just seeing the color blue promotes feelings of well-being, "producing physical, cognitive, and emotional benefits" similar to the effects of dopamine on the brain.[9]

A Stanford University researcher analyzed fMRI results and found that engaging nature stimulates the same area of the brain as does food, sex, and money. Studies in Europe and North America continue to show that either viewing nature or engaging in outdoor sports, especially when involving oceans, lakes, or rivers, calms us and elevates positive emotions. It also promotes attentiveness, concentration, and creativity.[10] In addition to steadying human emotions, being near water has proved to have curative effects on many health problems, including PTSD, depression, addictions, autism, pain, anxiety, stress, and attention disorders, and to hasten healing from surgery, illness, and injuries. As marine biologist Wallace Nichols observes, "Nature is medicine; this is an idea now reiterated by modern science."[11]

Almost thirty years ago, when I was a graduate student at Duke, I was plagued by extreme anxiety. Graduate school is, admittedly, an anxious environment for many people. Unlike most of my stressed classmates, however, I could not eat, lost thirty pounds, had trouble sleeping, and was consumed by worry. Concerned friends suggested all manner of things, including medication. One insisted on a simpler cure: "Go to the beach."

I went to Emerald Isle, North Carolina, and stayed right on the ocean in an old, weather-worn house nothing like the mansions more recently built on the Outer Banks. For hours, I watched the waves from a bench built into the wooden walkway that connected the cottage and beach. I walked at the edge of the ocean, looking for shells mostly. It was therapeutic.

Of all the shells, I liked the pink conch best. There were only conch fragments on the beach. A friend told me that it was exceedingly difficult to find an unbroken one in these waters. But one morning, while wading in the surf, I caught a glimpse of a large pink conch in the waves. Not a fragment—a whole one.

I dove for the shell. It slipped through my fingers. I dove again and reached, saltwater stinging my eyes. I felt it in my hand and grasped it tightly as a wave knocked me off my feet. When I came up from the water, I was still clutching the shell. Wet and pearly, it was perfect.

I sat on the beach, holding it close to my chest. I found myself repeating, "Thank you, thank you, thank you." Thank you? I realized that I was not only glad to have found the shell, but also grateful. I had forgotten that life was a gift. "Thank you" was a prayer of remembrance and healing. I felt at peace, somehow sensing a spiritual turning point. Years later, I learned that Buddhists believe that the conch symbolizes awakening, that it shakes us from slumbers of ignorance and propels us toward the journey of self-discovery and serving others. On that day, sitting in the sand and uttering fluid prayers, I felt bizarrely happy for the first time in a long time.

A new interdisciplinary community of scientists, environmentalists, health researchers, therapists, and artists is coalescing around an idea: *neuroconservation*. Embracing the notion that we treasure what we love, those concerned with water and the future of the planet now suggest that, as we understand our emotional well-being and its relationship to water, we are more motivated to repair, restore, and renew waterways and watersheds. Indeed, even as water is threatened, or perhaps because of the threat, public interest in water is very high. We treasure it—or, perhaps more accurately, we spend our treasure to access water for pleasure, recreation, and healing. Wealthy people pay a premium for houses on water, and the not so wealthy pay extra for rentals and hotel rooms sited at the oceanfront, on rivers, or at lakes. Those into outdoor sports, especially fishers and hunters, are fiercely protective of it and have founded numerous environmental organizations designed to protect water habitats for fish, birds, and animals.

Over the last two decades, spas have become a sort of modern equivalent to ancient healing wells. As an industry, spas are a global business worth about $60 billion, and they generate another $200 billion in tourism. In 2013, there were 20,000 (up from 4,000 in 1999) spas in the United States producing an annual revenue of over $14 billion (a figure that has grown every year for fifteen years, including those of the recession), and tallying 164 million spa visits by clients.[12] Ecotourism provides water adventures and guided trips, often in kayaks, rafts, or canoes. Ocean and river cruises are big business. Cities are creating urban architectures focused on waterscapes, happiness, and sustainability. Museums and public memorials of all sorts often feature water to foster reflection and meditation. And many communities are working to transform industrialized and polluted waterfronts into spaces that are pleasant, environmentally sound, and livable.

It's easy to see how water makes us feel better physically and emotionally, but there is a spiritual benefit as well: neurological studies about water bear a striking resemblance to studies conducted on prayer and meditation. Indeed, people who are near or in water express higher levels of happiness and often demonstrate better health outcomes; so too do people who pray and meditate.[13] Wallace Nichols, who never overtly writes of religion in his book *Blue Mind,* connects water with meditation, edging toward the territory of theology:

> Several years ago I came up with a name for this human–water connection: Blue Mind, a mildly meditative state characterized by calm, peacefulness, unity, and a sense of general happiness and satisfaction with life in the moment. It is inspired by water and elements associated with water, from the color blue to the words we use to describe the sensations associated with immersion. It takes advantage of neurological connections formed over millennia, many such brain patterns and preferences being discovered only now, thanks to innovative scientists and cutting-edge technology.[14]

Today science explores the objective dimensions of water and wellness, but the interplay between water, wellness, and spirituality was well known to our ancestors. Primal myths shared this ancient wisdom, and creation stories extolled the divine nature of water. Past generations built healing wells, spas, and baths, and archaeological remains still testify to their faith in water. Great religions created their rituals around water. Science can now map our neural pathways when we gather at the river, and psychologists can demonstrate the connection between happiness and water. But they are only proving something our souls have always known.

Water holds deep wisdom; it keeps our ancient memories of origins and our creaturely dependence. But we forget. From time to time, we need to be reminded that water is essential to health and happiness. Looking up from my desk, I see the conch on my bookshelf, close by and always visible, as it has been since that day on the beach, a token of God, of healing and grace.

The Threat to Water

In March 2014, the disappearance of Malaysian Airlines Flight 370 led to the largest and most expensive multinational sea search in history. For a month after the plane was lost to radar, investigation experts and sophisticated naval teams from the world's most developed countries spread out over the Indian Ocean in a desperate search for the airliner. The media covered it 24/7. Millions watched, hoping for some sign of the doomed airliner and the lost passengers.

At an early stage in the search, an excited news anchor broke into CNN coverage reporting that satellites had picked up a large "debris area" at a distant location in the South Indian Ocean. For hours, experts speculated about and analyzed this news, hoping for confirmation that the airliner had been found. Then came word from the searchers: no airplane. Rather, the large debris field was floating trash, as one commentator said, "just garbage."

For a short time, the experts switched from the plane crash to an environmental story. The world's oceans are full of garbage. Some of it is visible, like cargo that falls from ships carrying goods around the world, and some is less visible, like tons of plastics and chemical sludge washed—or purposely dumped—into sea currents from the world's watersheds. This debris clusters into oceanic gyres, creating large floating trash heaps of human-produced waste in some of the most remote locations of the planet.

CNN showed video footage and photographs taken by search crews. There it was: a massive tangle of human garbage, including thousands of the now ubiquitous plastic water bottles. Hours of news coverage that promised word of a downed airliner wound up being wall-to-wall analysis of stuff that washed down the planet's storm drains and formed itself into islands in the South Indian Ocean.

The news about the airliner was worrisome and sad, but somehow the news about the ocean struck me as equally depressing—especially since the commentators did not seem particularly fazed by the fact that these heaps of trash—"just garbage"—are largely toxic. As the trash degrades, it contaminates the food chain that begins in our oceans and sickens fish, birds, animals, and eventually us with chemicals no living being was ever meant to ingest. The problem of ocean trash is so bad that garbage clogs sea-lanes and ports in many parts of the world. Indeed, the U.S. Army Corps of Engineers picks up approximately ninety tons of trash every month from the San Francisco Bay alone.

But it is hard to see the ocean. Even though I was well aware of the problems of toxic trash at sea, the CNN reports startled me. As the old adage goes, "Out of sight, out of mind." Or, as naturalist Aldo Leopold once wrote, "We can be ethical only in relation to something we can see, feel and understand, or otherwise have faith in."[15] The South Indian Ocean may be out of my sight, but other problems are not.

In February 2015, I was driving in California from Santa Barbara to Solvang on a scenic road that passes Lake Cachuma, a huge constructed lake that serves as the major source of drinking water for Santa Barbara County. Although I used to drive that road frequently, it had been about four years since my last visit. When I came around a bend, expecting to see the bright blue water against the rocky hills, I was shocked. No water. At least not much. Instead, large swaths of devastated shoreline were visible. The ground was dry and cracked. Docks had collapsed at what used to be the water's edge. Hulls of old fishing boats lay stranded on rocks. At capacity, Lake Cachuma holds almost two hundred thousand acre-feet of water. Because of the drought occurring in eleven of the last fourteen years, the reservoir is at nowhere near capacity. Down to a quarter of its maximum water supply, it will be empty of usable water by October 2015, state experts say. Santa Barbara is moving toward reactivating its expensive saltwater desalination plant in order to help the city survive the current water crisis.

California is a drought-prone place. But scientists say that this is the worst dry period in more than a thousand years; the last such time occurred in the Middle Ages. It provides evidence of what is expected to be a widespread "megadrought" across the American Southwest. Deserts are creeping northward, and researchers like Columbia University's Jason Smerdon worry that "the twenty-first-century projections make the [previous] megadroughts seem like quaint walks through the Garden of Eden."[16] With the Sierra Nevada snowpack at its lowest level in recorded history, California instituted water restrictions on residents and businesses while attempting to find a way to keep water flowing to its farms. The state is draining its underground aquifers, some of which have been contaminated by industrial waste and others of which are "nonrenewable" sources of water. These natural aquifers are essentially large reservoirs created millions of years ago, deposits of ancient rain and runoff known as "fossil water." When that water is either polluted or depleted, it cannot be replaced. Stanford University estimates that 60 percent of California's water needs are currently being met by underground water pumped by increasingly expensive wells. The water table is falling; supplies of even this hidden source are rapidly shrinking.[17] Business news network CNBC reports that some experts are beginning to suggest that the United States may have to "migrate people out of California."[18] And it is not just California. More than forty states are anticipating freshwater shortages in the next decade.[19]

Even where there is water, there is still trouble. On a late July morning in 2014, as I walked along the Potomac River, I noticed that the water was green in spots. An anomaly? Odd light? As the weeks went by, the green turned an almost florescent lime and spread throughout the marsh. Herons, duck, and geese fled. The water was essentially dead, the birds' food contaminated by phosphates and nitrates. The fish and other marine creatures either have moved to safer waters or are dead. The toxins that killed them come mostly from industrial waste (much of it from illegal dumping), chemical farming, and lawn-control products upstream. In the decade that my family has lived here, there had never been such a sizable algal bloom. And it is not only the Potomac. Around the area, toxins have shown up in other streams and rivers—and in drinking wells—throughout the Mid-Atlantic. The Potomac, as beautiful as it can be, is one of the ten most threatened rivers in America. I see it each morning with my own eyes, and it weighs on my mind and heart.

Although some face more immediate dangers than others, most of the world's waterways and watersheds are endangered.[20] The Potomac flows into the Chesapeake Bay. The bay struggles for life as chemical-laden waters run into it from farms and industries along its rivers and streams. A coal-mining accident in West Virginia? That water eventually winds up as part of the Chesapeake. Water used to cool nuclear plants in Pennsylvania? To the Chesapeake.

Chemical crop fertilizers, some even under threat of EPA ban, bleeding off fields into a stream? Straight to the bay. Lawn fertilizer from new waterfront developments? Fish kill. Flush the toilet? Run the dishwasher? All that domestic water comes from the Chesapeake Bay watershed and returns to the bay. For all its beauty and the life and livelihood it has given to generations who dwell on its shores, the Chesapeake watershed functions as a giant industrial and domestic toilet. The remains of everything that seventeen million people and their businesses do, whether intentional or not, winds up in creeks and streams and travels down the rivers and out to the bay.

Of course, it is not just California or the Chesapeake Bay watershed. Where water is not plentiful—or where it was once plentiful—watersheds are actually drying up, becoming both siltier and saltier, more subject to damaging floods and erosion, more threatened by mining and drilling, and they face uncertain effects from global climate change. Where water is still plentiful, it is increasingly polluted or poisoned to the point of being unusable. We are facing great uncertainty regarding the future of water. In California, there is talk about migration. The same is true on the Chesapeake Bay— where the disappearance of oysters and crabs has led to a collapse of fishing towns and the dislocation of entire populations.

The problems multiply beyond North America and Europe, continents with extensive (even if polluted) watersheds. The Indus River is one of Asia's most important rivers, key to life and stability in China, Pakistan, and India. Yet, as a result of shrinking snow packs, industrialization, and deforestation, the river no longer flows as it once did, having become polluted, full of sediment, and more saline. Evidence is mounting that the course of the river is actually reversing itself. And the loss of natural wetlands has resulted in more violent inland effects from storms. In the Punjab breadbasket, farming and fishing are in radical decline. Thousands of young men who once could depend on meaningful work in those vital industries find themselves with no future. There has been an exodus of the young unemployed from the Punjab to cities such as Karachi, where the disaffected have become prime targets for conversion to Islamic radicalism.

The Indus crisis illustrates that threatened water can lead to threatening religion. From the Indus to Gaza to the U.S.-Mexico border, water is the source of great political and religious tension, and often war. As water recedes or becomes unusable and as food supplies become endangered, conflict will increase. This, combined with population growth and the need for agricultural water, may make many agree with science journalist Fred Pearce that "without a second agricultural revolution that targets water, a 'blue revolution,' the gains of the past generation could be wiped out as rivers run dry, underground water reserves are exhausted, and fields are caked in salt."[21] One need only look at any great river to see such problems; even the world's most isolated rivers and watersheds struggle to survive. From the humble oyster and low reservoirs to islands of floating trash and global terrorism, the future of water is the human future. And it may well be the future of God too.

Let Justice Roll On Like a River

In the eighth century BCE, a Jewish farmer named Amos railed against the rich who were manipulating credit to seize land from small landholders. The woes of Amos's time were real. Traditional farms fell into disarray, as the poor were kicked off their native lands. An extended drought had reduced agricultural production, and people had little water to drink: "One field would be rained upon, and the field on which it did not rain withered; so two or three towns wandered to one town to drink water" (4:7–8). Amos gives voice to those suffering, drawing attention to the link between abundant water, productive fields and vineyards, and economic justice. He calls for the rich to act on behalf of the poor. At the height of his lament, he contrasts the sporadic rains with the ever-flowing current of God's presence and care for the world. He cries out: "Let justice roll on like a river!" (NIV).

It is an important ancient story, reminding us that rivers serve as a powerful spiritual metaphor for our lives in God and that they are the actual source of sustenance and economic vitality. God's presence is like a river: God's justice flows like the waters. To tend to the waters reminds us of the source of life and gives practical expression to addressing our environment and the needs of the poor.

For three years, I lived in Memphis, Tennessee. There the Mississippi River runs wide and fast. From Mark Twain onward, the Mississippi has inspired story and poetry. But perhaps no one ever depicted it better than poet T. S. Eliot, who referred to the river as a "strong brown god":

> *I do not know much about gods; but I think that the river*
> *Is a strong brown god—sullen, untamed and intractable,*
> *Patient to some degree, at first recognised as a frontier;*
> *Useful, untrustworthy, as a conveyor of commerce;*
> *Then only a problem confronting the builder of bridges.*
> *The problem once solved, the brown god is almost forgotten*
> *By the dwellers in cities—ever, however, implacable.*
> *Keeping his seasons and rages, destroyer, reminder*
> *Of what men choose to forget. Unhonoured, unpropitiated*
> *By worshippers of the machine, but waiting,*
>   *watching and waiting . . .*
>
> *The river is within us, the sea is all about us.*[22]

It is easy to forget the river. Sometimes we consider water to be in our way, a barrier between us and where we want to go. Or just water under the bridge. As T. S. Eliot so eloquently noted, we ignore the "brown god" that runs underneath.

Watching the Mississippi, I realized I had never seen a river so powerful. A brown god, indeed. I realized why people in Memphis lived inland. The Mississippi is hard to contemplate. This river swelled into one's soul, demanding total attention. It was a consuming vista, that river—*Let justice roll on like a river.* The Mississippi does not allow for dreamy visions of distant promise. It insists on the here and now.

Many spiritual speculations have understood rivers as the way to the afterlife, forgetting about the water itself. Ancient Greeks passed over the River Styx, ancient Egyptians floated their rulers on barges down the Nile, and Indians burned the remains of their loved ones at the Ganges. If the river is the primal entrance to the underworld, the current that takes us to the grave, it is no wonder our faith traditions have tempted us to want to skirt the waters. Perhaps such spiritual disregard has led to a certain human carelessness about our watersheds, leaving us unable to gaze deeply upon these waters and consider them, in some meaningful way, significant for what they are.

But what if the power of the river is, as with the Mississippi, here and now, a fluid faith in the world? Not a distant divinity whose water ushers us to eternal life, but a swiftly flowing God whose justice surges downstream in the currents of the world? The river is not a place to die, but a place to live and share life with others.

When I first started walking along the Potomac, I fell in love with the wild irises that bloomed in the spring. How beautiful they would look in a vase at home! Without a moment's hesitation, I stepped off the path and headed toward the edge of the river. With the first step, I felt the spongy land. A few more steps, and it was squishy. I stretched for the flowers, took another step, and I was up to my ankles in watery mud. The irises were still just beyond my reach. I stood there, ruined shoes and all, wondering what I should do—walk deeper in or turn back to the path without the blooms.

My Potomac sojourn has deepened my spiritual vocabulary. Initially, I did not understand about riparian zones, seeing them as a mucky barrier to the river. The irises taught me that the riparian zone seems an apt metaphor for life. Neither the surety of firm ground nor the excitement of clear current, the muddy edge of the river is its most vital feature. Generally, it is not very attractive, especially in our world of polluted waterways. Yet without it nothing survives. The riparian zone is remarkably like what some faith traditions refer to as liminal space, the uncertain territory between two more certain realities. How often times in my own life are like what happens in the riparian zone: the ground under my feet softens, my steps turn tentative, and I become unsure of where or how to move ahead. This is the geography of trust and transformation, where the safe shore dissolves and we feel disoriented as we consider what we should do next.

Buddhists talk about stepping into the river, of going with the flow of the universe. But standing in the mud, I realized how messy and difficult it is just getting to the water to step in! Stepping into the river means stepping into an uncertain space. Going with the flow is not only rafting down a river on a pleasant summer day. Rather, it means beginning with the creeks of the watershed far away from the river. Going with the flow means moving with all the waters as they flow toward the main river leading to the sea. All the tributaries, the small waterways that seem so insignificant, merge to become the beautiful Potomac, the flooding Nile, the mighty Mississippi, or the godlike Ganges. And the great rivers themselves marry, mingling together to form the seas.

90

This is a vibrant spiritual vision—knowing God as water is not only about clarity and flow, but consists in great part of the muddiness of our own lives, for the river is a territory of doubt and desire. And we must walk through this riparian environment to reach the clear waters, where we might flow with the current (a flow that is not always safe or easy) and make our way toward the oneness of the great sea. Rivers are not a barrier to be breached or boundary to be overcome; rather, they are the living waters. They nourish us; they are our fluid way to health and happiness. Medieval mystic Hildegard of Bingen once envisioned a time when "rivers of living water are to be poured out over the whole world, to ensure that people . . . can be restored to wholeness."[23] Our lives are like a watershed, where everything flows toward the oceans; and the watershed is the metaphorical setting for the journey.

Rivers, however, are more than metaphors. Although watersheds provide a powerful language of spiritual insight, they are also real endangered places that demand our ethical attention. The world's waterways call us to practice social justice—to restore them, to make sure rich and poor alike have access, and to manage water in drought-stricken lands with creativity and foresight.

At a gathering of the Massachusetts United Church of Christ, a senior minister handed me a plastic water bottle—not one of those throwaway bottled waters from the grocery store, but a refillable bottle, complete with a reusable straw. It is a conference giveaway that I actually use. Religious communities are increasingly aware of water issues. A pastor from New Brunswick, Canada, started the global nonprofit Water Project to provide clean water and sanitation to disadvantaged communities. The organization partners with local groups in Sub-Saharan Africa to increase access to water and educate and train people in water issues. As it says in its mission statement, "We believe that providing water to those who need it most is a natural and humble expression of our faith that teaches us to love all and serve the poor."[24]

Congregations often serve local communities by mobilizing for watershed cleanup and education days. Many theological seminaries and divinity schools have initiated programs of study on faith and ecology, often with water as a major emphasis in the curriculum. Theologian Benjamin Stewart points out that "for as long as humans have prayed, they have probably prayed at water-places" and that God "*acts like* nourishing water flowing through our world," even as people of faith thank God "*for the actual water*" that flows in the world.[25] New Testament scholar Ched Meyers writes of "watershed discipleship" and invites Christians to "re-inhabit" the watersheds in which we live and see these places as the primary location of caring for the environment and our neighbor.[26]

At the November 2013 World Council of Churches assembly in Korea, religious leaders representing Christian, Muslim, Hindu, Jewish, and Buddhist faiths poured water into a common vessel signifying their unity, the importance of water in religious traditions, and their shared commitment to water justice.[27] Global Christian churches have formed the Ecumenical Water Network, which, drawing its commitments from biblical principles of creation, is dedicated to "equitable distribution" of safe, clean water for all the world's people.

But the ethics of water is far from the latest religion cause. For almost two hundred years, people of faith have been aware of the interconnected concerns of environment, health, economics, and water. In the nineteenth century, for example, British Christians led the political movement for public water fountains. Believing that fresh, clean water was a right for all and horrified by the fact that doctors encouraged mothers to give their children beer or whiskey to drink because public well water had become polluted by industrial waste and most domestic water was not safe, Church of England priests, Nonconformist Liberals, politicians, and activist laity pushed for the introduction of safe public drinking fountains, so that all could have free access to good drinking water. Indeed, they often justified this as promoting "communal purity and cleanliness," an earthly manifestation of the New Jerusalem, where a river runs from the throne of God. Many public drinking fountains throughout England were inscribed with Revelation 22:17: "Take the water of life freely" (KJV).[28]

In the same way, many contemporary water-justice initiatives are faith-oriented, including the work of theologians, preachers, activists, and congregations, all of whom are rediscovering the spiritual and sacramental aspects of water. With an issue of such global concern, however, Christians are not the only ones concerned with water justice. In Islam, to withhold water from a thirsty traveler is considered an affront to Allah, who is the giver of water to all people.[29] Indeed, an eighth-century imam is reported to have said, "There is no joy in life unless three things are available: clean fresh air, abundant pure water, and fertile land."[30] Muslims are forming organizations such as Green Muslims to connect Islamic communities with environmental activists on a range of issues, including water. Through the auspices of the United Nations, Christians, Muslims, Jews, Buddhists, Hindus, and secular people work together on UN Water, an international community committed to issues of freshwater, sustainability, sanitation, and water management. In addition to projects and programs across the globe, UN Water sponsors World Water Day on March 22 to draw attention to the role that water plays in all our lives.

The United Nations work is both important and essential. But the water movement is, at its heart, local. It is about the water in our own cities and neighborhoods, learning to reconnect with the liquid source of life. Across the United States and Canada, people are learning and teaching about the future of water, churches have installed wells and water barrels to collect rainwater, and congregations of all sorts regularly host watershed cleanups. Many churches and synagogues have banned plastic water bottles at events, choosing instead to serve water in glasses or cups. They are conducting water audits, planting drought-resistant landscapes, or installing low-flow irrigation systems. GreenFaith, a national environmental organization, runs Water Shield, a certification program for congregations and religious organizations that "conserve water, protect water quality, and mobilize its members and community to do the same at home."[31] Programs like Water Weekends and Water Wise educate faith communities regarding water issues. According to Adelle Banks of Religion News Service, "Water has become more than a ritual element used in Christian baptismal rites or in Jewish and Muslim cleansing ceremonies. It has become a focus for worshippers seeking to go beyond water's ritual symbolism and think more deeply about their relationship to this life-giving resource."[32]

Across the planet, people are learning their rivers and working for water. The green movement is becoming a spiritually hued blue.

The River of God

I still walk along the Potomac. But some days I sit by it. Those are rowing days, when I watch my daughter's crew team race on the river.

The young women are dedicated. They spend the winter months training, working out for hours on erg machines and running. In the spring, they get on the water, perfecting their form and rowing together as a team. And they learn the river, figuring out winds and currents to their advantage. In effect, the best boats become one—a unity of rowers and river as the team works together and with the Potomac. It is not an individual sport where people can jockey for attention; nor can rowers fight the river. Rowing embodies strength, control, and flow, the spirit of the waters. My daughter says she "feels alive" on the river; it has, in many ways, become her teenage church, a place where she meets the divine.

Watching my daughter row on the Potomac, I wish I were stronger, younger, a rower. Because I think I understand what she loves out there, over the riparian edge, racing on the currents. The river is a religious experience. "Throughout the whole of religious tradition," remarked poet Ted Hughes in an interview, "rivers have been gods. Water has been the soul. And water is the ultimate life . . . the divine influx."[33]

The Bible begins with the deep, when God's spirit sweeps over the waters. From wind and the seas comes all of creation (Gen. 1:1–2). For Christians, the Bible also ends with water: "Then the angel showed me the river of the water of life, bright as crystal, flowing from the throne of God and of the Lamb through the middle of the street of the city." The final scene in the book of Revelation is the river of God, the water that heals and washes away all sorrow. "Let everyone who is thirsty come," the last words of Jesus invite, "Let anyone who wishes take the water of life as a gift" (22:1–2; 17). Water in the beginning, water at the end. God is the Alpha and Omega of the wells, rivers, and seas.

Sky

We are stardust,
We are golden,
And we've got to get ourselves
Back to the garden.

—Joni Mitchell

Growing up in a large city, I never really knew the sky. In Baltimore, trees and buildings kept the sky from view. To see it, you usually had to look straight up. The sky did not meet the earth at a far horizon; indeed, you could only rarely see where they touched. No one has ever considered calling Maryland "big sky country," for it is not. The sky is small, a backdrop to urban landscapes or wooded hills.

My first real acquaintance with the sky came in 1972, when my parents moved our family to Arizona. We left Maryland in early November, on a cloudy morning, and headed west for a five-day journey in our brand-new yellow Ford station wagon. Two parents, three kids, and one Old English Sheepdog. The three of us quarreled about who got to sit in the far back boot with the dog and the suitcases—a private little world distant from adult conversation and cigarette smoke. As the eldest, I often won the battle. I liked being surrounded by windows, instead of confined in the middle seat. The back offered a better view.

As my father drove across the Appalachians and into the midwest, the landscape was still familiar. The first part of the journey took us through recognizable scenes of woods, small towns, and family farms. Then somewhere past St. Louis things started to change: trees were smaller and farther apart, the land was flatter, farms were bigger. And the sky suddenly became part of the landscape. The farther west we traveled, the bigger it became. Until west Texas. There the land seemed to disappear, and the dry earth, marked by cattle ranches and oil rigs, seemed an insignificant backdrop to the blue that swaddled everything. Riding in the back of the station wagon, I lay down and positioned myself to see only the sky, and I felt as if I were floating on a raft in the clouds. I wondered if twelve-year-olds in Conestoga wagons or Pullman cars felt the same when they sojourned west with their parents. The sky was huge, with a life-giving force of its own. For someone who grew up under the protective shelter of trees, it was overwhelming.

When we arrived in Arizona, our new house was an odd bit of eastern architecture: it had two floors. Our living room was upstairs and looked out above the surrounding suburban ranch-style houses. The living-room window looked west to Camelback Mountain; the kitchen windows faced east to the Superstitions. On any given day, you could look out and see seventy or so miles into the distance, where craggy mountain peaks carved into the cloudless turquoise horizon. The local weatherman (and they were only men in those days), for lack of anything else to say—as the weather rarely changed—reported on the sky: "Tomorrow we will have unlimited visibility." In Phoenix, the sky was all-encompassing, the home of the day's relentless sun and night's welcome canopy of stars. I could understand why the ancient peoples searched its vast vistas for signs of rain, sought shelter from its endless burning light by building their homes on cliffs for shade, and used the stars to mark holy places and guide the pilgrimages of the dead. No wonder they worshipped the sky deity as creator and giver of life.

"Where Is God?" and the Sky

The question "Where is God?" appears several times in the Bible, perhaps most famously in the book of Job, but it occurs frequently in the Psalms as well. Psalm 115 offers a lyrical meditation on the question:

> Not to us, O LORD, not to us, but to your name give glory,
> for the sake of your steadfast love and your faithfulness.
> Why should the nations say,
> "Where is their God?"
>
> Our God is in the heavens;
> he does whatever he pleases . . .
>
> The heavens are the LORD's heavens,
> but the earth he has given to human beings. (115:1–3, 16)

God is in heaven; God inhabits the sky. It is an ancient and universal answer, so ancient and universal that we do not know when or where human beings first articulated it. And it may well be the first answer that most people know in their own lives—learned in Sunday school or taught by parents or heard on the wind. Simple, right?

The psalmist's words, "Our God is in the heavens," actually unveil far more complex spiritual possibilities. Unlike the ground and water, sky is beyond our comprehension. Where does it begin or end? How large is it? It is both visible, as the location of heavenly orbs and clouds and colored light, and invisible, as atmosphere and wind. It is a vast cosmos and big skies; it is sunlight warming our face or wind blowing our hair. The sky is multilayered: it consists of a five-layer atmosphere and then outer space. The atmosphere is the world's protective covering, keeping the planet safe from the icy terrors of the deeper heavens. The sky touches the earth, yet its outer edges are infinitely far from us. It is where we always are, what we always breathe, yet at the same time it is a place we can never go without oxygen and special suits and flying machines. We breathe the sky in; we make wishes on stars whose names we do not know. The sky is the most intimate inner space and the most incomprehensible outer reaches of the universe. It is something we see; it is something that remains an invisible presence in our lives.

What does it really mean to say that God is in the heavens?

Every other year or so, my family goes on retreat to a place called Ring Lake Ranch outside of Dubois, Wyoming, in the Wind River Range, a couple of hours east of Yellowstone. On our first visit some years ago, the director warned us to bring flashlights and be careful after dark, for city dwellers were unused to night without electric lights. I was not entirely sure what he meant.[1] But when the sun completely set, it seemed like a thick wool blanket had been pulled over my head. All light disappeared. I had forgotten my flashlight, and I feared I would not make it back to my cabin. Trying not to panic, I sat on the lodge stairs and wondered what to do.

In a few minutes, my eyes adjusted to the night's lesser lights. The moon was bright, but it was not the only source of light. The sky was nearly pulsating with millions of stars, more stars than I had ever seen, some still, some in familiar patterns, some shooting past others toward destinations unknown. I trembled. The cold perhaps? A sudden shock at the power of the night sky? Without a moment's reflection, the words of an old hymn sounded in my mind: "Consider all the worlds thy hands have made."

Consider. Indeed, the word "consider," which comes from the French and literally means to "observe the stars," now serves as a call to reflect upon or study intensely. Consider the sky. That night in Wyoming, I understood that the sky was much more than I knew. It was compelling and frightening. I considered not only my strange insignificance, but I considered God, the one who is Light and made the lights. It was easy to see why thousands of generations of humankind believed God—or the gods—lived in the stars or dwelt in distant realms as a sky deity. In our time, the night sky has become less familiar, as city lights compete with heavenly ones to brighten the dark. But beyond the city, the night sky still dazzles, as it has since before our existence, and will for billions of years to come. The Milky Way, the Northern Lights, constellations north and south, millions of distant planets and moons and suns and comets, all dancing in the dark to some primal pattern that physicists seek and poets extol.

We can also consider the day sky with its clouds and colors. Clouds, of course, are water vapor, part of the great water cycle of rivers and seas and rains. Atmospheric conditions create different sorts of clouds. When water vapor gathers in particular patterns and at particular levels above the earth, these clouds form various kinds of storms from gentle rains to thunderstorms and violent cyclones. Clouds are one way that we "see" the atmosphere, the way in which otherwise invisible currents create these massive puffy pockets of water. Perhaps nearly everyone across the globe, young and old, shares the experience of looking up and seeing shapes in the clouds.

101

Like the stars in the night sky, they are what we see when we gaze up, the first thing we notice above.

During the day, we also see light. The sun is the primary source of daylight, the closest fiery star that warms the world and sends light that we might see. Unlike the dazzling night stars, it is easy to take the day's star for granted; it is a necessary yet oddly ignored fact of life. Yet light, as a spectrum of radiant energy, is the source of our vision. Without the wavelengths of light that strike our retinas and initiate nerve impulses, we would not see at all. Thus, light both enables the mechanism of human seeing and is something we see. This energy, whose primary source is the sun, interacts with our eyes and makes visible all that we perceive. We see because of the light in the sky, and we see the light of the sky. "Then God said, 'Let there be light'; and there was light. And God saw that the light was good" (Gen. 1:3–4). That God "sees" light is a spiritually compelling image. No wonder ancient creeds refer to God as Light from Light.

Thus, the sky, both night and day, makes itself known by what we see. But the skies hold things that are mysteriously unseen as well: dark matter and wind. Indeed, Genesis also speaks of the dark, which exists when light is separated from it, also created by God. The far reaches of space contain what physicists call "dark matter," unknown subatomic particles that cannot be seen and whose existence is inferred from mathematical models of the universe. Dark matter emits no light, yet its invisible presence accounts for gravitational effects on bodies that are visible in the universe. Scientists believe that 84 percent of the entire universe is composed of dark matter and dark energy combined, things that can only be seen by their effects. In the lower reaches of the sky, wind functions in a similar way. It cannot be seen, but we can see what it does. We measure wind by its impact, not by seeing the actual wind. Dark matter in outer space, wind in the layers of atmosphere—powerful yet invisible to us, these forces are part of human experience with the sky.[2]

The sky is not static. The firmament is not fixed. Instead, a dynamic sphere of activity surrounds us. Sometimes we pay attention to it and sometimes not. To say that God is in the sky is *not* to imply that God lives at a certain address above the earth. Instead, it is an invitation to consider God's presence that both reaches to the stars and wafts through our lives as a spiritual breeze.

Consider the Stars

Outside of Guelph, Ontario, is an old Jesuit monastery. There are only a few monks left, but the place still hums with energy. Rechristened the Ignatian Spiritual Centre, the complex includes offices for nonprofit organizations, an organic farm, an old-growth forest that is being restored, and a retreat house. Beyond the old monastery building, at the edge of the farm, there is a walking path for meditation. Traditionally, such paths at a Catholic monastery would trace the final steps of Jesus before his death, the walk called the Stations of the Cross. More recently, such walking paths have been labyrinths, a mazelike walk without any specific biblical reference. But here the path is unique: the Stations of the Cosmos.

The day is crisp, after a warm September the first truly autumn day in Ontario. I was glad for the jacket loaned to me by my hosts. I paused at the entrance. A sign explained:

> Thomas Berry, Passionist priest and cultural historian, argues that our culture needs a "new story" to guide it into a less destructive ecological age. Such a story would integrate the scientific account of the emergence of the universe with an understanding of its inherent sacredness.

The Stations of the Cosmos tells such a story by way of a spiral meditative walk. A spiral representing the entire 13.7 billion years of our cosmic and evolutionary journey is laid out on the ground. Major milestones are marked at a proportional distance along the length of the spiral. Each station presents key points in the universe's time line alongside beautiful photographs that celebrate God's magnificence as revealed in Creation.

I entered the spiral. At the center was a fire pit, symbolizing the big bang, the moment the universe flamed forth. I walked, circling out slowly to the next station, quite far from the center. At this station, a sign appeared marking the clustering of matter into gases and clouds. And so it went, the spiral and the stations of creation. Seventeen stations went by before human beings appeared. Seventeen stations without us—of the walk's twenty-five stations. I looked toward the sky, feeling both amazed and insignificant at the same time. The cosmos is more than we imagine.

Interest in the cosmos is not confined to a spiral walk built by a monastic order. In June 2014, *Time* magazine reported: "Every Sunday night for the past three months, millions of Americans chose to spurn *The Bachelor* and instead accompany astrophysicist Neil deGrasse Tyson on an hour-long trip across the universe."[3] With more than three million viewers per week for three months, Tyson's *Cosmos,* an ambitious television program about the big bang, black holes, dark matter, and climate change, topped all other shows during its run. As the reviewer wrote, "Not terrible for a country where a quarter of the population doesn't get that the earth revolves around the sun."[4]

Critics love ridiculing the large number of Americans who reject scientific ideas. Indeed, a regular feature in American polling is showing how many people do not believe in things like evolution or a multibillion-year-old universe. Such persistent ignorance is regularly blamed on a combination of bad teaching and bad religion, the latter of which is generally thought to issue from fundamentalist preachers and politicians. But the popularity of *Cosmos* points in another direction, that, indeed, large numbers of North Americans—religious, spiritual, and secular people alike—are fascinated by science. Although not much mentioned in the general media, if you want to start a conversation these days on science and faith, in most circles Darwin is passé. Instead, people in thoughtful faith communities are talking about the big bang and multiple-universe theories. They are taking their cues from the likes of *Cosmos,* geneticist Francis Collins, and physicist and priest John Polkinghorne, and they are even reading skeptics like Richard Dawkins and Sam Harris. The North American cultural conversation about science may not always be academically well informed, but it is lively. And much of it centers on science and spirituality.

For more than a decade, people attending events where I speak have asked me questions about physics, emerging understandings of science, and Christian faith. They were not hostile questioners—they were curious and eager inquirers. Since my training is in history and theology, I could not imagine why people were addressing such questions to me. But then I realized that they did not want me to answer the questions. Instead, they wanted to tell a roomful of people that the territory of faith and science was changing and that it was no longer at war. And I could also intuit that these new understandings of faith and science were changing their conception of God.

In one such room, a Presbyterian minister stood up holding the book *Field of Compassion,* by Judy Cannato. "Do you know this author?"

I shook my head no.

He went on, "She's a Roman Catholic, and she writes about how the 'new cosmology' is transforming our spiritual lives."[5]

A new cosmology? Cosmology is the science of the origin, structure, and fate of the universe, an academic discipline of physics, astronomy, mathematics, and philosophy that seeks to explain, well, everything. Cosmology looks beyond the immediate sky toward the distant deeps of space, wondering about where we came from, why we are here, what mysteries are revealed in the stars. Because we cannot directly experience the far reaches of the universe, human beings developed scientific tools to observe, chart, and explain the order of things. Physical cosmology has always had to contend with religious cosmologies, the body of mythologies and doctrines about creation, divine order, and the earth's destiny as related by faith traditions through time. Often physical cosmologies have supported—or been supported by—religious cosmologies. But scientists habitually unsettle theological convention and have found sometimes, especially throughout modern history, their research at odds with customary creation accounts.

That is what makes the big bang so interesting: it presents a cosmology that brings the disparate strands of science and faith back into conversation with one another, with fascinating implications for both. The theory argues that once the universe did not exist. Then, at a particular moment almost fourteen billion years ago, everything that now exists came into being as a singularity of infinitely dense and hot matter. Only seconds after this singularity appeared, it began to expand, flaring forth tiny bits of matter; as the particles and dust cooled, they formed clouds of gases that eventually coalesced into larger bodies, creating the stars, galaxies, planets, and moons. The big-bang theory replaced an older view— the steady-state theory, which had posited a static universe that

constantly produces matter—as the prevailing explanation of physical cosmology at the center of contemporary physics.[6]

The theory was first proposed by Georges Lemaître, a Jesuit
priest, in 1927, two years before Edward Hubble proposed the same
idea. In 1951, the pope suspected that the big-bang theory reopened
the door to Genesis and hailed the theory as scientific proof of Catholicism. Lemaître, however, insisted his was a neutral scientific
theory plain and simple, with no apologetic intention involved.
The big-bang theory coincided with the biological and theological
work of another Jesuit scientist, Pierre Teilhard de Chardin, who
suggested that the cosmos was unfolding in a spiritually purposeful
way, an evolutionary expansion that would culminate in a communal human awakening of complexity and consciousness in what he
called the Omega Point, another way of speaking of God.[7] At times
his work seems to press at the edges of Christian theology toward
new interpretation, yet even theologically conservative Pope Ben-
edict XVI warmly commended Teilhard and praised his insights.[8]
Pope Francis appealed to Teilhard's work in his encyclical on the
environmental crisis.[9] Teilhard de Chardin was a much better theologian than scientist, the opposite of Georges Lemaître. Taken together, however, their work has conspired to a reimagining of
Christian theology, cosmology, and the environment.

The big bang's simplest insight, and the one with the most profound implication for understanding God and contemporary spirituality, is straightforward: everything that exists was created at the
same time; thus all things are connected by virtue of being made of
the same matter. That matter burst forth seconds after the singularity appeared and is all the matter that will ever exist. Throughout
time, that dust has formed and reformed itself into gases, worlds,
and living beings. As theologian Elizabeth Johnson explains:

Out of the big bang, the stars; out of the stardust, the Earth; out of the matter of the Earth, life. Out of the life and death of single-celled creatures, an advancing tide: trilobites, fish, amphibians, insects, flowers, birds, reptiles, and mammals, among whom emerged human beings—mammals with brains so complex that we experience self-conscious intelligence and freedom. According to this scientific theory, everything is connected with everything else. British scientist and theologian Arthur Peacocke explains, "Every atom of iron in our blood would not be there, had it not been produced in some galactic explosion billions of years ago and eventually condensed to form the iron in the crust of the Earth from which we have emerged." *Quite literally, human beings are made of stardust.*[10]

The first time I ever heard anyone in church say that we are "made of stardust" was in an Ash Wednesday sermon. It had been a long time since I had taken college science, and I was not entirely sure I believed the preacher. So I started reading and paying attention to new discoveries in physics, about the big bang and the inflating universe, about dots and strings. Not only were we made of stardust long ago; every day more than sixty tons of cosmic dust fall to the earth, where it mixes with existing soil and enters the food chain. Stardust is a source of ongoing creation. We eat and breathe stardust.[11] I am no scientist, but even I can grasp physicist Brian Greene's claim: "The reality we have known is but a delicate chiffon draped over a thick and richly textured cosmic fabric." There is so much that we cannot see, so much just beyond our awareness.[12]

As I walked through the spiral making up the Stations of the

Cosmos on Jesuit property in Ontario, I considered God. Somehow, God is beyond even this, the big bang, the process of creation, and emerging cosmology. Yet God is not distant from it either. And I wondered: Is God initiator, presence, and horizon, the one behind, within, and just beyond the cosmos?

The Breath of God

About 2.3 billion years ago, give or take a billion years, ancient organisms called cyanobacteria, sort of blue-green algae, appeared on earth. They were a surprising life form, quite unlike their neighbors, the anaerobic organisms that thrived in oceans under an atmosphere of volcanic gases like carbon dioxide, ammonia, and methane. Instead, the cyanobacteria survived by photosynthesis, using energy made from the sun and producing free oxygen as a by-product. The cyanobacteria were a successful little species. Over time, the oxygen they created saturated the oceans and escaped into the atmosphere, where it accumulated. This was bad news for anaerobic creatures, because oxygen is toxic to them. Most of the earth's oldest inhabitants died off and were replaced by a new group of oxygen-breathing creatures. Scientists refer to this as the Great Oxygenation Event. And thus, the air that we breathe came into being. The newly oxygenated atmosphere supported respiration, the system that animals use for energy. The protective covering of the planet, made up of special molecules of oxygen called ozone, keeps life safe from harmful ultraviolet radiation. With air, biological diversity flourished and the earth as we know it was born. The atmosphere is humanity's womb, and without it all terrestrial life would perish.

The second verse of the biblical book of Genesis reads, "The earth was a formless void and darkness covered the face of the deep, while a wind from God swept over the face of the waters." The animating agent of creation was the air, in Hebrew *ruach,* a word signifying "wind," "spirit," or "breath." At each stage of creation, God breathes new life into the world, the spirit speaks all things into being. The beginning of Genesis reads like a poetic version of the Great Oxygenation Event. God is literally the air upon which all earthly life depends. The breath of God creates a sacred environment, the atmosphere of existence.

The Abrahamic religions refer to God as Spirit, the holy wind animating life. Judaism and Islam understand God's breath as an extension of God's being in the world; Christianity refers to the Spirit as the third person of the Triune God, a full embodiment of God's generative character. In the Gospel of John, Jesus breathes on his followers and imparts the gift of the Spirit, thus signifying the re-creation of the world through the church. This is the mysterious presence, unseen but active, manifested across the world, giving life to all goodness and beauty. Richer than a metaphor, God's spirit is the air, the wind. For Buddhists, to breathe is to achieve mindfulness, the awareness of one's breath within the breath of all, a form of focused respiration that joins a practitioner to the central realities of existence and opens the path to attain nirvana.

Hinduism likewise emphasizes the divine nature of breath: "From Him springs forth the breath of life" (Mundaka Upanishad 2:1:3). Indeed, the Sanskrit word for faith, *visvas,* means "to breathe easy; to have trust and be free of fear." Like those of the Abrahamic traditions, Hindu sacred scriptures also place breath at the center of creation. The great Hymn of Creation in India's most ancient text, the Rig Veda, names the Absolute: "That One Thing, breathless, breathed by its own nature" (10:129:2). Breath not only supports life, but is life: "Every single movement in the cosmos is a movement of the *vishwaprana,* the Cosmic Breath."[13] Native Americans believed that wind spirits, from the four directions of the world, united all earthly things and that the wind also connected all things past and present, forming a universal spiritual community of humanity. Thus, the wind unifies the natural world with the human community, creating a single spiritual reality through which everything exists.

Indeed, in the biblical traditions, God is identified as spirit. Hebrew names this *Ruach ha-Kodesh,* the spirit of YHWH, or the Spirit of the Lord. This spirit is the sustaining force of the universe, the invisible presence necessary for all life, the breath of God at creation and through the words of the prophets. This spirit is often understood as the feminine aspect of the biblical divinity, and the term *ruach* can be rendered as either male or female. While an important part of Judaism, the notion of God-as-spirit comes to the fore in the Christian New Testament, where the Greek word *pneuma* is used almost four hundred times to describe a sacred wind, divine breath, or the holiness of life, imbuing the whole story of Jesus with spiritual urgency. *Pneuma* is personalized as the Holy Spirit, an embodiment of God's own life, represented most often as a dove or other bird, sometimes in the female form. In the book of Acts, a rush of wind gives birth to the church, the spiritual body intended to carry on Jesus's work in the world.

This short survey points to a startling characteristic of world spiritualities: it is impossible to think of God without considering the atmosphere. Our experience of God, our very life, cannot be separated from our need for air. "Air is an intimate element," wrote Catholic priest John O'Donohue. "It gets right into you through your breathing and your blood, into the heart of your life. . . . God [is] breath and tenderness."[14] In human experience, our understanding of atmosphere is both a spiritual and scientific reality, a concern of the soul and biology. In both cases, we are speaking of

111

what animates life. From the perspective of faith, God creates through God's breath, and we humans breathe the very spirit of God. And the scientific elegance of the Great Oxygenation Event underscores the necessary harmony between air and existence. Perhaps it is right to say that God is the very atmosphere of our lives.

What happens, however, if God can't breathe?

Consider the Skies

Although the air we breathe is the basis of life and spirit, it is surprisingly easy to take it for granted. The very phrase, "It is just the air that we breathe," indicates lack of attention, something so ordinary we fail to notice it. The sky is like that. After all, this atmosphere has sustained terrestrial life for about six hundred million years. With such an extended history, it is not hard to imagine that the atmosphere we have always known will always be here.

But the atmosphere is changing. In the same way that 2.3 billion years ago a species began throwing oxygen into the earth's climate balance, we human beings are now causing more carbon dioxide to be emitted into the atmosphere than can be absorbed. This has led to a 40 percent increase in carbon dioxide levels since 1750, with the fastest increases coming in the last three decades. The rise in carbon dioxide is throwing off the climatic balance, causing a rise in earth's average temperature, leading to elevated sea levels, warmer, more acidic oceans, and radically intensified weather patterns. NASA maintains a global climate change website that updates the planet's vital signs. As of 2014, carbon dioxide levels are at 399.60 parts per million (since the beginning of human civilization, our atmosphere has contained about 275 ppm of carbon dioxide); global temperature is up 1.4 degrees Fahrenheit since 1880;

arctic ice is down some 13 percent in the last decade; the earth is losing 250 billion tons of land ice per year; and seas are rising at a rate of 3.18 millimeters per year.[15] None of this is good.

Indeed, it is very bad. We refer to it as climate change. But British journalist George Monbiot calls that a "ridiculously neutral term for the biggest potential catastrophe humankind has even encountered," saying we should rename it "climate breakdown." Others have suggested "climate disruption" or "climate collapse."[16] And 97 percent of the world's climate scientists say that we caused it, mostly by burning fossil fuels—oil, coal, and gas—and throwing their emissions into the atmosphere for the last two hundred years. Fossil fuels have made human life easier and more prosperous, but as environmentalist Bill McKibben explains, they have fundamentally altered the air we breathe:

> It's also, of course, why we have global warming and acid oceans; in essence we've spent two hundred years digging up all that ancient carbon, combining it with oxygen for a moment to explode the pistons that take us to the drive-through, and then releasing it into the atmosphere, where it accumulates as carbon dioxide. That cloud of carbon is nothing more than a ghostly reflection of the pools of oil and veins of coal where it once dwelled—each gallon of gasoline represents a hundred tons of ancient plants.[17]

Changing the atmosphere is changing the planet, transforming our "cozy, taken-for-granted earth" into a "a planet, a real one, with melting poles and dying forests and a heaving, corrosive sea, raked by winds, strafed by storms, scorched by heat. An inhospitable place."[18] Are we, as McKibben suggests, "running Genesis backward," decreating the world?[19]

The ground is the earth's body, water its lifeblood, and the atmosphere its lungs. And the planet is sick. Or, as the *Millennium Ecosystem Assessment* report concludes, the earth is "wearing out and will soon become exhausted, incapable of supporting life as we know it."[20] Scientists call this new epoch in world history the Age of the Anthropocene, a period in which we human beings have decisively reshaped the environment, mostly through our addiction to fossil fuels. A recent article in the *Economist* explains how we arrived at the Anthropocene:

> Although the natural fluxes of carbon dioxide into and out of the atmosphere are still more than ten times larger than the amount that humans put in every year by burning fossil fuels, the human addition matters disproportionately because it unbalances those natural flows. . . . A small change in income can, in the absence of a compensating change in outlays, have a disastrous effect. The result of putting more carbon into the atmosphere than can be taken out of it is a warmer climate, a melting Arctic, higher sea levels, improvements in the photosynthetic efficiency of many plants, an intensification of the hydrologic cycle of evaporation and precipitation, and new ocean chemistry.
>
> All of these have knock-on effects both on people and on the processes of the planet. More rain means more weathering of mountains. More efficient photosynthesis means less evaporation from croplands. And the changes in ocean chemistry are the sort of thing that

can be expected to have a direct effect on the geological record if carbon levels rise far enough.[21]

In short, we have tipped the atmosphere's balance, not unlike the cyanobacteria did millions of years ago, when they managed to unintentionally alter the planet. The notion that we have changed the world in ways that threaten our own existence is both depressing and frightening. With oil, coal, and gas as our bricks, humanity has built a carbon tower of Babel, now poised to crash down.

There are those who deny, yes. And some of them use religion to back up their claims. But something else is happening as well. Growing awareness of the crisis has motivated many—many millions—to act on behalf of the atmosphere. Over the last decade, thousands of people in churches and synagogues have quizzed me regarding climate issues. One of the most significant conversations occurring in faith communities is that concerning climate change—especially as it relates to theology, spirituality, and social justice for the planet. People shared stories of reading groups studying climate change, gave me brochures about nonprofit organizations they had started in their communities to reduce carbon emissions, and told me how they turned plots of unused church land into soil farms and local food gardens. It was like a secret legion of green activists building solar panels, teaching "creation care" to their children, and marching against the Keystone pipeline.

Jim Antal is president of the Massachusetts Conference of the United Church of Christ and a well-known activist on issues of climate change. Jim became fascinated with the sky when, in 1957, he and his older brother skipped school to photograph the transit of Mercury across the sun. That day, the sky came to symbolize freedom and limitless imagination. When he later read Rachel Carson, Aldo

Leopold, Barry Commoner, Jacques Ellul, and Paul Ehrlich, he drew connections between environmentalism and faith, saying, "The more I learned about life's interdependency and fragility, the clearer my vocation became." As a pastor and denominational leader, his vision is clear:

> All of life is connected. We are all in this together. We all live at the same address—and at this moment, the address found above every door, on every dwelling, is 400 ppm [400 parts per million of carbon dioxide in the atmosphere]. There was a song we used to sing at disarmament rallies in the 1980s. The refrain went: "We're all a family under one sky, we're a family under one sky." It's even more true now than it was then, and we need to work to prevent that beautiful sky from falling down.[22]

In 2013, Jim drafted his denomination's policy on fossil-fuel divestment, guaranteeing that money from the United Church of Christ would no longer support companies that contribute to global warming.[23] He still serves as the Massachusetts conference president while also teaching other denominations, nonprofit organizations, colleges and universities, and individual investors how to divest from fossil-fuel companies.

Mallory McDuff, a professor of environmental studies, calls people like Jim Antal and the many congregations involved with saving the skies "natural saints," those who have woven together their own spiritual lives with the life of the planet.[24] Paul Hawken's *Blessed Unrest* explores the larger dimensions of such engagement and reports that more than a million organizations—many faith-based, many not—are now working worldwide toward "ecological sustainability and social justice." What I have witnessed are people forming such organizations related to their religious communities, Roman Catholics, evangelicals, liberal Protestants, Jews, Muslims, Hindus, and Buddhists. Thousands of other groups, however, are more broadly spiritual, pluralistic, or humanist in nature. Hawken claims that we are now in the midst of the largest social movement in human history, with tens of millions of people involved in mostly grassroots communities trying to address issues of climate change. It is an organic movement to "restore grace, justice, and beauty to the world," thus constituting a global spiritual revolution to save (from Latin *salvus,* meaning "to heal") the earth.[25]

As people are working for earthly salvation, they have begun an equally organic process of reinterpreting their theologies to be more sensitive and aware of creation. In some cases, such theological reflection is the work of trained scholars and religious leaders, issued as books and position papers from university presses or denominational headquarters. However, most of this work is coming from the grass roots. In a natural expression of the spiritual revolution, people are seeking to relocate God and understand their sacred stories in the context of climate disruption. If we humans created the Age of the Anthropocene, we can certainly reimagine how our cherished faith and wisdom stories can help us navigate the rough weather ahead. The new vision knits spirituality, science, and social justice into an earthy fabric of meaning and faith. And it is arising from many religious traditions at the same time, as if carried on the currents of the atmosphere itself.

The winds of worry are howling. Yet if one listens carefully, there is evident the whisper of God. Change is in the air.

Vertical Faith

On a visit to Kentucky, a minister acted as my host, driving me to events and making sure I was comfortable and fed. Friendly and knowledgeable about a wide range of subjects, he talked about good bourbons, local farming, climate change, and the poems of Wendell Berry. I asked him to tell me about the church he served.

"The church building is one of those intimidating ones—it goes straight up. The first time I saw it, I got neck strain," he said, laughing. "The walls are high, with towering white pillars, and it has a very tall steeple. And it sits on one of the highest hills in the county."

He paused for a moment, thinking before he went on.

"Everything about it is vertical: the building, the theology," he continued. "It orients people away from the earth; it's about 'me and God' and being with Jesus after death. The architecture points toward heaven." And then in a compassionate, not critical, tone he added, "Their faith is vertical too."

In some ways, the architecture of a temple pointing toward the sky represents humanity's most primal spiritual impulse. Religion itself most likely began when some ancient ancestor looked up to the sky, perhaps a glorious sunset or a jeweled night, gasped in wonder, raised her hands in worship, and uttered a word that came to mean God. Sky gods and goddesses are regular features in almost all world religions from the earliest ones until now; a heavenly father or queen of heaven has occupied the heights of human spiritual imagination for eons.

A tall church does not end up on a high hill by accident. For centuries, churches with soaring steeples have pierced the sky. This vertical architecture symbolized the fundamental structure of an old theology: God was in heaven, and humankind was here on earth. A gap existed between God and us, and the church served as mediator between the two realms, communicating the word of God down to us and providing a pathway of salvation up to God. In a very real way, churches have functioned like elevators of divine things; the top floor is, as it were, life's last trip.

In the Hebrew and Christian scriptures, the word "heaven" often means the sky. The Hebrew word for "heaven," *shamayim,* referred to everything in both the earth's atmosphere and outer space. The writers of both the Old and New Testaments thought that the universe had three closely stacked tiers, an underworld, this world, and the heavens. The top tier, the heavens or the "high place," was considered God's habitat, and the Bible occasionally depicts God as seated on a throne there. But heaven was far more than a cosmic throne room. The sky is a sacred space, endowed with divine character, giving light, warmth, wind, and rain to the earth. In an interesting theological twist, "heaven" became interchangeable with "God" in rabbinic tradition; *shamayim,* without the article, became a regular expression for the name of God. Indeed, there are many places in the Hebrew Bible where it is difficult to tell if the writer is speaking of the sky or of God, for heaven, like God, issues decrees, directs the destiny of humankind, and answers prayers.

Heaven is both a location in the larger cosmos and a spiritual geography that represents divine attributes and intention. Judaism and Christianity urge followers to seek heavenly things, to model their lives on heavenly virtues, and to have hope in heaven. In the New Testament, heaven most often appears as the "kingdom of heaven," God's political and social vision for humanity, an idea that Jesus uses to criticize the Roman Empire's oppressive domination system. Jesus's own prayer, "Thy kingdom come. Thy will be done, on earth as it is in heaven" (Matt. 6:10), seeks to align earthly ethics with the divine order of God's dwelling. According to Jesus, heaven is an intrusive reality, the realm of God hovering all around, sometimes even synonymous with God.[26] The Bible says the kingdom of heaven "has come near" (Matt. 4:17), and if heaven is nearby, so is God. Heaven is here-and-now, not there-and-then.

To speak of heaven, therefore, is another way to speak of the earth. But the vision for the earth that "heaven" presents is not in keeping with the world's violence, oppression, and injustice; rather, it is an alternate vision of peace, blessing, and abundance, the world as God intended it to be. Because heaven embodies the sort of virtues that human beings long for, it is depicted as a place of perfection, a paradise. But heaven has also been pictured as far away, unattainable in this life, a blessed reward for having lived with patience and grace in the suffering of this world. Accordingly, the best we could get here is a foretaste of heaven, a glimpse of the glory that awaits after death. For centuries, we have distanced heaven, placing it beyond reach and making it impossible to experience. If you think about it, however, heaven is not far away at all. We may walk on the ground, but the rest of our bodies move through the sky all the time—the troposphere, the layer of the atmosphere that extends upward from the earth's surface to about thirty-five thousand feet. The sky begins at our feet. Thus, we actually live in the heavens now, in the space in which earth and sky meet. God's "heavenly" presence is the air we breathe.

Some people, I suppose, might worry about losing a sense of the mysterious and transcendent aspects of God by making the divine presence too immanent, overly identified with the world (and sky) around us. Vertical theology was very good at maintaining the separation between God and us, thus preserving God's unknowable sanctity, the distant wonder of the divine. There is a point to be made here, one even understood by the most passionate mystics. God is not completely accessible to us.

To say that God is the air we breathe or in the sky that surrounds us does not negate the mystery of God. There is another location where earth and sky touch: at the horizon. The horizon is strange; it is the line where heaven and ground touch, but it moves when you approach it. Physicists talk about a "cosmic horizon," the edge of the universe past what we see. Horizons retain an aspect of mystery, even a sort of transcendence. They are never quite where they once were; they always shift. To speak of God and sky is to speak of intimacy, but it also hints at a different sort of distance as well—not like God sitting far above the world, but perhaps more like God at the horizon. Just beyond what we can see, there is more. Not God above, but God at the edge, the edge of the visible world, the horizon of mystery.

When I think of the far-off qualities of God, I no longer think "up"; instead, I consider God beyond the horizon, just beyond the place where sky meets the ground. The Spirit calls our gaze outward, to lift our eyes to the edge. The spiritual revolution is the shift from a vertical God to God-with-us. Dirt and water are understandable and tangible, icons of earthy sacredness. But we need to sky to remind us that no matter how close God is, God is still the One who hovers at the horizon.

"What did you do to try to shift their awareness from a vertical faith to a more horizontal one?" I queried the Kentucky pastor.

"We planted a garden," he replied. "We grow food. Lots of food. For the local food bank. We've studied the soil and learned about global warming. We're finding God in the garden. It isn't quite as vertical as it used to be. Heaven is getting downright earthy."

And that, of course, is another vision of heaven: a garden. Where dirt, water, and air all come together to feed us, to heal the earth, to produce the atmosphere we need to survive. Paradise, really. Here and now.

John 3:16

For several years at most American sporting events, there would be someone in the crowd holding up a large sign: "John 3:16." The New Testament verse reads, "For God so loved the world that he gave his only Son, so that everyone who believes in him may not perish but may have eternal life." The sign holders intended this to be an evangelistic device, a witness to their faith. John 3:16 acted as a code word for a sermon meant to convince people to give their lives to Jesus and get born again. I have not seen the sign for a while, though. It offended many people, especially those who are not evangelical Christians, leading me to wonder if stadium owners and television producers finally found a way to ban it.

But I am sort of sorry that they did. The word translated "world" is the Greek term *kosmos*. John 3:16 is not a call to personal salvation or revivalist fervor. Instead, it offers a glimpse of Christianity's central cosmology. The emphasis is on the first line, and the verse essentially says, "*God so loved the universe,* that God entered the *cosmos* in the form of a gift, the gift of Jesus, that we might trust in this divine presence and experience abundance." It is not a story of getting saved from hell—unless that hell is the one we are making through our destruction of the atmosphere. Rather, it is the Christian way of saying that God dwells in the universe we also inhabit, that we might experience the life of heaven here and now.

Danish theologian Niels Gregersen refers to this as "deep incarnation," the manifestation of God "in, with, under, and as" flesh, with a human body, a body made from the same stardust that makes up all other bodies. Elizabeth Johnson explains Gregersen's "deep incarnation":

Born of a woman (Gal. 4:4) and the Hebrew gene pool, Jesus of Nazareth was a creature of earth, a complex unit of minerals and fluids, an item in the carbon, oxygen, and nitrogen cycles, a moment in the biological evolution of this planet. Like all human beings, he carried within himself the signature of the supernovas and the geology and life history of the Earth. The atoms comprising his body once belonged to other creatures.[27]

The heavens live in us, with us, as the reality under all things, as part of creation. In Christian theology, Jesus brings together sky and earth, the God who dwells with us. John 3:16 proclaims that this divine indwelling is life. Other religions say similar things in different ways—God is closer than we imagine, and the ever active spirit is animating the world.

The sky is sacred: the sphere of dynamic forces and mysterious emptiness. Looking toward the heavens, I think of Jonathan Edwards's words from the eighteenth century: "When we behold the light and brightness of the sun, the golden edges of an evening cloud, or the beauteous rainbow, we behold the adumbrations of His glory and goodness, and in the blue sky, of His mildness and gentleness."[28] We cannot love something without seeing it, and it is hard to see the sky. Yet love it we must. For loving the atmosphere, knowing that it is God's abode and God's breath, will give us the courage to save it.

If we fail to comprehend the sacredness of the sky, that the heavens are the spiritual currents of life, then how can we survive? Without breath, we die. So will earth as we know it. Or, as noted in a remark attributed to Hildegard of Bingen almost a thousand years ago: "If we fall in love with creation deeper and deeper, we will respond to its endangerment with passion."[29] God really does love the cosmos. And so must we.

Dirt, water, and sky are three of the four classical elements (the fourth is fire) that ancient people believed constituted the cosmos.[30] This simple taxonomy provided a map of meaning that enabled our ancestors to better understand the world. The four elements formed the basis of science and philosophy, but reached their most elegant expression when describing God and spirituality, the territory where the sacred met the mundane. Indeed, these earthy elements were understood as gifts of the gods, icons of holiness, or aspects of the divine being.

With the advent of modern science, when the four elements were rightly replaced by more sophisticated understandings of geology, biology, and physics, the spiritual dimensions of earth, water, air, and fire receded from our imaginations. Sacred traditions replete with metaphors of God in the elements were replaced by modern theological arguments—about facts and religious texts, correct doctrine, creation versus science, the need to prove God's existence, how to be saved, and which church offers the right way to heaven. These are the questions of vertical faith, the mechanics of elevator church.

Although some people are still interested in those modern theological questions, many more are not. They are turning away from religious institutions that insist on asking them. The spiritual revolution is, in part, a rejection of the theological questions that have shaped Western religious life for the last four centuries or so.

But to turn away from something also means to turn toward something new. The turn from the vertical God has redirected our spiritual attention toward the world, the horizons of faith. Seventy years ago, C. S. Lewis wrote a book called *Mere Christianity;* for years, I have joked with friends that any such theology today should be called *Here Christianity*. In turning, there is also a returning—to a deep spiritual memory of earth, water, sky, and fire. In these chapters, I have pointed out how contemporary people are finding God in and with dirt, water, and sky—as the fire of the Spirit illuminates the way throughout. This is the spiritual revolution.

Despite the fact that it is contemporary, it is not really new. It is a recovery of something very old—discovering the ancient spiritual subtext of the world's religions. That subtext has always been the thread of faith, too often obscured, but sometimes it becomes visible again when people are brave enough to ask the question, "Where is God?" During the 1640s, for example, when England was torn apart by a civil war, Robert Herrick, an Anglican vicar and poet, wondered where to find God in a time of violence and religious extremism:

TO FIND GOD

Weigh me the fire; or canst thou find
A way to measure out the wind?
Distinguish all those floods that are
Mixed in that wat'ry theater,
And taste thou them as saltless there,
As in their channel first they were.
Tell me the people that do keep
Within the kingdoms of the deep;
Or fetch me back that cloud again,
Beshivered into seeds of rain.
Tell me the motes, dust, sands, and spears
Of corn, when summer shakes his ears;

Show me that world of stars, and whence
They noiseless spill their influence.
This if thou canst; then show me Him
That rides the glorious cherubim.[31]

Earth, water, sky, and fire. There is God. A spiritual revolution and ancient awareness. Our natural habitat.

Part Two

HUMAN GEOGRAPHY

———

Without stories, the land turns into real estate.
—*Mark Abley*

When we entered the front door of the house on Autumn Avenue, we felt we had come home. The American foursquare-style house, built in 1912, sat behind overgrown azaleas on a quiet street in Memphis. We were on a short visit from California, my new husband and I, preparing to move to Tennessee, so I could take up a position at Rhodes College. We had looked at many houses already, and none seemed right. We arrived at this one and walked up the path to the wide porch. A white porch swing hung there, swaying just a bit in the afternoon breeze, like an invitation to sit, sip iced tea, and chat. I squeezed my husband's hand, and I could swear I felt the baby kick. The front door was original, beautiful aged oak with leaded stained glass.

Stepping across the threshold, we found ourselves in another world. The entryway was nearly as big as our apartment; the carved wooden staircase curved gracefully toward the second floor, where a window seat was stationed under a stained-glass window on the landing. An oaken beam and columns framed the wide door into the living room, where a fireplace with the original pottery tiles and wooden mantle served as the room's focal point. Floor-to-ceiling pocket doors separated the living room from the large dining room, whose main feature was a bay window designed to showcase the Christmas tree. None of the wood had ever been painted. The floors, beams, columns, doors, and moldings were original to the house, aged like fine antiques.

Beautiful, yes. But also worn. She was shabby-chic to be sure. Original light fixtures had been replaced by modern ones, the doorknobs looked like the cheapest choice from a home-improvement store, and plywood closets had been carelessly installed in bedrooms. There was no heat in the kitchen or laundry room, the windows needed to be washed and reglazed, and a second-floor bathroom sagged perilously above the living room. There were problems here, lots of them, hidden behind those walls.

But this house had spirit. And we loved it.

We moved in August 1997, a few weeks before our daughter was born. The first thing we did was to remove the haphazard closets and create a nursery. We would do many things to the house— restore fixtures, strip old floors, make the place more habitable—but we never painted the glorious wood. Mostly, however, I learned its stories. The house was built as a mirror twin to the house next door; the pair were gifts to two maiden sisters, the daughters of a prominent Memphis doctor. Our house was clearly outfitted by the more romantic of the two girls, with its pink rose windows and round columns; the neighboring house was more modern and edgy in its color choices and square appointments. The sisters shared the driveway. Stairways faced one another from the matching front porches, providing easy access across the drive to each other's homes without going out to the street.

The house was a gift, and it always felt like one. After the sisters died, our house went on to be owned by a pastor with many children, and then another family. Through the early twentieth century, the house was full of energy and laughter and even history, as its inhabitants contributed to the life of the city and a few had gone off to war. Someone had even run a small school in the living room for a time. It would be impossible to count the number of people who went in and out that front door, for mundane purposes, social visits, or bearing news. Thousands, I imagine. In the garage, there was a jumble of things people had left behind—old license plates, broken baby carriages, gardening tools, boxes of useless dishes, once stylish chairs, and auto parts. I thought of it as an archaeological tell. A possum, however, thought of it as her home.

In the 1960s, however, the neighborhood was scheduled to be torn down to make way for a new freeway, part of the vast interstate highway network. Similar houses on streets all around Autumn Avenue fell to the wrecking ball until the citizens of Memphis rebelled against the plan and challenged it all the way to the U.S. Supreme Court in an effort to save the historic neighborhood. For twenty years, the future of our house hung in the balance, the streets all around consisting of empty lots where grand houses had once stood. Our house had been neglected and occupied by a series of uncaring renters but had somehow survived. Eventually, a man— who worked for Habitat for Humanity and loved old houses— bought it and coaxed it back to life. And thus began a new chapter for the house on Autumn Avenue.

Our daughter was born in October 1997, and we brought her home to the nursery, which had peach-colored walls. The neighbors came with casseroles, offering food to the newborn's family as a gesture of welcome. People from church stopped by while out walking or to just to chat. We befriended other parents as they navigated baby strollers down Autumn Avenue's bumpy sidewalks. When I returned to work at the college, my students would come by the house to work on papers or projects or play with the baby. And I often held classes in my living room. Coworkers would stop by from the college, and we would talk while sitting on the swing, the little one on my lap.

Family and friends visited from other states. We held dinner parties and birthday parties and hosted church groups. We lugged a ten-foot Christmas tree into the dining room and wrapped the stairway with pine boughs. We added new stories to the tales of Autumn Avenue, like the time our porch furniture was stolen in broad daylight while I sat in the living room or when our neighbors turned out en masse to search for our lost dog. Of course, they are probably still laughing at my bemoaning the fact that the *New York Times* did not deliver in Memphis, my thwarted attempts to grow tomatoes in the backyard's hot red clay, or my discovery that the words "fresh" and "vegetables" were a bit of an oxymoron in local restaurants. I never really understood Memphis, the world of the Old South, where we found ourselves.

But I loved that house, this wonderfully hospitable home that both sheltered my new family and opened itself so generously to the world, a storied place of habitation. Somehow we knew we did not own it; rather, the house seemed to own us. We were its stewards, its caretakers for a time in the longer history of its life. We planted a tree in the front yard to honor our daughter, an October Glory maple, in celebration of her birth month. We put down roots.

And then, unexpectedly, my husband got a job offer in Washington, D.C. Just three years after we arrived, we left. We wondered if it was possible to take the house with us.

I have not returned very often. But I keep up with some of the old neighbors. They tell me that the maple is tall, full, and healthy—the most beautiful tree on the street. Every October, when it blazes red, they remember the couple from California and their baby girl who lived in the house with the open door.

Roots, home, neighborhood, and community—these are the geographies of our lives, the places where God dwells.

Roots

We return to the lives of those who have gone before
us, a perplexing mobius strip, until we come home,
eventually, to ourselves.

—*Colum McCann*

One summer vacation, my husband and I were visiting historical sites on Maryland's eastern shore. Armed with a list from the Internet of historic houses, graveyards, and churches, we followed back roads and traveled by ferry to little-remembered locations of early American history. The Maryland counties between the Chesapeake Bay and the Atlantic Ocean are among the oldest settled parts of the United States. Once home to the Choptank Indians, they are marked by tiny Colonial towns and made famous by James Michener in his novel *Chesapeake*.

After exploring an old Episcopal church, my husband asked, "What next?"

"There's a Quaker meetinghouse not far from here," I replied. "Outside of Easton. Let's go there."

We drove up a country road toward Easton. Before we entered its historic downtown, a modest sign pointed off the road: "Third Haven Meeting House." We turned into the property, bounded by an aged brick wall, onto a rough driveway lined with even older trees. The summer sunlight fell through the foliage upon a white clapboard building with green trim, neat and simple. We were the only people on the property, and a sort of profound quiet engulfed us. If it had been a Catholic church, monks would have been chanting. But it was a meetinghouse for the Society of Friends, also known as the Quakers, the most radical of seventeenth-century Protestants, those who eschewed all outward ritual and religious hierarchy in favor of silence and finding the inner light within.

"It is old," I said. We parked and walked up to the front porch. "I wonder if it is open."

My husband looked through the window, not the smooth modern kind, but glass pocked with imperfections and rippled patterns. "Pretty," he said. He tried the latch.

The door swung open to reveal a cathedral of simplicity. The scent of old wood overtook me; the vision of light falling across rows of plain benches made me gasp. The building was both empty and full at the same time, inviting all seekers to come and sit and listen. Surely, if God spoke, God spoke within these walls.

We stayed for more than an hour, perhaps longer, exploring every corner of the place. Climbing stairs to the loft, sitting on the elders' bench, running our figures over the glazed windowpanes. We read the history pamphlet provided to visitors, "Old Third Haven Meeting House 1684," and learned that George Fox himself, founder of the Friends, had visited Quakers in this area about ten years before the meetinghouse had been constructed. Those who met here, initially in houses as "meetings" and then in this building, had been among the first English settlers to oppose slavery, championed complete equality in God, and contributed to making religious toleration a reality in the colony.

I did not want to leave. I wanted to stay forever, embraced by the spare holiness. I sensed a connection with the place, the strange sensation of once having been there, even though I had never even entered a Quaker meetinghouse before.

"Do you want to go?" my husband asked.

"Not really," I replied. "It feels like . . . like . . . a kind of spiritual home. I feel like I'm home."

We left reluctantly, placing a donation in a small box by the door. We walked around the large churchyard, peeked in the "new" building (dating from Victorian times), and then departed.

"Do you want to go somewhere else?" he asked.

"Where could we possibility go after that?" I said. "What a remarkable place."

Three years later, I was doing genealogical research into my mother's family. I had tried many times to trace her roots on Ancestry.com, but had failed. After abandoning the project for a year, I returned to the website to look at added information, a new family tree. The line reached back in history: my mother, her father, her grandfather, his father . . . to one Andrew Orem, who was born in Scotland, came to Maryland, and married a woman named Eleanor Morris at the Third Haven Quaker Meeting in 1678.

The Easton Quakers were my ancestors. Those who began my family in the New World had left behind their familial Anglicanism or Presbyterianism to join the ranks of the Friends in Maryland, where they listened to George Fox preach on the inner light. They were the very people who formed that society, constructed that building, fell in love and formed families, listened to God within, and learned to follow Jesus's way sheltered by those clapboard walls. Hidden by layers of history, now recovered to sight. I found them.

But, of course, I already had. Three summers before in the silence of an old meetinghouse. I may never have been there before, but they had been. And I recognized it in my bones. I found my roots.

"Where Is God?" and Roots

My search for family had begun a few years earlier, shortly after I turned fifty. I had returned home from a business trip exhausted. Tired of airplanes and hotels, I blurted out to my husband, "I wish somebody would just ground me."

As soon as the words came from my lips, I felt an overwhelming need for connection, an urgent desire to know where my family had come from and what their lives were like. My own parents had died and had left only snippets of family stories. I felt as if I had inherited a few puzzle pieces, with no larger picture to guide me in putting them together.

My husband looked at me quizzically.

"Maybe I don't need to be grounded," I continued more deliberately, "Maybe I just need to find my roots—the ground from which I came, what really grounds me." Thus, the journey to find my ancestors began. And I quickly realized it was about more than biology. It was about my soul.

Honoring ancestors is a nearly universal spiritual practice. In some religions, it appears as ancestor worship or praying to those who have gone before. In biblical traditions, the call to attend to our roots takes the form of a commandment: "Honor your father and your mother" (Exod. 20:12). This is an injunction not only to respect our immediate parents, but to appreciate and remember—or, as it says in Leviticus (19:3), to "revere"—our fathers and mothers, who went before. This forms a spiritual thread of family through time; honoring our ancestors is an obligation of faith.

Just as God is found in the immediate experience of the world around us, God is also with human beings through history. Finding God-with-us is a spiritual practice of memory, connection through time with our ancestors—Christians call it the "communion of saints"; Jews refer to this as *l'dor va'dor,* "generation to generation." Knowing these roots ultimately roots us in God, who is Father and Mother of us all.

But how can we revere those we do not know?

Rooting Around in History

The *New York Times* refers to ours as a "genealogy-crazed era." Surprising genealogy stories involving celebrities make headlines: Barack Obama and Sarah Palin are distant cousins; Emma Watson, star of the Harry Potter movies, is related to an actual sixteenth-century witch; a white supremacist learns—on a television talk show—that he is 14 percent black. Television shows like the international hit series *Who Do You Think You Are?,* America's *Finding Your Roots with Henry Louis Gates, Jr.,* and *Faces of America,* and Canada's *Ancestors in the Attic* trace the family trees of politicians, authors, and movie stars and share the findings with eager viewers. PBS recently added *Genealogy Roadshow* to its lineup, a program on which regular Americans submit DNA samples and have their family trees traced back multiple centuries. In June 2014, a cover story in *Harper's* magazine featured "America's ancestry craze," saying that with genomic testing "a new world has opened up for adoptees, African Americans, the descendants of Holocaust survivors, and anyone else cut off from her origins" to trace their roots.[1]

Every year, 14 million or so people sign into the global website Ancestry.com to search out their familial past, a number that doubled between 2009 and 2012. Ancestry.com is far from the only online genealogy community; there are thousands of such tools, with some sites attracting large numbers of amateur and professional researchers. In December 2010 alone, the top ten genealogy websites combined exceeded 17.5 million visitors. Global Industry Analysts (GIA) estimates that 84 million people spend anywhere from $1,000 to $18,000 a year on genealogical research, including pricey DNA tests to find a physical connection to their past. Bloomberg Business reports that "genealogy ranks second only to porn as the most searched topic online," claiming that some online sites can "easily" develop "into an addiction."[2]

Of course, this is not entirely new—one can think of Alex Haley's 1976 novel *Roots* and the award-winning miniseries of the same name tracing the family saga of Kunta Kinte, the final episode of which can still claim fame as the third most highly rated American television show ever broadcast. Or the Mormons' Family History Library and records vault in Utah, one of the largest world's genealogy collections. Then, of course, there are vast peerage records for English noble families; lineages of kings and queens from nations around the world; and the line of popes of the Catholic Church stretching back to the apostle Peter. Human beings are keepers of family lists stretching back through time. And when the lists are lost, destroyed, or damaged, we go looking for them.

Why do we do this? Keep those lists? Search for them? Spend time, energy, and money tracing who we really are?

Some point out that records are kept for economic reasons, to support patriarchy, maintain tribal or racial purity, or prove political legitimacy.[3] True enough. Genealogy is used for all those purposes. But how do we account for our surprise when we gaze at an old photograph and see our own face? Our squeal when we find the name of our first ancestor to make her way to a new nation in digitized forms like old passenger lists or immigration records? Or our smile when, by fluke or luck, we find the citizenship papers of a great-great-grandparent in a library? Those moments are more than economic inheritance or patriarchal lineage. They are moments when our hearts seem to stop, when we sense a connection through time and fall silent in the mystery of the past and who we are in the present.

Why this interest in ancestry and lineage? Few of us will discover that we are heirs to a great title, a vast estate or wealth, or even a legacy of fame. Most people come from humble roots, are descendants of farmers and shopkeepers and soldiers and peasants and slaves. The humble status of the majority our ancestors is the very reason the roots are not known; had they been royalty or movie stars, they would have been remembered. Indeed, many family histories are riddled with scandal, purposefully hiding what were once undesirable connections, membership in an outlawed religion or radical political party, or offspring from a forbidden tryst. Surely we could be content with the old adage, "Let the dead bury the dead," and move on. Yet we do not. Millions spend energy, time, and money stitching together their past, trying to uncover who they really are.

Ultimately, the quest to connect with the past is a spiritual quest. For contemporary people, history, memory, and family connections have been largely severed—we live, as one French philosopher says, in "amnesic societies." At first this phrase seems odd. In addition to the craze for genealogy, there is an equally intense interest in old things, a passion for collecting pieces of the past. The wealthy invest in old furniture and paintings, historical items, and autographs; the rest of us content ourselves with digitizing family photographs or picking up odd pieces of grandmother's china on eBay.

All this hunting and gathering underscores a surprising problem: we save things, but have little sense of how they fit together or what they might mean to our own lives. We hoard history, attaching ourselves to mementos and minutia almost as a sort of emotional packing material against the larger forces of forgetfulness endemic to the modern world. Historians recognize this contemporary paradox—we have more information about the past, but less actual connection to it than those in previous ages. Lack of historical knowledge is a perennial news story. Built into the very structure of Western society is bias against the past—the idea that what is new is better. "Now" is superior to "then." And the energy of the young trumps the wisdom of age.

Foundational to our way of seeing the world, the notions that newer is better and history is progress are relatively recent ideas and would have been unthinkable to our ancestors. Before the eighteenth century, most people lived with different senses of time and history than we do now. The world has only followed a universal standard of time since 1884; before that, time was local and random based on custom and observation. As an academic discipline in the way we conceive of it, "history" is also quite new, having developed only two or three hundred years ago. Before that, most cultures, even western European ones, had senses of time and history that interwove or overlapped, without clear scientific distinctions. Human ancestors generally believed that time existed of a single fabric without divisions between past, present, and future; there was only what was before and what might be after. Thus, the world was inhabited by all sorts of forces that lived beyond history, such as saints, angels, ghosts, and demons, all hanging about and forming a vast community of memory in which those living in a particular time would find meaning. Contemporary philosophers and historians refer to this as the "enchanted universe," a worldview that accommodated visible and invisible realities as a unified whole.

Well into the nineteenth century, even as definitions of history and time changed, people would talk to saints or deceased relatives as if they were still alive. Equally real was the penetrable veil between good and evil, especially on days like All Hallows' Eve or at the time of death, when malevolent forces interrupted daily life. Philosopher Charles Taylor refers to this older world as "boundless," that is, a reality with no divisions between past, present, and future, forming a single, miraculous universe of both wonder and fear. Those who preceded us lived with and, in many cases, were haunted by memories of those who went before.[4] In religion, this was expressed through ancestor worship, commemorations of the dead, and the celebration of saints and heroes.

In contrast to our ancestors' world as "boundless" in its understanding of time and space, ours is "bounded," says Taylor. Indeed, that is the very point of modernity—to delineate, define, categorize, and systematize knowledge in an attempt to understand, predict, fix, and control material reality according to the standards of science and academic inquiry. The shift from a boundless world to a bounded, scientific one has contributed to everything from human rights to democratic government, increased agricultural production, and longer life spans. For all its remarkable gains, however, there have been losses as well. History, for example. Once, history was a living sense of community, a reality in which one participated in everyday activity; now history is a subject to study, learned facts of dates and interpretation. Modern history gave us the gift of knowing more *about* our ancestors, while it eroded our capacity to dwell *with* those who have gone before. Combine this philosophical shift with the massive immigrations of the modern world—everything from European settlement of North and South America, to indigenous displacements and slavery, to movement due to war, economic opportunities, and climate change—and it is easy to understand why and how we have forgotten who we are and whence we came. We have become nomads in time.

Thus, the "chain of memory," as one French writer insists, has broken, shattering our sense of the belonging into thousands of individual and disconnected shards.[5] So we go about as historical scavengers—picking up random names, dates, bits of odd information, souvenirs of the past. But the larger picture is gone, save what we reassemble.

And this is troubling. If we do not know where we came from or where we are in a story, it is difficult to imagine that we can grasp the meaning and purpose of our own lives.

Generations of Faith

The book of Genesis opens with a natural genealogy, referring to creation as "the generations of the heavens and the earth" (2:4).[6] The first chapters reveal a primitive history of the earth: God created light, separating day and night; next came water and sky; from water and sky, land; land brought forth vegetation; in the skies appeared the sun, moon, and stars; the waters brought forth living creatures; the earth, mammals; and finally God created humankind.

The first human genealogy in the Bible is in Genesis 5:

> This is the list of the descendants of Adam. When God created humankind, he made them in the likeness of God. Male and female he created them, and he blessed them and named them "Humankind" when they were created. When Adam had lived one hundred thirty years, he became the father of a son in his likeness, according to his image, and named him Seth. The days of Adam after he became the father of Seth were eight hundred years; and he had other sons and daughters. Thus all

the days that Adam lived were nine hundred thirty years;
and he died. (5:1–5)

The chapter continues on in the same manner for twenty-seven more verses, tracing Adam's family to Noah, at the time of the flood. There are two dozen such lists in the Hebrew Bible, some very lengthy, some short; and there are two major genealogies in the New Testament, one in Matthew and the other in Luke.

Although searching for online family history may be a big business or an engaging addiction, it is also a deeply spiritual preoccupation. For people unfamiliar with the Bible, it may be surprising to discover that ancient scripture is full of genealogies; for those who know the Bible, the genealogies, the "begats," are considered the boring bits to jump over to get to the real story. And both Judaism and Christianity take genealogy beyond the Bible, basing entire traditions of interpretation, schools of doctrine, and great communities of synagogues and churches on descent from particular wise teachers, saintly practitioners, or spiritual masters.

Islamic scriptures and traditions trace the genealogies of Ishmael, the prophets (including Jesus), Muhammad and his descendants, and early heroes and teachers of faith. Buddhists track the lineage of *dharma,* the teachings, of particular schools and teachers as well as the genealogies of gifted gurus and leaders. It is possible to view reincarnation itself as a genealogy of sorts—a spiritual line of enlightenment manifesting itself through generations. And most tribal religions throughout the world base their existence on their lineage from creation as well as their spiritual leadership through families of shamans. Genealogy is one of the most significant, perhaps even universal, aspects of the phenomenon called religion. Since the dawn of time, human beings have believed that spiritual insight, power, and piety somehow passes down through generations.

Despite the fact that most people find them dull reading, the Bible's genealogies have sparked much debate through the centuries. Skeptics insist that these lists, with their omissions, contradictions, and incomprehensibly long life spans, are not only irrelevant; they undermine scripture's historicity and veracity. Conservative Christians claim the lists are accurate in every detail, including, of course, that Methuselah had a son when he was 187 years old and lived another 782 years and that the priest Melchizedek had no parents whatsoever. Thus, doubters use genealogy to disprove the Bible, denying its veracity, while the devoutly literal use the same texts to prove fantastical tales, demanding that faith entails accepting dubious history and science.

Genealogies were not, however, considered dull in their original context. Indeed, genealogy was a common feature of many ancient religions and their sacred texts. Like their neighboring Sumerians, Assyrians, Babylonians, and Egyptians, the Hebrew people secured political or priestly legitimacy through kinship. These records established lines for passing on possessions and property, along with role, rank, and authority. Religious genealogies are not just economic or political, however. They also register the handing down of religious practices or wisdom, that is, "tradition." In the Bible, the genealogies are not really about who was the father of whom; they are part of the larger story of how sin and evil are transmitted through the human race from Adam onward and how God's promises are secured through righteous heroes and rulers.

In an odd way, critics and biblical fundamentalists are right— genealogy is controversial. These lists were controversial even when they were written! Since lineage confers political and spiritual authority, genealogy was a high-stakes literary enterprise. To claim that one was a son of a blessing, like Jacob, or a son of a curse, like Esau, made a huge difference in the ancient world; quite literally the success or failure of a tribe or king rested on the claim to the right ancestry. Thus, biblical genealogies tend to conflict with one another. When a particular ruler came to power, the ruler's family legitimized authority by claiming ancestry from a "good" patriarch; when he lost power, the next ruling family would do the same.

The Bible's genealogies, and the contradictions in them, actually reveal a long history of struggle and political conflict, a process by which different groups valorized their ancestors and thereby valorized themselves. And not everyone accepted everyone else's version of ancestral authority, so they wrote their own equally glowing accounts of family. As a result, competing lists actually wound up in scripture—such as the competing ancestry lists of Jesus found in the Gospels of Matthew and Luke. Sometimes new religious leaders or dissenters would simply propose a new sacred text with a different set of genealogies—as Muhammad did with the Qur'an or, much later, Joseph Smith did with the Book of Mormon—to claim political or spiritual authority on the basis of their lineage.

Genealogy is not what skeptics or fundamentalists make it out to be; it is not historical or biological fact. Every sacred tradition, every sacred text, every religious denomination has contradictory genealogies. Genealogies reveal the quest of ancient people to find a place in the universe and claim divine favor. Such an enterprise is inherently risky and of necessity involves conflict with those who discern different patterns through time. This conflict is often invisible to modern people and is almost always invisible to those outside of specific faith traditions, because the argument is the way that competing stories, practices, and interpretations of God manifest themselves in the lives of our heroes, shamans, and saints. Genealogies,

145

therefore, are less about historical accuracy and more about the aspirations of the people who wrote them.

Jesus's genealogies in Matthew (1:1–17) and Luke (3:23–38) serve as good examples of this dynamic. The writer of Matthew presents Jesus as the king of the Jews: "An account of the genealogy of Jesus the Messiah, the son of David, the son of Abraham" (1:1). The claim is big and bold, directed toward a Jewish audience seeking both political liberation and spiritual empowerment during a time of oppression. Matthew proclaims that this Jesus, whose story he tells, embodied both King David's royal authority and the covenantal authority of Abraham. All God's promises to Israel are fulfilled in Jesus, who appeared to be the son of a carpenter, but was in actuality both King and Savior.

Luke's story is far less regal than Matthew's. It does, of course, include King David (since ancient prophets said the Messiah would be of the line of David), but it also includes a host of lesser-known characters, some of whom do not appear anywhere else in the Bible. Gone is the triumphant line of kings. Who was Joda, son of Joanan, anyway? Or Cosam, son of Elmadam? Never heard of any of them. Luke also traces Jesus's line back as far as it can go—through faithful Noah, back to Adam, through his gentle son, Seth. The point is obvious: Jesus is from good spiritual ancestry, clearly blessed of God through so many generations (as evidenced by all these sons!), related to some heroes like David, Jesse, Jacob, and Isaac, but, like all of us, a child of our first parents, created by God. Luke's is a universal genealogy, emphasizing the unity of the whole human family. Yes, there were some amazing people in the family tree, but much of the story is about regular people who were faithful to God.

The two genealogies underscore a fundamental struggle in early Christianity, a conflict that runs through the texts of the New Testament: Was Jesus the Jewish Messiah or the Savior of the whole world?

The "begats" are not boring at all. They tell stories of belonging, of our sacred location in God. And sometimes those stories surprise us, especially when they reveal conflicting spiritual impulses in our own souls.

Spiritual DNA

Knowing the stories of our ancestors makes a difference in how we act, the choices we make, and how we understand our own lives. When I was growing up in the Methodist Church, my least favorite hymn was "Faith of Our Fathers," emphasizing genealogy and faith:

> *Faith of our fathers, living still,*
> *In spite of dungeon, fire and sword;*
> *O how our hearts beat high with joy*
> *Whene'er we hear thy wondrous voice!*
>
> *Faith of our fathers, holy faith!*
> *We will be true to thee till death.*

There is a good reason I disliked this particular hymn. When I was a girl, the dominant family story was that of my father's family. My father descended from relatively recent German immigrants who arrived in America around 1876. They first settled in Philadelphia, but within a decade moved to Baltimore and opened a florist shop. My father and his brother and sister were fourth-generation florists in this line and heirs to the same shop that had been founded by their original immigrant ancestor. Genealogy, lineage, and inheritance were incredibly important to them.

As far as I knew, we were German. My grandfather still used occasional German words (mostly to curse, I suspect). And on Sundays we gathered around a large table at his house for a family dinner that consisted of mostly German-American food. My grandfather was as much a patriarch as it was possible to be in the 1960s, as he tried to maintain the sort of authority and power his own grandfather had brought with him on the boat from nineteenth-century Germany. Truth be told, he was not very nice. He did not like Jews or African Americans and had deep contempt for women. He bellowed and threatened and tried to control the lives of everyone and anyone he could. The family history was one of hierarchy, authoritarianism, bigotry, exclusion, sexism, and racism—everything I came to reject and work against in my own life.

For many years, I felt ashamed of this ancestry. When people asked me where I grew up, I would joke, "Nineteenth-century Germany." But something deeper nagged at me: I could not figure out how I fit into their story. I did know that my views on race, gender, equality, and politics were much more like those of my mother's than my father's relatives. And, like her, I had what my father's aged aunts called "gumption" (a most undesirable quality in a girl), and they regularly warned me that I would get myself in trouble by reading too much. "Just like your mother," they would shake their heads. "She voted for Kennedy. And all that civil rights business." My father's family disapproved of both my mother and me.

My mother's family was more mysterious. Her father's parents were divorced in the 1920s, leaving my grandfather to be raised by a childless aunt. My mother's mother was estranged from her mother, evidently because my grandmother had become pregnant when an unwed teenager. My mother's family was lost in a tangle of secrets and poverty. They, whoever they were, were mostly invisible to me. I loved my maternal grandparents, but they rarely spoke of the past. My mother did not know much about her ances-

tors, a grandfather from Pennsylvania and some other family ru-
mored to have originated on the eastern shore of Maryland.

When she died, I went looking for them. And that led me to
Easton, Maryland, and the Quakers at Third Haven Meeting
House.

My mother's ancestors were among Maryland's first settlers.
Since Andrew Orem was from Scotland, he may have come to
Maryland as a Presbyterian, perhaps seeking his fortune, then converted to Quakerism when he (or his parents, who apparently came
as well) heard George Fox preach.[7] Or perhaps they converted in
Scotland to the new Quaker religion and came to Maryland to find
religious toleration. That part of the story is, indeed, lost. But whatever the case, he threw his spiritual lot in with the people who
believed that every person—male or female, rich or poor, slave or
free—possessed the inner light of Christ and was completely loved
by and equal before God. No hierarchy or patriarchy in the little
church he helped build. Instead, the "church" consisted of all God's
people; none had the spiritual authority to rule over another. God
spoke directly through the Spirit to the hearts of all gathered in
silence in a community where "authority" was based on one's
openness to spiritual experience, faithfulness, and following the
way of Jesus.

When I found the marriage record of Andrew Orem and Eleanor Morris at the Third Haven Friends Meeting, everything made
sense.[8] Without knowing it, my mother had inherited Quaker values. And without knowing it, so had I. For most of my life, I tried
to fit into my father's family genealogy, a story that made me a
rebel, a dissident, an outsider. But when I learned of my mother's
ancestors, I discovered a genealogy of social justice and spirituality,
the very things that had animated my life. I was not a rebel rejecting

a family tradition of exclusion; I was being faithful to the ancestors I never knew. There was spiritual DNA entwined with all the other inherited traits. I found a faith from my mother's fathers, and it was worth singing about it.

The Great Web of Belonging

I am not alone in wondering about my roots. Discovering where we come from gives us a sense of where we belong. As a young man, Barack Obama could never put together the strands of his own life—black and white in America. After his long-absent father died, Obama went searching for meaning through the stories of his family. This eventually took him to Kenya, his father's homeland, where he began to learn about his father and grandfather. "It had all started with him," Obama wrote of his paternal grandfather. "If I could just piece together his story, I thought, then perhaps everything else might fall into place." As he retraced his grandfather's footsteps, learning the ways of his African homeland, Obama felt that "every touch and breath and word carried the full weight of my life; that a circle was beginning to close, so that I might finally recognize myself as I was." And then finally he heard a genealogy recited by his Granny: "First there was Miwiru. . . . Miwiru sired Sigoma, Sigoma sired Owiny." The lineage was accompanied by stories, mostly of betrayal and abandonment, that revealed to the young man a new understanding of his life:

> I felt the circle finally close. I realized that who I was, what I cared about, was no longer just a matter of intellect or obligation, no longer a construct of words. . . . All of it was connected with this small plot of earth an ocean away, connected by more than the accident of a name or

the color of my skin. The pain I felt was my father's pain.
My questions were my brothers' questions. Their struggle, my birthright.[9]

Ultimately, the search for ancestry is a quest for connections—
for something that is underground in the roots of our families.
Whether it's my own discovery of Quaker ancestors or Barack
Obama's of his Kenyan forefathers, when we bring hidden connections to the surface, we discover subconscious motivations, clarify-
ing the meaning of our lives, and find new directions of vocation.

But genealogy is not just about individuals or personal stories,
for tracing our roots leads to a conclusion that we do not often consider: every family tree intersects with other family trees. Our roots
are intertwined. We are all related to each other. We belong to each
other.

The math is intriguing. Because of the exponential nature of
family (two parents, four grandparents, eight great-grandparents,
etc.), after ten generations all lineage reaches "the inflection point,"
where, according to science writer Steve Olson, "the number of
your ancestors explodes to be most of the population living in a
specific part of the world." For example, almost all European-
background individuals share at least one common ancestor in the
last five centuries.[10] Based on mathematical models and DNA com-
parisons, scientists speculate that most living human beings are all
somehow related through a "recent common ancestor" who may
have lived as recently as five thousand years ago.[11] Science journalist
Carl Zimmer explains it this way:

When you draw your genealogy, you make two lines
from yourself back to each of your parents. Then you
have to draw two lines for each of them, back to your

four grandparents. And then eight great-grandparents, sixteen great-great-grandparents, and so on. But not so on for very long. If you go back to the time of Charlemagne, forty generations or so, you should get to a generation of a trillion ancestors. That's about two thousand times more people than existed on earth when Charlemagne was alive. The only way out of this paradox is to assume that *our ancestors are not independent of one another.* That is, if you trace their ancestry back, you loop back to a common ancestor. We're not talking about first-cousin stuff here—more like twentieth-cousin. This means that instead of drawing a tree that fans out exponentially, we need to draw a web-like tapestry.[12]

In the ancient and medieval worlds, people believed the universe was structured as a "great chain of being." The "fan" of reality began with God and cascaded downward through all of creation from high to low: angels, humanity, animals, plants, and minerals. This "fan" formed a pyramid, with the most important beings at the top. Each category was further subdivided into hierarchies. Within "humans," for instance, the king ranked highest, followed by princes, nobles, free men, peasants, and slaves. Men ranked higher than women, and certain races ranked higher than others. This pyramid structure, the great chain of being, was believed to be the sacred pattern of the universe, in which authority, power, and knowledge flowed downward. Everyone and everything had a place. Yet in a deeply spiritual way everything was also connected to God, since God was the head of all. To stay in one's place ensured earthly protection and eternal salvation. Hence, ancestry was important—it located every person in this spiritual superstructure, securing each a place in God's divine order in this life and beyond.

But there is another way of seeing a spiritual pattern to the universe. Through the search for our ancestors, we discover that the branches of our family trees are entangled. When we make our way through the thick canopy of the past, we discover that lineage is anything but a line. It is looks far more like a web.

The great chain of being has been replaced with by a "web of life" or "web of belonging." The phrases "web of life" and "web of belonging" began to appear in discussions of human society in the 1980s and 1990s, increasing rapidly through the first years of the 2000s. This makes sense. "Web" has emerged as a compelling way to understand the structure of the world—from the "webs" of ecosystems to those of the digital world. Our conception of reality has shifted from top-down chains of authority supported by technical expertise and mechanical organization toward living systems of interrelationship and interdependency knit together in a web of life.[13] It is only a few short steps from scientific webs to cultural webs to a web of the spirit: the great web of belonging.[14]

Throughout all major world religions is a subtext of this alternative, the insight that creation is not bound by a divine hierarchical order but is, instead, a circle or dance or tapestry, where God, humanity, and nature participate together in community. Indeed, the ancient biblical creation stories relate a tale of intimacy between God and the world, an intimacy that becomes broken but that nonetheless is the primary relationship between God and creation from the beginning. Religion, with its cycle of rituals based upon Sabbaths, months, and seasons, was intended to reconnect God with humanity and nature.

Ancient monotheism had more in common with what we now call tribal religion—which is decentralized, local, relational, and nature-oriented—than any modern religious institution. In the Bible, God is not mediated through structures; rather, structures provided ways for people to participate in the divine realities that infused the world around them. "The whole earth is a living icon of the face of God," wrote John of Damascus in the seventh century.[15] It is possible, even desirable, to read the Bible as a story of a deep web of interconnection. As Barbara Brown Taylor, Episcopal priest and writer, puts it:

> There is another way to conceive of our life in God, but it requires a different worldview—not a clockwork universe in which individuals function as discrete springs and gears, but one that looks more like a luminous web, in which the whole is far more than the parts. In this universe, there is no such thing as an individual apart from his or her relationships. Every interaction—between people and people, between people and things, between things and things—changes the face of history. Life on earth cannot be reduced to four sure-fire rules. It is an ever-unfolding mystery that defies precise prediction. Meanwhile, in this universe, there is no such thing as "parts." The whole is the fundamental unity of reality.[16]

This has most often been the minor key of religion and theology, but similar insights are found in reformers and mystics of all sorts— those who lived at the fringes of institutional religion and protested established hierarchies. And reclaiming this wisdom has often been the source of spiritual reform movements.

Archbishop Desmond Tutu writes of the same: "The first law of our being is that we are set in a delicate network of interdependence with our fellow human beings and with the rest of God's creation."[17] This is the African concept of *ubuntu*—"I am because you are." *Ubuntu* empowered the struggle against apartheid and continues to inspire movements of equality in Africa and beyond. To understand that we are connected, that we belong to one another, is a powerful deterrent to fratricide, terrorism, slavery, and violence. We are not warring tribes. We are the same tribe. *Ubuntu* is an African way of expressing the great web of belonging. Each one of us exists through others. But *ubuntu* extends beyond personal existence: "We are because we all are." And to family: "My family is because your family is." Or, perhaps better stated: "My ancestors are your ancestors too."

The shift from God at the zenith of the great chain of being toward God with us in a great web of belonging is the heart of today's spiritual revolution. The web of belonging originated in the big bang, when all matter burst forth across the universe, and it is experienced in the natural world in the ecosystems of dirt, water, and air. But it is also encountered in human experience through the complex relations humanity has made through time, the brotherhood and sisterhood of humankind. As the American Catholic bishops insisted, the earth and the human family are linked in a "natural ecology and social ecology," "the web of life."[18] That vision includes a spiritual ecology as well. The great web is the woven world of the planet and the people and the God who dwells therein.

God is not a far-off Weaver of the web, like the earlier Watchmaker God, who assembled creation and left it to run on its own. No, God is part of the web, entangled right here with us.

Tangled Webs

Webs are not neat. They can be sticky messes and, for some, a death trap. And that goes for our ancestral webs as well. What if we do not like our families? What of dysfunctional relationships, control, and even abuse? Our families might be a great source of delight, but very often families are also the source of our deepest insecurity and shame. Indeed, the very idea of a "web" of belonging conjures up one of the most famous lines of English-language poetry: "Oh, what a tangled web we weave / When first we practice to deceive!"[19] During much of recent history, people have had to escape their ancestral lands and families in order to find freedom and make their own way in the world. Entire political systems have been built on the right of individuals to create their own destinies. In Western culture, to be truly oneself often means stepping outside, or even rejecting, the webs constructed by ancestors.

Escaping family is not an easy thing to do, because we carry our ancestors within. Even when we move across the planet, take a new identity, adopt a new religion, and make an entirely "new" family, we often still act as if we live in the world of our first relationships. In recent decades, psychology has increasingly explored the idea that our personhood is intimately related to and dependent upon the personhood of others in a circle of "relational selfhood" and that we all live within systems of emotional interdependence modeled to us by the families into which we were born.

Contemporary therapy often explores the negative aspects of these family systems, empowering individuals to "differentiate" from unhelpful relationships and form healthier bonds with siblings, parents, and spouses. People who engage in such therapy are encouraged to draw emotional genealogies of their extended families in order to discern how pain, shame, abuse, anxiety, addictions, depression, and mental illness might have been present—an exercise that is frequently reported as a significant step in personal self-discovery.

In other words, not only is it important to know who our ancestors are; we should know something of what they did and how they lived their lives. Ancestry is more than pedigree; it is a handing down of patterns of faith, doubt, joy, and despair. To understand these patterns and the interrelatedness of sadness and even sin often opens new paths of mental, emotional, and spiritual healing.

The concept of the relational self, an identity constructed within webs of interdependent people through time, has proved so powerful that emotional genealogies have been employed as a tool to understand organizations, congregations, and institutions as well as nuclear families. If anything, psychology has moved in the direction of poetry, as it increasingly discovers that no person is an "island." Rather, we are dependent upon relationships and connections that saturate our understanding of ourselves.[20] And the more honest we are in telling the stories of our ancestors in the web, the more we will be able to understand ourselves and the possibilities carried in our emotional DNA for our future.

Thinking about the possibility of spiritual DNA opens up Jesus's genealogies in a new way. Returning to Matthew's pedigree of Jesus the Jewish Messiah, for instance, attentive readers should be startled. Jesus's ancestors include Jacob, the son who stole his older brother's birthright; Tamar, the woman who tricked Judah, her father-in-law, into getting her pregnant; the son of Boaz and Ruth, an illegal immigrant who seduced her future husband; King David's son Solomon, who was the offspring of a relationship that began in adultery; King Uzziah, who tried to usurp the priesthood and was subsequently struck with leprosy; and of course Joseph, Jesus's mostly ignored stepfather. And this is the genealogy that presents Jesus in a positive light!

Matthew's genealogy does two things. First, it provides Jesus's legal pedigree. He is the son of David, in Israel's royal line. Matthew's family tree is a bit like presenting evidence for admission into the

Daughters of the American Revolution. But Matthew has a second purpose. His genealogy tells readers that Jesus's ancestry is the human story of faith and faithlessness, of good deeds and wicked ones, of saintly actions and dubious intentions, of marital fidelity and sexual duplicity. In other words, Jesus may be a "king" in the royal line of David, but his family is pretty much the same as everyone else's. Matthew puts it out there—Jesus, son of Joseph, has a family genogram that could keep a therapist occupied for years. When ancient Christian thinkers insisted that Jesus was fully human, they were not kidding.

Other biblical genealogies are the same, full of stories of relatives you would rather forget. But they also underscore one of the great spiritual insights of human experience: pettiness, sin, evil, and suffering are somehow passed through generations, but the graciousness of God's blessings overcomes what seems an insurmountable and inherited curse. God's mercy flows, apparently, through the actions and despite the choices of our ancestors: "I the LORD your God am a jealous God, punishing children for the iniquity of parents, to the third and fourth generation of those who reject me, but showing steadfast love to the thousandth generation of those who love me and keep my commandments" (Deut. 5:9–10).

According to Hebrew teaching, the inheritance of human beings is not primarily sin but blessing, as the ramifications of goodness last many thousand times longer than those of evil. Catholic priest and theologian Diarmuid O'Murchu refers to this as "ancestral grace," the belief "that God has been with humanity on the whole evolutionary journey of seven million years" as the "great gifting power" that nourishes and sustains all being.[21] We live and move and have our being in a great web of belonging whose connective tissue is grace.

158

The Book of Life

Since discovering my Quaker roots, I have learned that Quakers were meticulous record keepers. Every Monthly Meeting, the basic unit of administration in the denomination, had at least three books: the men's minutes, the women's minutes, and the book of marriages, births, and burials.[22] Indeed, most Quakers also kept books of their own families, as Howard Brinton, one Quaker leader, noted in his autobiography: "As I take down from library shelves the Smedley Book, the Sharpless Book, the Brinton Book, the Kirk Book, the Darlington Book, and the Cox Book and look at these solid, serene, strong faces expressing a simple but carefully worked out mode of life, I feel that I can understand them."[23] Evidently, Quakers regularly joke about their tendency toward "ancestor worship." Brinton continues:

> A common modern American way of thinking which holds that every tub stands on its own bottom, that every man is an isolated individual and responsible for his own ability and character is not true biologically, psychologically, nor spiritually. Those who have preceded us are bone of our bone, flesh of our flesh, and we can no more separate ourselves from them than a plant can separate itself from its roots.[24]

The books, like old photographs and journals, ancestral altars, or days of remembrance, remind us that we belong. Belonging, however, is far more than a list—a pedigree that might guarantee admission to a historical society or determine a noble heritage. To belong is not about joining an exclusive club based on one's bloodline. Rather, as Howard Brinton insists, ancestry links us to a "pattern of life," a spiritual culture that cannot "be reduced to a theological system."[25] The old Quaker books are a practice of memory keeping, what Thomas Aquinas once referred to as the "well-furnished memory."[26] Belonging is an intentional practice of remembering that we are *joined with* the lives of our ancestors.

Ancient Jews and Christians taught that there was a Book of Life listing all the names of the righteous. This book, sometimes known as the Book of Remembrance, also records good deeds. Several apocalyptic texts depict God reading the book at the end of days, admitting all there listed to eternal life. There is a second book as well, the Book of Death, holding the names of all destined for hell. Those who read scripture literally believe that God has two actual books, waiting to be opened on the last day. The books determine your eternal fate.

Most modern people dismiss a literal interpretation of a Book of Life. But the books are a metaphor—as is the idea that the books serve as a ticket to heaven. Going deeper, the idea of a Book of Life is both humorous and beautiful. Did God forget the names of all the faithful? God needs a list? The same God who can number the hairs on your head cannot remember your name on Judgment Day? Who cannot laugh at the idea of God needing a contact list of those destined for eternal life?

The Book of Life is not a tally of human holiness. It is a spiritual analogy for human memory—the need to inscribe the names and acts of our ancestors in a place of eternal remembrance (or, as ancient tradition would have it, to wreak vengeance upon the cruel ones by blotting them out of the Book of Life). The Book of Life is a biblical version of walking through a graveyard and reading the names of those who died in faith, rows upon rows of names carved in stone, the names of our ancestors, all awaiting the resurrection of memory. The book is another way of speaking of the web. And that is what we are called to do. To find connections we did not know, to pass stories down from generation to generation, to strengthen our memories of those who have gone before. We must seek out ways to honor the ancestors we remember, our more distant ancestors, and those who might only be spiritual ancestors. And, above all, we must live fully aware that we are all of the same family.

In the end, it is no accident that human beings bury the dead, that we return our parents and loved ones to the earth, for these are our roots. And tending to the roots ensures healthy growth in our own lives. Seeing under the surface is part of the spiritual journey of self-knowledge that leads to God.

In January 2014, my sister, brother, and I interred our parents' ashes. When they died, they left no directions about where they wished to be buried. They were both native Marylanders who had made their way to the great southwestern desert and lived the end of their lives in Arizona. We did not know if they wished to be scattered in the vast sands of the desert or taken home to the waters of the Chesapeake. Eventually, we laid them to rest at a Methodist church near Phoenix, in a garden that blends the desert and water. We read scriptures promising that dry lands will become springs.

Standing at the desert columbarium, looking toward the rugged peaks of the Superstition Mountains in the distance, I thought of far-off Easton, of Andrew Orem in Scotland and of his coming to America, of convinced Quakers building their farms on the mealy soil of Maryland's eastern shore, of their generations of offspring, and of my mother and my father, lifelong spouses, being laid to eternal rest in the Arizona dust.

I read a poem:

slack water,
the tide neither rising
nor ebbing;
for the moment I wonder if
I too can walk on water

Let me
steep myself
in the briny breach
and be born
anew this day

this beach
charges me nothing
to walk among
the sea rack and
shards of memory

stitch my shroud
tie granite to my ankles
bury me
deep in the heart
of the Chesapeake[27]

I picked up a rock from the desert garden. I sometimes hold it in my palm and remember my parents, their names inscribed on a marble plaque, now under the desert sun, burning brightly in the Book of Life. One day, when my roots feel more deeply established, I will take the stone and bury it in the graveyard next to an old meetinghouse in Maryland.

CHAPTER

❧ 5 ❦

Home

The ache for home lives in all of us, the safe place where
we can go as we are and not be questioned.

—*Maya Angelou*

In a somewhat vain attempt to tidy a cluttered storage room, I
excavated a box of treasures from adolescence: old pictures, a
couple of scrapbooks, high-school newspapers, ticket stubs from
Disneyland, a program from an assembly. Among the mementos, I
discovered my copies of Laura Ingalls Wilder's *Little House* books.
As I flipped through the worn and yellowed pages of paperbacks
forty-plus years old, they smelled just as pages in old books should.

Instinctively, I clutched one volume against my chest, feeling a
little like Laura hugging her ragdoll, Charlotte. How I loved these
stories of a nineteenth-century girl and her restless pioneer family.
No wonder they had been saved in this precious carton of mementos. I must have read them a hundred times, practically memorizing
the Ingallses' journey from one little house to another as they made
their way on the American frontier.

The stories are adventures of moving west, full of tales of crossing rivers, violent storms, failed crops, and Indian wars, told from the perspective of a little girl. At their core, however, they are stories of home. A few years after I first read them, on the first episode of the television series based on the books, Laura's character distilled this essence when she famously remarked, "'Home' is the nicest word there is."

Oddly enough, the Ingalls family did not stay in any one home for long. Indeed, they moved from Wisconsin to Missouri and Kansas, back to Wisconsin and then to several towns in Minnesota, to Iowa, and then to the Dakota Territory. Laura Ingalls lived in at least a dozen houses before she was eighteen, when she married her homesteader neighbor, Almanzo Wilder; she moved a few more times as an adult, including a brief sojourn in Florida. Hers was not a settled existence.

Laura's tension, clear in the books, is between the impulse to move and the desire to stay, being torn between her sedate mother and unstable father. So the comment, "'Home' is the nicest word there is" (which does not, to my knowledge, actually appear in the original books), raises a surprising question: What constitutes "home"?

For Laura, every house became "home" when Ma unpacked her china shepherdess, the beds were made up, and Pa pulled out his fiddle. Whether it was a cabin in the woods, a sod house on the prairie, or a wood-frame building in town, "home" had a surprisingly fluid meaning for this nineteenth-century family. Home happened in numerous geographies, in a number of different dwellings, a constantly changing reality. Home consisted of some familiar treasures, an appreciation of place, and closely knit relationships between loved ones. Home meant working together with new neighbors, welcoming unexpected guests, and providing shelter for others on a journey. Home was as much a disposition as a building, the place of ultimate hospitality, where everyone was accepted, and a respite in grace. It is a sense of peace and fulfillment, of knowing one is in the right place. On the final page of the final book, the author reflects of newlywed Laura, "She knew she need never be homesick for the old home. It was so near that she could go to it whenever she wished, while she and Almanzo made the new home in their own little house."[1]

By the time I was eighteen, my family had lived in seven different houses in two states, moving back and forth between Maryland and Arizona. And by the time I was thirty, I lived in seven more houses in four additional states. Laura's understanding of home proved invaluable to me. I learned to pack and unpack boxes, place familiar things on new shelves, make up new beds, and sing songs of welcome. Moving from place to place was hard. But making a home was a spiritual work of inhabiting new places well and knowing how to open the door to strangers—something not easy to achieve, but necessary to fill the ache that dwells in human hearts to belong.

"Where Is God?" and Home

My mother was less sanguine about moving, however. In 1969, she and my father had built their dream house in the Maryland countryside. Set on almost two acres of woodland, the house was big and welcoming, accommodating not only three active children and a huge dog, but also my grandmother and hordes of friends, neighbors, and relatives. To my parents' delight, several other families from the "old neighborhood" bought lots nearby and built as well. We had made a communal exodus to the country and found ourselves in my mother's promised land.

We only lived there for three years. In 1972, my father became ill, had a falling out with his own father, and could not remain at the family business. My parents decided to make a new start by moving again. They chose somewhere both warm and far away—Arizona.

It felt like a marvelous adventure to us children, but to my mother it was like being exiled to a desert wilderness. The dream home sold, and we moved into a tract house. Acres of trees were replaced by a front yard full of cacti. No lifelong friends, no neighbors dropping by, no relatives visiting on Sunday. Just five of us and the dog, a tiny band of settlers in a tough new world.

We younger ones adapted quickly, making new friends and finding a place for ourselves in Arizona. And my father loved it—for him it was a place of healing and freedom. But my mother never really adjusted. She missed the seasons. It was too hot. The mail was slow, and letters from back home were fewer and farther between. There were no trees. Everything was brown. Within a year, she was in despair. I asked her what was wrong.

"I don't feel like I belong here," she replied. "I miss home."

Homesickness is not an illness. It is a sort of dis-ease, the queasy feeling that we are somehow out of place. Questions about home are almost inevitably "where" questions: Where are you from? Where is your home? Where do you live? The query anticipates something far more than an address. Home is more than a house. It is a sacred location, a place of aspiration and dreams, of learning and habit, of relationships and heart. Home is the geography of our souls. The "where" questions of home naturally open to the spiritual question: Where is God?

Philip Sheldrake, a scholar of Christian spirituality, makes the case that "place" is more than physical: " 'Place' is location with particular significance because of its connection with the people who live there rather than somewhere else, or because it evokes something of significance." It involves history, memory, practices, story, and ritual. And place imparts identity and meaning, "bound up with moral and social values," and helps orient us in relationship with other people and the world.[2] Home is a place where we belong. No wonder my mother missed home.

Place is what grows from ancestral roots, that sense of well-being and connection arising from the soil of our lives. Until recent centuries, most people lived where their ancestors lived. But now? It is hard to imagine how many millions of people have moved away from their native lands. The modern world consists mostly of immigrants, massive numbers of people dislocated by war, famine, conflict, religious migration, climate change, economic hardship, or cultural curiosity. People are out of place. Transient moderns make their homes in new places.

There is something elusive about place, something my mother struggled to find in Arizona. The places we come to know as "home" involve an intangible flash of recognition, a soul connection that brings forth a different sort of knowing about God, nature, or oneself. Home is a place where God somehow meets us—where we belong. In my own life, I experienced that sacred sense in several places. Maryland and the Chesapeake, my birthplace and ancestral place, serves as a spiritual template of my identity; the sense of belonging I have to its land, temperament, and history goes with me wherever I go, a ghost of locality haunting every landscape I encounter.

But other places have been significant to me as well, turning into "my place" as I moved through the world. The American Southwest, with its deserts and sunny skies, speaks to me deeply, almost as the spare spiritual yang to Maryland's watery yin. Santa Barbara, California, has been a home to me, a city and landscape that gifted me with passion and vocation, where the weather wraps one like a garment of grace. On the beaches of North Carolina I have found healing more times than I can count. And the tiny Scottish island of Iona, with its Celtic Christian history and rugged hills, has wormed its way into my soul like few other places. These are all places I call home. All these places compose my "place."

And that is the funny thing about place in contemporary society: we make it from shards of memory and experience, and it typically involves some sort of spiritual dimension. Few of us have exactly the same place, but I suspect that our "soul mates" and closest friends are often those who come from, at the very least, similar places. Indeed, to say, "We are coming from the same place," expresses solidarity, shared vision, spiritual unity, and common purpose with others. In recent years, perhaps in part due to the economic downturn, there has been a surprising social shift around place. We are still a mobile society, but people stay home more, travel fewer miles, and move less often than in the past. Sociologist Richard Florida notes that attachment to place has become a wide cultural ethos, especially among young adults who "no longer ask, 'What do you do?'" when meeting new people, but instead ask, "'Where do you live?'"[3]

Place is an expandable and retractable concept. We might feel at home "in the universe," in any number of cities or landscapes, or in a particular neighborhood. The most intimate answer to the question, "Where do you live?" is to reply with an address, a specific physical location of one's abode, the place where one returns and lays one's head at night. But "Where do you live?" is ultimately a sacred question. French philosopher Gaston Bachelard writes, "Our house is our corner of the world. As has often been said, it is our first universe, a real cosmos in every sense of the word."[4] To him home is the cradle, the most intimate of all places. If life begins well, "it begins enclosed, protected, all warm in the bosom of the house."[5]

A house may be a physical place, but home is "inhabited space." Home is the location that shelters our lived experience, but also holds our memories and shapes our desires. As Bachelard points out, a house is also a metaphysical thing, the realm of spirituality, dreams, psychology, and poetry—the place where we center ourselves.

Where is God? We dwell at home. And God dwells there with us. In a very real way, we inhabit God.

God's Dwelling

Home is a central theme in the world's great religions: Jews seeking a homeland with God; Christians proclaiming that God dwells within our hearts; Muslims facing home to pray; Buddhists finding a true home in enlightenment; Druids and Wiccans worshipping gods who make their home in the seas and trees. Human beings build temples to shelter God's presence, we mark sacred places with shrines, and we bury, float, or burn our dead that they might find their way home to God.

The overarching narrative of the Bible is that of humanity searching for home. In the beginning, God created the beautiful earth as our home, but we carelessly misused it, resulting in exile from our natal place. The rest of the story recounts how we either faithfully sought God's homeland or sinfully abused it, with consequences of blessing or curses. Throughout, a spiritual interplay emerges: not only did God create our earthly home, but God is our home. A letter on Catholic teaching sums this up:

> The whole universe is God's dwelling. Earth, a very
> small, uniquely blessed corner of that universe, gifted

with unique natural blessings, is humanity's home, and humans are never so much at home as when God dwells with them.[6]

It is a powerful story, rich in literary ambiguity—the earth, us, home, and God are almost interchangeable characters in this ancient record of humankind's aching search to dwell.

In addition to this large biblical narrative, specific stories also relate tales of us, home, and God. Perhaps none does so more beautifully than the book of Ruth. Ruth, a Moabite woman married to a Jew, is widowed. Instead of staying in her own homeland after her husband's death, she pleads with her mother-in-law, Naomi, to be allowed to accompany her to Israel to find a new home:

> Where you go, I will go;
> where you lodge, I will lodge;
> your people shall be my people,
> and your God my God.
> Where you die, I will die—
> there will I be buried. (1:16–17)

Home is the relationship between two people, a physical place, and God. This is sacred dwelling. Place, presence, and family make home.

In the Bible, "place" is the land of Israel and "presence" is that of Israel's God. "Family" is actually the most confusing aspect of the story. Who makes up our home? The biblical answer encompasses a surprisingly wide diversity of family arrangements and relationships. Biblical understandings of the family include a naked couple cohabiting in a garden without benefit of state-approved union, polygamous tribal patriarchs, despotic kings with their harems, women who baited men (including by incestuous measures) to impregnate them or who shamed them into marriage using sexual wiles, people tricked into unwanted marriages, and the shockingly unmarried rabbi Jesus (son of a teenage unwed mother), who urged his followers to leave their fathers and mothers to follow him and embrace a life of chastity for the sake of God's kingdom.

Jesus's followers made a great deal of trouble when they redefined "home" to include women and slaves, upsetting the traditional Roman family everywhere they went. Ancient Christian practices of family shocked good Romans. Early believers created such an inclusive understanding of "home" that it resembled, for all intents and purposes, a spiritual form of communism. Christians had a disturbing tendency to eschew state-sanctioned and arranged marriage in favor of having their unions blessed by priests or bishops (thus angering the Romans even more). Or they avoided marriage completely, placing themselves outside of familial arrangements of protection and inheritance, opting instead to live with spiritual brothers and sisters in shared houses. Still others chose a state of utter singleness as holy hermits intent on finding their home in God alone. One could read the Bible and study church history for weeks on end without coming across any home that even vaguely resembles the domesticity of the Victorian family or the twentieth-century American ideal. Indeed, the complexity and theological messiness of "home" in our own time is much more like what our ancestors experienced in biblical times than almost anything preached in a fundamentalist church.

The people who make up a household, those who create a home, are not always related by blood, nor do they always form customary legal or religious bonds. But making a home together is intended as a grace, a place of sacred habitation, a sign of God's intent to dwell with all humankind.

Who's at Home?

Sometimes wisdom is found in the oddest places, for example, in a real-estate blog. Blogger David Marine writes:

> The English word "home" is from the Old English word *hâm* (not the pig), which actually refers to a village or estate where many "souls" are gathered. It implies there's a physical dwelling involved, but the main idea is that it's a gathering of people. One dictionary I came across online had an interpretation of the modern definition of home that I really like. It states that home is "the abiding place of the affections." To me, that sums it up like nothing else. It's not a building or a room, but a place where your love dwells. *Home is the abiding place of the affections.*[7]

We all know that "home" has to do with family, the people with whom we live. Indeed, homes comprise people, who together create a place with some expectation of provision, warmth, and security.

For much of the last two hundred years, the Western cultural ideal of home was the domain of the patriarchal family: father, mother, and children, with an occasional extension of familial relations to include grandparents or a spinster aunt, perhaps a trusted servant or dear friend.[8] Home was populated thus, a seemingly sacred order of men, women, and children, governed by rules and roles to ensure shelter and safety for the souls therein.

The ideal might seem like a historical absolute, but in reality it was always messy. Nostalgia sometimes prevents us from remembering how complex the meaning of home could be. Even in the most traditional of arrangements, there were often second wives and stepchildren, because so many women died in childbirth. There were secret offspring, born to unwed women, sometimes raised within a family but more often not. There were children of masters and slaves or servants, conceived in forbidden love or forced sexual encounters across socially taboo boundaries. There were always widows and orphans, eccentric cousins, "bachelor" uncles, and aunts who lived with "special friends." The size of families shifted over time, as couples had fewer children when they moved from farm to city. And, as time went on, extended family transformed into nuclear family, leaving those in the larger group to find their own homes, at first near the original family or in the old neighborhood, but eventually farther away.

Perhaps the biggest challenge to the old ideal, however, came when women claimed equality with their husbands and demanded respect for their work (whether at home or in the workplace). In the 1970s, the patriarchal family, which had already been stretched and strained in many directions, gave way to a new vision: that of the family of mutual exchange, created around the values of shared love, empathetic participation, and freely accepted obligations. Thus was born the contemporary family, built upon affection but with no set structure of authority, gender, religion, ethnicity, race, or even legal contract to regularize it. There are a multitude of types of contemporary unions and, as a result, a multiplicity of the types of homes we are making.[9]

In addition to the variety of unions, marriage is also undergoing significant demographic change. In the United States, women now marry at the average age of twenty-seven, men at twenty-nine; in Canada, women at twenty-nine and men at thirty-one; these are historical highs for both genders. This shift toward late marriage is occurring in all the world's wealthiest nations; Sweden posts the highest marriage ages, women at thirty-three and men at thirty-five.[10] While delayed married is on the rise, so is cohabitation. In the United States, approximately half of marriage-age women reported having cohabited with a partner between the years 2006 and 2010. Although some of these relationships resulted in marriage, others did not.

All this results in changes regarding children as well. A University of Virginia team reports, "At the age of twenty-five, 44 percent of women have had a baby, while only 38 percent have married; by the time they turn thirty, about two-thirds of American women have had a baby, typically out of wedlock."[11] Thus, a large number of American women are already mothers when they enter into their first marriage, and when they do settle into families, the number of children tends to be smaller, because the focus is on "quality" of parenting rather than "quantity" of children.[12] Divorce rates are down, mostly because delayed marriage is up. But there are plenty of families headed by single parents, about 30 percent, whether those parents are female or male, straight or gay.

Delayed marriage is also referred to as "capstone marriage." For many years, marriage was considered the beginning of making a home. When a man and woman wed in their early twenties, their relationship served as the foundation for decisions about where to live, what house to rent or buy, the path of careers, committing to a religious community and civic organizations, and raising children. Early marriage was the "cornerstone" of everything that followed. Now, however, the pattern has been reversed. Through their twenties, young adults finish school, choose a place to live, begin a career path, explore social, civic, and spiritual options, form friendships, and sometimes become parents—all before marriage. Getting married is the "capstone" of the journey of early adulthood, not its prerequisite, as it once had been. Thus, by the time a couple marry, the partners may have already made a home, or perhaps several, either with someone else or alone. Making a newlywed home becomes the work of merging previous homes, more akin to the sort of homes created through divorce and remarriage in previous decades.[13]

In addition to changes regarding heterosexual marriage, same-sex marriage is transforming American homes. According to the 2010 U.S. Census, almost 650,000 gay or lesbian couples shared households, a rise of 80 percent in just ten years. Of those families, 25.3 percent were raising children. These numbers are sure to increase as the Supreme Court extended the right of marriage to same-sex couples in June 2015, making the United States the twenty-first nation to do so. Not only is marriage equality legally protected, but a growing number of religious and faith communities now define marriage as a sacred commitment between two equal partners, not as a relationship between a man and woman.

Added to the dizzying mix of cohabitation, civil unions, marriages (early or delayed), and single-parent households are single people. More than half of American adults are single, and roughly one of every seven adults lives alone, making up 28 percent of the nation's households. One sociologist notes that single-person households "are now tied with childless couples as the most prominent residential type—more common than the nuclear family, the multigenerational family, and the roommate or group home"—and tend to be clustered in urban areas. In New York City, one million people live by themselves, many in residences designed as "one-person dwellings."[14] Evidently, people living alone like living alone with others who live alone, thus creating a new sense of "home" beyond the walls of residential buildings and more conventional domestic relationships. In a sense, for singles, public space itself becomes a home, expanding the definition of "home" into workplaces, bars, cafés, coffeehouses, gyms, parks, health clubs, social

justice and political causes, and virtual communities and social networks; singles are often "at home" on the web. Thus, the single
household is not necessarily an isolated one. Instead, singles are
constructing new forms of connecting with others, "creating new
possibilities for [their] personal, romantic, and social lives" by making a variety of homes over time with coworkers, friends, compan-
ions (both human and animal), and lovers.[15]

Added to the list of creative possibilities of home are those of
our spiritual lives, for it is pretty clear that any domestic divinity
can no longer just be depicted as a father presiding at the head of his
nuclear family's dinner table. The emerging types and demographics of partnerships and marriage reveal that the entire concept of
home is changing. Religious institutions are scurrying to articulate
ancient theologies and spiritual practices in ways that offer meaning
to new possibilities of sexuality, relationships, and marriage. These
denominations are not simply attempting to be relevant; instead,
they know that home and faith are interconnected. The domestic
revolution is a spiritual revolution. And the way we make a household opens up new questions about the God who is with us at
home.

Domestic Danger

When I was a young teenager, my parents took in an uncle who
was continually struggling to find work. Although they knew he
was difficult, they did not understand that he was a violent and
abusive person, haunted by extreme mental illness complicated by
a history of substance abuse. His presence ripped through our
household like a meat cleaver, leaving behind emotional turmoil
and damaged relationships. Whenever he was under our roof, home
was anything but a shelter. Instead, for the months of his residence,

it was as if our house were possessed. My siblings and I learned how to make quick exits from explosive rooms and find relief in the pages of books or behind locked doors. Home's promise of security and acceptance degenerated into a precarious tightrope walk between survival and threat.

For all its promise of grace, home can be a horror as well. Too many people have experiences of a home that shelters sickness and addiction, of homes that deteriorate from carelessness and neglect, or homes broken apart through willful violations of the relationships in them. The news is full of reports of domestic violence and abuse, and most people are aware that a woman is far more likely to be killed by her lover or husband than a stranger. Home is a vulnerable space, offering possibilities of care and tenderness to be sure, but also an open pathway for those who choose to take psychological, emotional, or physical advantage of its privacy and shelter. Indeed, home-centered violence can be so destructive that some social scientists refer to it as "intimate terrorism."

There is a vigorous debate as to whether religious people engage in domestic abuse and violence more or less often than the general public. If some use religion to justify or excuse such acts, it is in clear violation of the fundamental principles of faith. Indeed, ancient writers understood the potential for the home to become a house of horrors instead of a sacred dwelling, and even cultures that were rigidly patriarchal still held up high standards for the spiritual disposition of the home.

Throughout Jewish history, marriage has been understood as sacred, and the home that a couple makes is expected to be governed by harmony. This ideal is expressed in the Hebrew term *shalom bayit,* meaning "peace in the home." *Shalom bayit* signifies completeness or wholeness achieved through nurture, respect, and *chesed* ("loving-kindness"). Thus, the home is the place of most intimate fulfillment. A harmonious household makes both husband and wife happy, provides for safe rearing of children, and becomes a sanctuary of God's presence.

Early Christians extended the principle of *shalom bayit* to include the ideals of spiritual equality and mutual submission. According to Paul, "there is no longer male and female" in Christ (Gal. 3:28); therefore husband and wife should "be subject to one another out of reverence for Christ" (Eph. 5:21). In a New Testament passage on the order of households (Eph. 5:21–33), the primary call is to love, tenderness, kindness, and a practice of honoring the body, which is a spiritual disposition of physical reverence toward each other. Domestic tranquility is the goal, in which thoughtfulness and regard replace threats and violence as the path toward orderly relations.

Islam likewise emphasizes kindness between husband and wife, a disposition extended to the entire household. Ibn Abi al-Dunya reports a saying of the Prophet: "When Allah loves the people of a household, he introduces kindness among them." In the Hadith husband and wife are described as shepherd and shepherdess over their flock, and the Qur'an stresses attributes of mercy, affection, and enjoyment between members of a household (30:21). Kindness thus begins at home and is a divine gift to a faithful household; the well-disposed home then serves as example for the rest of the world to see the truth of the Prophet's teachings.

Home is a vulnerable place, the location of the most tender practices of human relationships, where kindness is essential for the safety and growth of all those within a household. Within the structure of genuine kindness, people develop the ability to trust, to receive from others, to dream and create. Many spiritual leaders have noted the connection between vulnerability and human flourishing. As Buddhist monk Chögyam Trungpa notes:

Real fearlessness is the product of tenderness. It comes from letting the world tickle your heart, your raw and beautiful heart. You are willing to open up, without resistance or shyness, and face the world. You are willing to share your heart with others.[16]

The world first enters into our hearts at home, where we learn to live with others and experience the power of mercy. If one learns kindness at home, it is much easier to practice kindness in the world. If one learns violence at home, it is harder to resist doing the same in the world. Of course, kind people may go astray and wounded people may be healed, but what happens at home becomes a sort of emotional script for the rest of our lives. That is why Mother Teresa once said, "We must make our homes centers of compassion and forgive endlessly."[17] Compassion may begin at home, but it does not stay there. Peace in the home extends to peace for the world.

Spiritual Habits of Home

One of the first phrases I remember to describe spiritual practices came from John Wesley, the eighteenth-century founder of the Methodist Church: "holy habits." A keen observer of human nature, Wesley saw that bad behavior and moral failings were practiced acts, often taught by and reinforced through the surrounding environment. Quite simply, unethical conduct was a habit, personal to be sure, but also a habit shaped by the larger community in which one lived or worked or worshipped. Habits of moral transgression might arise by accident, through ignorance, carelessness, or willful imitation, but they were always reinforced by spiritual inattentiveness. Having noticed the relationship between bad habits and environment, Wesley reversed the formula. Could virtue become habitual as well? He went on to teach that men and women must practice "holy habits" in mutually supportive homes and communities in order to know God and create a more just society; and a more just society would naturally foster habits leading people to a deeper spiritual awareness. Habit and habitat went together. To ignore the relationship between the two imperiled both the soul and the social order. To be intentional about habit and habitat, however, was salvation.

The words "habit," "habitat," and "inhabit" all come from the same Latin root meaning "to hold or possess" or, in a related sense, "to dwell." The terms refer to customary actions or conditions, such as repeated acts or comfortable environments, all involving a sort of unreflective regularity. Habits and habitats are ordinary things often taken for granted. Thus Wesley's genius, and the genius of many other spiritual masters, was to develop ways for people to pay attention to habits and habitats, practicing love, acceptance, and kindness in ways that focus spiritual attention and transform lives. Instead of dwelling in whatever happens to be of the moment, paying attention to what we do and the shape of the environments where we do things can transform regular things and customary acts into the stuff of human spirit, the soul of community.

When it comes to understanding home, faith traditions have emphasized relationships over physical location, often recognizing that those who dwell in the same household constitute the nearest of neighbors. Home incubates our first habits, the repeated actions that form character. What happens at home does not stay at home, however. The home is a training ground for spiritual and ethical habits that we take out into the world as adults. Because households nurture habit, they can be schools of intentional spiritual practice. Things like sharing, eating together, praying, conversation, critical thinking, acceptance, forgiveness, and charity can become habitual. Home can be a genuine community, where love overcomes isolation. In recent years, researchers have discovered that people and families who engage in spiritual practices at home are generally happier, more involved in the community, and healthier. Thus, churches, synagogues, temples, and mosques have placed greater emphasis on spiritual practices in the last two decades, encouraging the faithful to assume domestic responsibility for the moral formation of their families.

This may sound old-fashioned, like family Bible reading or saying grace around a table. But the new awareness of domestic spiritual practice does not focus solely upon familial devotions. Instead, in many faith communities, the emphasis is in on moral practices. And two locations have emerged as particularly sacred: the front door and the table, the physical places at home where we form the spiritual habits of hospitality and gratitude.

A door is the place of coming and going, of safety and protection, and of welcome. At the first Passover, Moses had the people sprinkle their doorposts with blood to protect them from the harm coming to Egypt. As commanded in scripture, Jews still place a small decorative case called a mezuzah on their doorway, inside of which are verses from the Torah beginning with, "Hear O Israel: The LORD is our God, the LORD alone," and continuing through the promises that follow for God's abundance and "houses filled with all sorts of goods" (Exod. 6:4–15). When entering a house, Jews recite a blessing or touch the mezuzah as a gesture of prayer. The doorway is a reminder that God dwells with Israel and that God's words are a sanctuary.

Jesus, well aware of the spiritual importance of the door in Judaism, would later say, "I am the door" (John 10:9, KJV), inviting his followers into a life of safety and abundance. Later Christians would elaborate on this image by placing Jesus at the door, as a guest seeking entrance into our homes, "Behold, I stand at the door, and knock" (Rev. 3:20, KJV). Some Christians place crosses above doorways as a token of Jesus's presence at the entrance.

In other traditions, spiritual talismans of all sorts mark doorways and windows to drive evil spirits away and keep good ones in. Practices like feng shui and Native American smudging are similar; furniture is arranged and space purified to welcome, bless, and heal. Doors keep out danger, but also usher guests and strangers into the sanctuary that is home. The doorway serves as a moral stage for the practice of hospitality, an architectural reminder of how we receive others into the inner places of our lives.

The table is another school for holy habits, perhaps the lessons and practices we most remember from our childhood homes. Kitchen tables, dining-room tables, picnic tables, these are communal gathering places for family, where we celebrate one another and, very often, participate in sacred rituals at home. Around tables we learn what to eat and how, ways to set a table for special meals or guests, how to share customs and traditions through generations, and how to serve others. At the family table, many learn how to pray—whether through Shabbat liturgies or a traditional grace or in extemporaneous prayer. All sorts of manners and rules, some formal and many informal, govern tables for the enjoyment of all those gathered for a meal. The table is the earthy manifestation of God's presence, the "heavenly feast," where all are fed and sustained and no one suffers want. German theologian Dietrich Bonhoeffer wrote of the "festive quality" of the daily table:

> It is a constantly recurring reminder in the midst of our everyday work of God's resting after His work, of the Sabbath as the meaning and goal of the week and its toil.

Our life is not only travail and labor, it is also refresh-
ment and joy in the goodness of God. We labor, but God
nourishes and sustains us. And this is reason for celebrat-
ing. . . . Through daily meals [God] is calling us to re-
joice, to keep holiday in the midst of our working day.[18]

Thus, the table reminds us that the center of our lives is a feast in
which we celebrate the gifts of food and community and remember
our ancestors and the Giver. The habits we bring to the table can
make or break the party.

"Home is where we figure out primary patterns of nurture and
productivity, habits of need and desire, forms of rage and forgiveness,
ways of 'taking time' and discovering the people who 'count' for us,"
writes Sharon Daloz Parks, formerly a senior researcher at Harvard
Business School. "Our households are anchoring places where, over
time, we craft the practices by which we prosper or fail to prosper."[19]
At our doors, we craft practices of welcome; at the table, we craft
practices of thankfulness. Doors and tables offer the promise of community. In both places, we form habits that will take us beyond the
walls of our private homes to a more meaningful shared life in our
planet home. Hospitality and gratitude need to be habitual in a world
where far too many people are willing to violate the trust of the
home. Do we dwell together well or poorly? To build a house on a
good foundation may save the planet. Our homes are a sort of spiritual training ground for what happens in our world house.

A Domestic Revolution

After a church service at which I had preached in Northampton,
Massachusetts, a parishioner came up to me and asked, "How did
you like the bread?"

The Communion bread that day was real bread, not small, tasteless wafers. The question was a bit odd, however. I had never been asked for my opinion about the flavor of the Lord's Supper!

"Ah, good," I replied.

"It was special," said the parishioner. "Made right here in Northampton."

Many people bake bread, I mused. Not all that surprising. But I must have looked a little puzzled, for she went on, "Not only made, but grown. Down the street. We're growing our own wheat again here in New England. This Communion bread was grown, harvested, milled, and baked right here."[20]

Almost three hundred years ago, in this same church, Jonathan Edwards preached to his congregation about the need for spiritual rebirth, stirring up a deeper awareness of God's presence and work in the world. Many in the small town responded to Pastor Edwards's plea. Word went out abroad that a great spiritual renewal was under way in Northampton, and soon other towns experienced the same. The event became known as the Great Awakening, a spiritual movement that transformed North American religious and political life, making society more democratic and inclusive.

These days something of an awakening is under way again in Northampton, but it is not taking place primarily in the church. Instead, it is a domestic awakening, a spiritual revolution taking place in farms and homes and small shops, led by people growing organic crops, raising livestock, brewing beer, making jewelry, weaving cloth, and making clothes. Northampton's downtown is abuzz; dozens and dozens of local businesses are part of a regional revival. Entrepreneurs have fostered vitality through creativity and attention to the local, not opting for quick fixes or sacrificing the environment for financial expansion. People are chatting about New England's "new culture," a kind of new old way of life.[21] The "old" are the domestic arts, local farming, and crafts linked with new technologies and informed by postmodern sensibilities, a commitment to ecological sustainability, and a protest against the concentration of wealth by corporations and global elites.

And it is not just in New England. The domestic awakening is under way across North America, with profound, deeply spiritual ramifications. I know pastors who brew beer, monks with vast organic gardens worked by their neighbors, women who have formed knitting groups at church, urban homesteaders raising chickens in their backyards, a doctor who does her own canning, and even a seminarian furniture maker. Friends are collecting water, generating their own power, and making their own compost. My office is in my backyard; my husband's in a downstairs bedroom. Once, not long ago, Christian fundamentalists were the only people involved in homeschooling. But now others are embracing the idea of home-as-school, and approximately two million American children now learn at home. Church has moved home too. Some estimates place the number of house churches in the United States around thirty thousand, not including the multitude of other sorts of non-Christian and spiritual gatherings that take place in domestic settings.[22]

The domestic turn shows up in the media as well. "Shelter shows," found in the United States on PBS, HGTV, and other domestically themed networks, rank among the most popular on television. Once such shows were confined to a few offerings on public television, but HGTV now dominates North American viewing as a primetime top-ten cable network.[23] Critics often attack shelter television as indicative of greed and status seeking. But I think this misses the mark—domesticity programs may actually point to important spiritual longings in American culture. While much of television veers between reality shows and the real horror of twenty-four seven global news, programs featuring houses serve to remind viewers of shelter and safety. In a world that appears to be falling apart, an hour of watching someone restore a house offers the refreshing possibility that things can be fixed. Even Hillary Clinton, when retiring from her position as secretary of state, said that she looked forward to watching television, especially home-improvement shows, her favorite being HGTV's *Love It or List It*. She confessed to the *New York Times*, "I find it very calming."[24] At first hearing, that may sound like escapism, but it is actually a comment laden with spiritual and social implications for habitation and rootedness, perhaps a longing for a remodeled American household.[25]

One writer refers to the domestic awakening as "radical homemaking" and points out that it is not a movement of separation and escape, but about "interdependence" and "interreliance" with family, friends, and community—a search for new order. The domestic awakening is about restitching a pattern of meaningful life that contributes to making the world more just and peaceable.[26] This revolution is not the outgrowth of conservative religions or a reformulation of 1950s ideals of womanly bliss. As journalist Emily Matchar observes:

> This current domesticity-mania is unique in that it signals a profound social change among educated, progressive Americans. It's part of a shift away from corporate culture and toward a more eco-conscious, family-centric, DIY lifestyle, a shift that has the potential to change the American cultural and political landscape. . . . New Domesticity is the embrace of the domestic in service of environmentalism, DIY culture, personal fulfillment. Though it may resemble your grandmother's homemaking, it's not—this is something new, different, perhaps even revolutionary.[27]

The current domestic revolution may be new, but history is replete with revolutions that began at home. Christianity itself can be understood as a domestic revolution. The first churches recorded in the New Testament met in homes, often overseen by women. Ancient Celtic spirituality was a domestic piety based on the daily work of rising, tending to the fires, serving meals, and performing farm tasks. Throughout the Middle Ages, groups of pious revolutionaries continuously challenged the church and the state by gathering in homes, away from authorities, to practice their own ways of faith and life, most often in service to the poor. All of these movements, despite their various historical times and cultures, were animated by the idea that God is with us, an intimate and domestic presence, empowering people to experience the world as a holy habitation. And they offered a powerful challenge to religious and political institutions—as well as oppressive economic systems.

The connection between the domestic and the spiritual revolution is most dramatic in the sixteenth century's Protestant Reformation. By 1500, many Christians wondered if the established church had any real meaning in their lives; it was a distant institution that drained local coffers and seemed to offer little in return. For them, "home" was a holy turn toward the local, a spiritual renewal of place and neighborly relations. Marriage became a protest movement against a church that practiced priestly celibacy, reading and writing empowered "even" women to engage theology and politics, and tending home and rearing children were redefined as God's work equal to the work of a priest in a parish church. This was a middle-class revolt against feudal politics and economics, with the home and the family shop as the focus of a new model of community and prosperity.

Protestants did something else shocking: they put pews in churches and encouraged families to sit together in holy worship, an innovation that allowed men, women, and children to actually share spiritual space. These revolutionaries ripped piety out of convents and monasteries and relocated it in the local church and the household. The faithful laity read the Bible, prayed, and sang hymns around kitchen tables during the week with as much devotion as was expected in the monastic office or Sunday worship. Historians note that Protestants' lusty attitudes toward sex made a "genuine break" with pre-Reformation practices and that their "new image of the family" amounted to a "radical redefinition" of the sacred.[28] The sixteenth-century domestic revolution laid the groundwork in Western culture for democratic forms of church organization, an elevation of women's roles in spiritual leadership, and universal public education. It is nearly impossible to imagine modern Europe and North America without the reformation that began at home.

Domestic revolutions did not cease with the Reformation. The fluid mix of spirituality, protest, and homemaking reappears throughout modern history. Before they built church buildings, Quakers and Puritans met in homes to share, teach, and preach their particular views of faith and social revolution. Women, like Anne Hutchinson in Boston, used their parlors as pulpits and proclaimed egalitarian versions of Christianity that challenged patriarchal traditions of the established church. Eighteenth-century Methodists made home meetings central to practicing faith. Such societies broke boundaries of race and class and functioned as an economic and religious corrective to the worst abuses of slavery and early industrial capitalism. Utopian communities like New Lanark and New Harmony revolutionized industry by linking work, education, spirituality, and domestic arrangements into prosperous communities. American writer Henry David Thoreau extolled the wisdom of the native and local, offering a stabilizing vision of home to a restless, mobile young nation. Catherine Beecher, sister of the author Harriet Beecher Stowe and daughter of a clergyman, developed a new field of intellectual and moral endeavor for women: home economics. Her work transformed the nature of homemaking by providing it a kind of domestic philosophy that integrated insights from science, nutrition, theology, and education and turned it into a profession. Social reformers like Jane Addams, Vida Scudder, and Dorothy Day established settlement houses and workers' homes to improve urban social justice, bridge the gap between rich and poor, and create economic alternatives to the prevailing forms of capitalism.

Sharon Astyk, a contemporary domestic revolutionary, writes of the need to "settle" in a place, to create a sustainable home as both shelter amid financial uncertainty and an economic alternative to consumerist culture. When she speaks of an "economy of love," based in trust, support, and needing one's neighbor, she echoes voices from past domestic and spiritual revolutions.[29] How widespread are such sentiments now? Take a look at the books in the home section at the local bookstore, where, tucked between expensive volumes on home decor, there are a host of guides to urban homesteading, domestic crafts, and turning one's suburban backyard into an organic farm. To transform home is to transform the world. Domestic revolts are spiritual and political ones as well.

God as Home

In 1679, my newlywed ancestors Andrew and Eleanor Orem bought their first home, a parcel of land called Bantry, in Talbot County, Maryland. Bantry is no longer a farm, but it still exists as a road outside of Easton, Maryland. I have been there, exploring the place they once inhabited. It is mostly woods now, with some houses off the road facing the water. An older home sits at the end of the road, but it probably does not date back more than a hundred and fifty years, and it is certainly not my ancestors' abode. In the woods, there is a foundation of a small house, stripped bare by weather and scavengers and time, cracked by aggressive roots and vines, overgrown and hard to see. Somewhere here, in this place, Andrew and Eleanor built my family's first North American home.

I do not understand why I feel compelled to find where they lived, as if by discovering the location of their house I will somehow find them and, by implication, learn something of myself. Houses loom large in memory, but physical houses last only a bit longer than human beings—a generation or two, maybe three, and most family homes disappear. From Bantry Road, I see woods. And water. Lots of water. The ground here is only three feet above sea level. Andrew and Eleanor's house is long gone, and one day in the not too distant future—their farm will be gone too. Underwater, I suspect, claimed by rising seas.

Great spiritual traditions insist that houses, however significant, are not really our home. Dwelling in a space with others and the practice of lingering in place are the things that make home. Indeed, theistic faiths insist that ultimately God is our home. God dwells with us, and we in God. In Judaism, one way of referring to God is *shekhinah,* meaning the dwelling or settling of the Divine Presence, a word that also is used to describe the nesting of birds. The ancient Hebrew prophet Isaiah spoke of Immanuel, "God with us," as the promise of shelter and safety for Israel, one of the names that Christians later adopted for Jesus.

According to Christian teaching, Jesus is the Son of God, the human form of the Divine One made incarnate through Mary and born into the world. For Muslims, the Divine Presence, "God with us," is the manifestation of tranquility, the spirit of God that extends shelter and blessing to the faithful. They believe that God dwells most specifically in the Ka'bah, the House of Allah, the physical portal in Mecca between the sacred and secular worlds, toward which they face when they pray. The Hindu Bhagavad Gita describes God's dwelling as a string of pearls (a particularly interesting metaphor in light of contemporary physics) as the divine within and connecting all living beings. Accordingly, God dwells in the world the way a soul dwells in the body.[30] Throughout all of human history, we have built houses for the divine—temples and shrines and tabernacles and churches and sanctuaries—all to provide God shelter and extend that shelter to pilgrims who pause under holy roofs.

The word "dwell" is related to an Old English word for "heresy" or "madness." Perhaps it is a sort of insanity to believe that God dwells with us. If so, the madness is the long-lingering hope of the human race, the dream to dwell. It is not only a hope, however; it is also hard work, this effort to shelter our souls. Perhaps making a home is both a divine madness and a human one.

Ultimately, physical houses go to ruin, but home is an ongoing spiritual promise. The contemporary mystical poet Gunilla Norris writes:

> I leave the bedroom . . . I begin walking
> through my house. I will traverse it
> many times today like a creature
> covering her turf. It is a journey
> that zigzags and returns upon itself . . .
> a circumambulation . . . a re-remembering of place.
>
> I know this is the way many ancients prayed—
> Circling a holy site to deepen their devotion.
>
> The floor in this house is wood . . . wide, old boards.
> When I walk I am walking on the wood and in the woods.

I am walking on the life of these trees.
They have been cut and planed . . . offered up
for this sheltering.

My foot falls. The ground rises to meet it.
A holy, ordinary moment is repeating itself.
All the time I am meeting and being met like this.
Your whole creation is ground.
Help me to remember that in this mutuality
we can become home for each other.
You are asking us slowly to become
Your holy site.[31]

Home, a holy habitation, a sacred space. We do not often stop to consider where we dwell, much less how it shapes us to move about in the world, for either good or ill. But somehow we keep searching for home, looking for a safe haven to reside and return.

To me, Bantry is a holy site, a place of origin. As I scour the woods for traces of an ancestral abode, however, I inwardly sense the rising tides of an uncertain future. How long will this place remain above water? Will the coming flood submerge my family history forever? Where will home be then? Perhaps I need to build an ark of memory. Then the refrain of an old hymn sneaks up, words first learned in my childhood Methodist church:

O God, our help in ages past,
Our hope for years to come,
Our shelter from the stormy blast,
And our eternal home.

Neighborhood

It's a beautiful day in this neighborhood,
A beautiful day for a neighbor.
Would you be mine?
Could you be mine?
I've always wanted to have a neighbor just like you.
I've always wanted to live in a neighborhood with you.

—*Fred Rogers*

On an early November Saturday, with the autumn leaves at peak color against a bright blue sky, I walked to St. Aidan's church, a small congregation near our house. The building was open for a contemplative morning of silence, prayers, and candlelight, during which the neighborhood could remember a young woman, one gone missing and then found murdered, who grew up a few blocks away.

When I entered the wooden sanctuary, the place was still, but dozens of burning candles remained as evidence of many who had wandered in. The sense of sacred sadness was thick—the priest later told me that forty or fifty people had shown up at various times during the morning—and tokens of their prayers remained, the lit candles, bouquets of flowers. Someone had laid a yellow bow, a ribbon recently tied around a neighborhood tree, on the altar. It had been placed on the table as a holy offering to God.

The girl we remembered was Hannah Graham, a student at the University of Virginia. In fall 2014, her face splashed on television screens and the Internet in a dramatic missing-person case. Many people followed the story; major media outlets carried the news. In a sense, she became everyone's neighbor, the familiar girl who lived on any suburban street. But as these things do, other stories eventually took top billing, and the case receded from public view. Except, of course, when your neighbor is missing. When it is your neighbor, you do not forget.

Until that difficult autumn, I never really understood the power of neighborhood. Although my family had lived here for more than a decade, our northern Virginia suburb had always seemed somewhat anonymous, almost like a stereotype, with its fenced backyards, neat lawns, and quiet streets. A friend jokingly calls it "Brady World," a reference to the 1970s sitcom of family Americana, a place of niceness and middle-class aspirations. The children walk to good schools, bike along the Potomac, play in safe parks, and attend one of a dozen neighborhood churches. Parents hold backyard barbecues, set off fireworks on July 4, hang holiday lights together, and plant rival political signs in front yards. But other than regular suburban activities, nothing much happens here. People go about their lives and business pretty much in private.

And then Hannah disappeared. A neighbor's daughter, formerly a student at the local high school, now a college sophomore. Gone. About a week after she disappeared, yellow ribbons started to appear on neighborhood light posts and trees, on porches and mailboxes. Parents fretted about how to talk to their children about the news; students tired of news cameras occupying the high-school campus; teary-eyed neighbors spoke in hushed voices about their fears at the local grocery store or while walking their dogs. No matter the news, or how many days went by, we kept tying those ribbons on trees. The yellow streamers signaled support and grief, bewilderment and fear, hope and persistence. "Bring Hannah Home!" proclaimed signs secured by large bows. Bring her home to our neighborhood, wrapped in yellow ribbons everywhere.

Weeks later, at the end of October, searchers found Hannah's remains in a dry creek bed in the woods outside of Charlottesville. She would come back to our neighborhood. Not, of course, as we hoped.

While walking out the door shortly after her body was discovered, I said to my daughter, "I guess we can take this ribbon down now." I fingered the yellow bow, faded and softened by weather.

"Don't, Mom. Don't take it down. Not yet."

She was right. We could not take it down. Those ribbons embodied our care for each other, for the tender ways our community was connected. The threads that tie our lives together had become visible, this fabric of neighborhood, incarnated in yellow florist ribbon. These quiet streets, with their modest twentieth-century houses, lined by trees and edged with trim lawns, made up a real place where neighbors mourned together and practiced loving one another. Quietly, painfully, unexpectedly, we learned that when one of us is lost, we all are. We are our sisters' keepers.

A woman who lives near St. Aidan's collected the ribbons. She made a wreath of them to give to Hannah's parents and honor their daughter as appropriate, a token of a neighborhood awakened to its heart.

"Where Is God?" and the Neighborhood

The English word "neighbor" comes from the Old English words *neah* (or *nigh*), for "near," and *gebur,* meaning "dweller." By 1600 or so, the word "neighborhood," which had meant the "state or condition of living in a neighborly fashion," came into its modern usage as a noun for a community of people who dwell near one another. Lewis Mumford, a distinguished urban historian, points out: "Neighborhoods, in some primitive, inchoate fashion exist wherever human beings congregate in permanent family dwellings."[1] Put simply, people create neighborhoods when they gather together beyond family ties, live close to others, and choose to share certain resources (in the contemporary world, those resources include, for example, electricity, schools, roads, places of worship, stores, and often a park or some other commons). Neighborhoods are born when people settle in a certain geographical space and turn it, in common effort with others, into a habitable place.

Although Mumford was probably not thinking about theology, his language—"congregate" and "dwelling"—signals a playful ambiguity with secularity and the sacred that is present in our experience of neighborhoods. Indeed, "abide," a term often used to describe God's presence, is essentially the same word as "abode," our home.

Of course, neighborhoods typically have churches, synagogues, temples, and mosques—important buildings in any community. Neighborhoods need spiritual gathering places as much as they need schools and shops. Yet God does not live at the neighborhood church. If God dwells within our individual household, then certainly God dwells next door as well. God abides with us as a gathered community of neighbors. When we live near others, even with only the thinnest of personal connections, we still belong to each other through the environment we share. Journalist Peter Lovenheim makes this point about his neighbors in Rochester, New York:

> On a summer night, if our windows were open, we fell asleep to the same sound of crickets; in the morning, we awoke to the same birdsong and din of distant traffic. We all resided, as it were . . . on the same farm; our soil was the same; our rainfall was the same; our sunlight, snow, and pollen index were the same. And we moved through this same physical miniworld, most of us, daily for years. Surely this shared physical environment, both below and above the ground, bound us as neighbors.[2]

Neighborhoods are ecosystems of relationships between people, a shared experience of the natural world we inhabit, and the ways we care for each other and the land. We might neglect or forget this, but the congregation of our lives with those nearby is sacred, a human geography in a spiritual habitat. To remember and to re-connect with our neighbors and neighborhoods is a life-giving, sane, and humane way of life.

All of the world's religions make neighbors the central concern of spirituality and ethics. Love of God and neighbor are absolutely intertwined. Jesus made this case succinctly when asked by the Pharisees to name the greatest commandment. Jesus responded: " 'You shall love the Lord, your God with all your heart, and will all your soul, and with all your mind.' And . . . 'You shall love your neighbor as yourself.' On these two commandments hang all the law and the prophets" (Matt. 22:37–40). If we understand that neighborly relations are woven into divine love, then we can grasp that God is, essentially, a near-dwelling God. We know God through our neighbors. And that is a good thing—for in recent years, we have turned our attention once again to the local. To reconnect with our neighborhoods and those nearby is truly a spiritual revolution.

The Sacred Next Door

On a late summer day when I was about seven years old, there was a commotion next door. We lived in one of three houses that shared a property line; another of the three was owned by my uncle. My mother ran outside, with me in pursuit, and we saw my cousin sitting in a huge tree on the property line with the third neighbor's yard. He was wielding a saw and an axe, hacking branches away, while our neighbor yelled up at him from the near the trunk. "Come down, right now! Get out of my tree!" My cousin yelled back and kept cutting and chopping. Each year, the old fruit tree dropped part of its ripened bounty on my uncle's driveway. As a result, it had created a sizable purple stain on the concrete. Having had enough of this and worried that his new car would fall victim to the fruit, my uncle sent my cousin up the tree to get rid of the branches overhanging the driveway. My cousin had been quite zealous in his task, taking out large sections of the tree. There was quite a racket, a good deal of cursing, and accusations about trespassing.

Another neighbor, a police officer, appeared on scene and calmed everyone down. My cousin descended from his perch, but still looked defiant amid the piles of branches at the base of the tree. The owner of the fruit tree demanded recompense, and my uncle, now also on scene, refused and laughed. The tree took the worst of it, looking every bit the victim of a chainsaw massacre. It never really recovered. Our neighbor and my uncle never spoke again. And although we did not know it that day, there would be no more pies made from the tree's fruit for the neighborhood.

My mother took the neighbor's side against her own brother-in-law. After everyone had left, we stood on our back porch. I was crying, so upset was I about the tree, and my mother held my hand.

"Your uncle was wrong," she insisted. "What if it was his tree? Would he like it if someone did that to his property?" Her lips tightened into a grimace. "He only thinks of himself, never others. I don't think he even knows the Golden Rule. He never considers his neighbors."

"Remember the Golden Rule from Sunday school?" she asked, as she squeezed my hand. "Do unto others as you would have them do unto you." She pointed to the sad remains of the once bountiful tree and said, "We must love our neighbors as ourselves. If we don't, that is what happens."

The Great Tree Slaughter introduced me to ethics, a field of philosophy that might be better called "how to get along with the neighbors."

The Golden Rule. Most of world religions and ethical systems teach the Golden Rule, a precept that makes the way we treat our neighbors central both to the good life now and to eternal life with God. On my office wall hangs a poster, entitled "Ageless Wisdom," that lists a dozen versions of this neighborly principle from ten major religions.[3] There is, of course, the Christian version: "Do to others as you would have them do to you" (Luke 6:31). And so it goes on. Hinduism: "This is the sum of duty: do naught unto another which would cause you pain if done to you." Taoism: "Regard your neighbor's gain as your own gain, and your neighbor's loss as your own loss." Zoroastrianism: "Whatever is disagreeable to yourself do not do unto others." Judaism: "You shall not take vengeance or bear a grudge against any of your people, but you shall love your neighbor as yourself" (Lev. 19:18); and "What is hateful to you, do not to your fellow man. This is the law: all the rest is commentary" (Rabbi Hillel). Confucianism: "Surely it is the maxim of loving-kindness: Do not do unto others what you yourself would find hurtful." Islam: "None of you [truly] believe until he wishes for his brother what he wishes for himself."

When my mother quoted the Golden Rule on the back porch, it sounded a bit old-fashioned to me. I did not like what my cousin had done to the tree, but the rule seemed a bit moralistic, perhaps out of step with the needs of the dynamic days of the 1960s—a little *Leave It to Beaver* in a *Mad Men* sort of world. But in recent years, as the borders between global neighbors become more porous and new neighbors move in to old neighborhoods, the Golden Rule has experienced a comeback, its principle of reciprocity stunningly relevant in a world divided by class, race, and religion. Contemporary historian Karen Armstrong argues that the Golden Rule "is the best idea humanity has ever had, and it can serve as the unifying ethical insight of compassion." She has helped to found an international movement to make peace through new practices of neighborliness. The movement's charter states: "The principle of compassion lies at the heart of all religious, ethical, and spiritual traditions, calling us always to treat all others as we wish to be treated ourselves."[4] Armstrong describes the Golden Rule as an "imaginative act of empathy" that can be practiced by religious and secular people alike.[5]

Armstrong is not the only contemporary religious leader calling for renewal of the Golden Rule. In his address to the world following 9/11, the Dalai Lama asked the world to embrace the rule as a way of healing:

> A central teaching in most spiritual traditions is: What you wish to experience, provide for another. Look to see, now, what it is you wish to experience in your own life, and in the world. . . . If you wish to experience

peace, provide peace for another. If you wish to know that you are safe, cause another to know that they are safe. If you wish to better understand seemingly incomprehensible things, help another to better understand. If you wish to heal your own sadness or anger, seek to heal the sadness or anger of another. Those others are waiting for you now. . . . They are looking to you for love.[6]

The Dalai Lama believes that this "common ground spirituality," based on the call to "love your neighbor as yourself," is the only path toward global tolerance and peace.[7] Pope Francis has made the command to love God and love neighbor the center of his papacy, insisting that Catholics must "welcome others as true brothers and sisters, overcoming divisions, rivalries, misunderstandings, and selfishness."[8] Author Deepak Chopra refers to it as "an injunction to live by grace."[9] Even Prince Charles, who will one day be the head of the Church of England, reminded an audience gathered to consider religious tensions in the Middle East "that the emphasis of the love of neighbor" and the Golden Rule "are the ultimate foundations of truth, justice, compassion, and human rights."[10]

Proximity is not only what makes a neighborhood. Simply living next to others is not enough. The spirit of neighborhood means practicing the Golden Rule, when near dwellers treat others the way they hope to be treated. When we love our neighbor as ourselves, we build sacred connections between the spaces we inhabit.

My mother would be so pleased.

The New Neighborhood

I am sitting in my neighborhood Starbucks, in a suburban box-store "retail community" less than two miles from my house. It is midday in the middle of the week. People are reading, doing business, talking on the phone, or playing video games. Four women are studying the Bible together. In my immediate vicinity, two people are white, two people are black (one is a woman wearing a veil and doing homework), and two are Hispanic. Even with a rotating staff and mobile clients, employees know many of these people by name, asking questions about their children, recent vacations, or work. For a couple of weeks, a young man ditching school occupied the same table every morning. I am not sure what happened to him, but I do know the manager was keeping an eye on him. When it is cold, the working regulars make room for the homeless folks, often buying coffee for them. A gay couple stand at the register, holding hands while ordering their lattes. I like writing here, feeling the company of others, even when we are all busy on our own projects. I may not know every one of them, but they are not really strangers. They are my neighbors.

Perhaps the oddest thing about my current neighborhood is that it is so close, about fifty miles or so, from the neighborhood in which I grew up. A short drive away is Baltimore, where my family was from and where I spent my childhood, in the middle-class neighborhood of Hamilton. We were white Protestants and Catholics, mostly from German families, with a few English and French in the mix. We were a neighborhood with picnics and parades, the PTA, schools, shops, and safe streets where everybody looked after everyone else's children. There was a coffee shop there too, bearing the oddly appropriate name The White Coffee Pot, where my grandparents and parents were regulars and where the neighbors gathered to work and socialize. Much of Hamilton's neighborliness was a function of being alike and often interrelation through marriage. Difference was not welcome. Nor were strangers. It was a tightly bounded place, an exclusive set, as it were, of family and faith. Put simply, the world of The White Coffee Pot is far more than fifty miles away. My local Starbucks and the old White Coffee Pot are a universe apart, neighborhoods of completely different sorts.

Neighborhoods are often spoken of with nostalgia or as in precipitous decline. Some people remember old neighborhoods like Hamilton lovingly and wish such communities would return. Theirs is often a romantic view of the past, seeing the streets through rose-tinted memory. To speak of neighborhood decline is often more academic—as scholars point out the erosion of "social capital" and communal connection. They demonstrate the link between failed neighborhoods and poor educational outcomes or crime. To speak of neighborhood in either way can be depressing, for both assume that our grandparents' neighborhoods were better than our own.

Although it is easy, and perhaps popular, to mourn the loss of old neighborhoods, the truth of the matter is that new neighborhoods have proliferated in global urbanized society. Neighborhoods have not so much declined as been transformed by massive population growth, economic disruption, and technology.

Some are healthy, many struggling, and more are simply surviving. Even with the full force of mobility and technology, people still choose to live near one another and, no matter how fragile or invisible the ties in such neighborhoods might be, we remain interdependent and connected.

Peter Block, writing about contemporary neighborhoods, argues that the problem is that people do not feel as though they "belong" to such places (even though they do), resulting in what he calls "an age of isolation" instead of being "grounded" through "the sense of safety that arises from a place where we are emotionally, spiritually, and psychologically a member."[11] Although we live near to one another in *neighborhoods,* we do not feel that we necessarily belong to one another, that we have *neighborly relations* with either place or people. We might live *in* a particular location, but it is hard to sense that our lives are *with* others. In a way, a neighborhood is simply the space where people reside near others; the challenge of re-creating vibrant, healthy neighborhoods is building connections between people and, in the process, turning isolated individuals into neighbors. Indeed, "neighborhood" is an empty concept without neighbors. Thus, the meaning of "neighborhood" is intimately caught up with an important question, one fraught with spiritual and ethical implications: Who is my neighbor?

In the twenty-first century, it can be hard to attend to our neighborhood and know our neighbors. People are busy. Most people are struggling to make it economically, and too many are just trying to survive. We might live nearby, but we have little access to other people's lives. And oddly enough, even though many people feel isolated, our understanding of neighborhood has expanded. We live in multiple layers of geographical and virtual neighborhoods. Those who are "nigh" include friends and family living across the nation or world, connected through social media, professional associations, or shared-interest groups. We are aware of neighboring cities, counties, states, and countries. Global media connects the planet into a vast neighborhood, where people from once distant cultures or religions, like the Dalai Lama, Malala Yousafzai, or Nelson Mandela, wend their way into hearts everywhere and become both our neighbors and our heroes. What we commonly call "celebrity culture" is an extension of neighborhood gossip, the technological equivalent of swapping stories of surprising or salacious behavior over the back fence. Perhaps we retreat into our own houses because the neighborhood is so large that it is intimidating. We do not know how to live with the neighbors.

Each morning, however, I wake up in a physical neighborhood—my house on a particular block in a particular town in Virginia where I say good morning to my family and look out the window to see if my neighbors are up and about. I open the *Washington Post* and read news from my larger urban neighborhood, the city, and other suburbs. Then my neighborhood expands: I check e-mail for correspondence from close family, friends, or business associates in my personal and professional neighborhoods. I go to social media and read posted updates online. I flip on cable news and cruise through several news sites to find out what is happening in our shared global neighborhood. During the first hour of each day, I check on many thousands of people, some physically near, many near to my heart, and many more who are near in my thoughts or concerns. I think of all of them as my neighbors—and the places where I meet them as the multiplicity of the neighborhoods in which I live.

Some critics would say that these are not neighborhoods—they are only digital connections, not the sort of ties of trust and relationship through which real neighborhoods succeed. If Lewis Mumford was correct, that neighborhoods are where people congregate for the purposes of making the world more habitable, then these layers of connections may be the yellow ribbons of our new neighborhoods, the inchoate architecture for emerging global neighborhoods. Indeed, technology may not be eroding our neighborhoods as much as stretching our understanding and experience of our neighbors and neighborhoods, creating new forms of congregating and new possibilities for neighborliness.

If I spent time in my old neighborhood, I suspect it would be far more like my neighborhood Starbucks than the old White Coffee Pot. In the part of Baltimore where I grew up, the physical landscape has not changed very much in the last five decades. But the people living there—and the ways in which they relate to the landscape—have. Those people are far more racially and religiously diverse than my grandparents could have ever imagined, and their diversity has made the old patterns of neighborly relations impossible. Yet at the same time the new neighborhood inhabitants have been (often unintentionally) building and practicing new connections of relationship. A new kind of neighborhood is forming. Even if you have lived in the same place your whole life, changes in economy, demographics, technology, and culture have moved almost everyone—and that is a global everyone—to a new neighborhood. The biggest issue of the twenty-first century is not necessarily the "decline" of neighborhood. It may be that we have all moved to a new neighborhood and have not learned how to get along with the new neighbors.

Who Is My Neighbor Anyway?

"Love your neighbor as yourself." "Do unto others as you would have them do unto you." Easy to affirm, but very hard to do. How do we love our neighbor as ourselves? What should we do in response to the Golden Rule? We do not always know how to move from principle to deeds, from the command to the concrete.

A second and perhaps more subtle set of questions follows these, and how we act upon the rule depends on how we answer them: How far does the principle of compassion extend? Who are the "others" in the Golden Rule? Who is my neighbor anyway?

Although the ideal of the Golden Rule might be central to human experience, it is also the case that people have often drawn a tight circle around the neighborhood, attempting to exclude those not of their tribe from the practice of compassion. This is especially the case when it comes to religion.

The tension between the Golden Rule and the boundaries of neighborhood forms the central question in one of the New Testament's most important stories, the parable of the Good Samaritan (Luke 10:25–37). In it, a lawyer challenges Jesus with a question, "Teacher, what must I do to inherit eternal life?"

Jesus knew this to be a rhetorical question, so he responds, "What is written in the law? What do you read there?"

The lawyer then quotes the two great commandments: "You shall love the Lord your God with all your heart, and with all your soul, and with all your strength, and with all your mind; and your neighbor as yourself."

Jesus replies, "You have given the right answer; do this, and you will live."

But the lawyer objects. He cannot do this until Jesus answers another question, "And who is my neighbor?"

Jesus replies with a story:

> A man was going down from Jerusalem to Jericho, and fell into the hands of robbers, who stripped him, beat him, and went away, leaving him half dead. Now by chance a priest was going down that road; and when he saw him, he passed by on the other side. So likewise a Levite, when he came to the place and saw him, passed by on the other side. But a Samaritan while traveling came near him; and when he saw him, he was moved with pity. He went to him and bandaged his wounds, having poured oil and wine on them. Then he put him on his own animal, brought him to an inn, and took care of him. The next day he took out two denarii, gave them to the innkeeper, and said, "Take care of him; and

when I come back, I will repay you whatever more you spend."

The Samaritans and the Jews were enemies, two tribes caught in an ancient argument about birthright and ethnicity who lived in seg-regated neighborhoods. By Jesus's time they were forbidden to have contact with each other, and violent squabbles sometimes erupted. The lawyer, who was a Jew, surely knew of both the informal cus-toms and formal laws separating the two groups. Samaritans and Jews were not good neighbors. Yet Jesus turns the ancient Jewish com-mand to love your neighbor into a story about these hostile groups. The man in the ditch, who is Jewish, is bypassed by those close to him by tribal ties (most likely the priest and the Levite were afraid the thieves were still about in the area and that they might be the next victim) and is eventually rescued by a Samaritan. Thus Jesus enlarges the sphere of neighborhood to include those we deem objectionable.

Turning to the lawyer, Jesus asks, "Which of these three, do you think, was a neighbor to the man who fell into the hands of the robbers?" Who is the neighbor?

The lawyer says, "The one who showed him mercy."

Jesus replies, "Go and do likewise." That is how you should act as well.

The Prophet Muhammad was also aware of the human ten-dency to shrink the size of the neighborhood. In a story told by his wife Aisha, an angel visited Muhammad teaching that neighbors, regardless of their race or religion, must be treated with gracious-ness and respect. Thus, the Prophet insisted that different kinds of people are actually neighbors in a wide circle of relationships and linked devotion, salvation, and compassion into a whole: "Worship God and join none with Him in worship, and do good to parents, kinsfolk, orphans, the poor, the neighbor who is near of kin, the neighbor who is a stranger, the companion by your side, the way-farer you meet" (Qur'an 4:36). In a twist on this, Muhammad also warned that if one wanted eternal salvation, "Let him not harm or annoy his neighbor" (Muslims believe it is a sin to merely annoy your neighbors).[12] In a notable story, one of Muhammad's compan-ions insisted his servant give a portion of a slaughtered sleep to "our Jewish neighbor." According to early Islamic teaching, neighbors may be part of your own tribe or another, but all deserve respect, communal protection of their property, help if harmed or hurt, provisions like food and water, the right of privacy, and freedom from annoyance. Islamic sacred texts are full of stories about neigh-bors and neighborly obligation, all pointing toward the under-standing that neighbors are essentially "extended family."[13]

That Christian and Muslims struggled with the question of the neighbor points to the origin of their ethics in Judaism. The com-mand to love one's neighbor is, as the lawyer related to Jesus, the culmination of the Jewish holiness code. Most of the religious rules and obligations of the Hebrew Bible, especially in the book of Le-viticus, detail what constitutes neighborly relations and who is re-lated to whom in what degree. The length and complexity of the ancient law only underscore the sacred seriousness of neighborli-ness, the principle on which all Jewish ethics was based. The ques-tion "Who is my neighbor?" appears both implicitly and explicitly throughout Jewish tradition, where scholars, kings, and rabbis con-tinually tried to come to terms with the breadth and scope of God's command to love others. The Hebrew scriptures can be seen as an extended argument about neighbors, in which some ancient writers insisted that communal bounds were based on tribe, blood, or reli-gious practice. But there is another understanding as well—as told in stories like those of Rahab, a prostitute, who helped the Israelites capture ancient Jericho, and Ruth, a foreign widow who became

King David's grandmother—that make the case for "neighbor" as a wide circle of relations based on virtues of hospitality, commitment, and mutual respect across boundaries of race or religion.

From even a quick survey of Jewish, Christian, and Islamic sources, it appears that one of the central dilemmas of Western religion is the issue of neighbors. The founders and great spiritual leaders all pushed the boundary outward, urging their followers to envision the world as a large neighborhood. Yet the religious forms that developed on the basis of those grand visions are often far narrower, typically defining neighbors as "people like us" or "those who agree with us." Should "neighbor" be universally defined or more narrowly so? Does the Golden Rule apply to everyone or only those of whom we approve?

Tribes and Clans

In the 1980s, when I was living in Durham, North Carolina, I attended a church in a neighborhood undergoing transition. St. Stephen's Episcopal Church had been built to serve Hope Valley, an upper-class neighborhood, an early twentieth-century enclave strategically positioned on the other side of the Durham county line, allowing residents to avoid racial tensions in town. By the late 1980s, however, change was afoot in Durham County. Huge planned developments sprang up, complete with schools, private pools, and associations. The new communities bore old-fashioned words like "chapel," "farm," or "woods" in their names, to give them an air of tradition. The old Hope Valley neighbors, who could be an exclusive lot, had a hard time with these pop-up communities, seeing the new people as interlopers and the new developments as intrusions on the landscape. At the church, a tribal war broke out between those who sought to maintain the old neighborhood and the newcomers who had begun to attend the church. In the short term, the old-timers won. It was, in a word, unpleasant.[14]

An odd thing, however, has happened since. The way of life that the older church members were trying to maintain, that of the historic houses and interrelated families, has pretty much vanished. They may have won the skirmish at the church, but the world was changing around them. Although old Hope Valley remains as a protected historic district, some of it was surrendered to infill and tear-down, and the newer surrounding neighborhoods, with their modern amenities, are now home to many thousands more people than the original neighborhood could have ever housed. The new tribe eventually took over. Thirty years ago, I thought that the conflict at St. Stephen's church was about theology. In hindsight, it is apparent that it was a conflict about sociology: the meaning and future of the American neighborhood.

What happened in Hope Valley was a microcosm of something happening all over the United States. Old neighborhoods, urban, suburban, rural, or small-town, have been challenged by new kinds of neighborhoods where new patterns of tribe were being formed. In some cities, liberal tribes were forming; in other American cities and counties, the same phenomenon was under way in a conservative direction, where people clustered around different economic or cultural patterns. Across the nation, neighborhoods became more homogeneous in taste and worldview, even while sometimes becoming more racially or ethically diverse. Although some people bemoan or ridicule the rise of gated communities (those neighborhoods surrounded by fences and guards), if truth be told, a large percentage of the population does not need actual gates in order to live behind the invisible fencing of "like-mindedness."[15]

And that is what a tribe is: people who are, in some way or another, alike and band together for common purpose. Human beings feel safer when they are near those who understand them, whose lives are enmeshed socially and economically, and who share a common outlook. Tribes are as old as human history.

Although "tribe" is often a negative word in contemporary usage, it is helpful to remember that "tribe" is a rich source of history, identity, and solidarity among native peoples. The problem is not the idea of tribe per se, but what happens when tribes become exclusive (when belonging is based on some form of superiority) and interested primarily in their own survival (when other tribes are viewed as a threat). Old Hope Valley is an interesting example. It began in the 1920s as a revolutionary experiment in community planning, a mixture of private and public spaces, with harmony between architecture and nature, based on the sensibilities of a successful Southern merchant class. Hope Valley was a tribe, and it existed within a world of Durham's other tribes: the lively Hayti neighborhood, the African American equivalent to Hope Valley, including its famous financial district known as "Black Wall Street"; the white working-class neighborhoods around the tobacco mills served by both social justice churches and labor unions; and the academic community of students and professors who lived on or around the Duke campus. Durham, like all dynamic cities, has a history of tribes clustering in community. For a city to succeed, however, tribes must work together.

When the tribes found a larger common purpose—like supporting education or building a successful local economy—the groups managed the tensions between the need to belong based on alikeness (as manifested in Durham's many neighborhoods) with the need for cooperating with people who were different (in workplaces and civic associations). In times of economic stress, however, cooperation could quickly turn to competition between classes and neighborhoods. The structure of racism was always in play as well.

At times, class and race served as meaningful bonds of neighborhood, but all too often class and race buttressed fear, thus turning places like Hope Valley into clannish enclaves. In the case of Hope Valley, what began as a radical rural experiment in making community quickly devolved into an enclave, a world unto itself, threatened by change. "Fear brings out the basest instincts," writes British political scientist Sue Goss, "and narrows our sense of belonging to self-preservation."[16]

Building strong neighborhoods will not necessarily make the world a better place. Old Hope Valley was a very strong neighborhood, with thick history and meaningful ties. Thirty years ago, however, those ties created an insular community of superiority and fear, and all of the worst aspects of tribalism came into play in the conflict at the church. Strong neighborhoods can be strong in the wrong ways, about the wrong things. But building communities on the basis of "likeness" is not really a problem either, for human beings have always built neighborhoods around some principle of "likeness." The difficulty arises when strong ties and likeness mutate into exclusion and conformity. Nostalgia for the old neighborhood often blurs the reality that it can be damned unpleasant to live in restrictive and close-minded places. Generations of Americans left the old neighborhoods to experience personal freedom with looser or fewer ties in order to find fuller, more meaningful lives.

Freed from old ties, however, we usually make new ones. Mobility creates the conditions for new neighborhoods to form. Unless one is a hermit, most of us naturally sort into groups of likeness. We hang out with those we like around shared concerns and similar tastes. That is the basis of friendship, the secret ingredient of neighborliness and community. That's the rub: human beings are tribal people. We always have been and always will be. Neighborhoods have always been places where people gather in small clusters to reside together in safety and mutual support, little "tribes" in a larger city or region. A fine line is crossed, however, when tribes become clans and neighborhoods become enclaves. Clans almost always have the compulsion to fight other clans; enclaves typically feed on paranoia about the outside world. In the twenty-first century, some tribes act more like clans—looking inward for approval and outward with accusation. Too often, our chosen neighbors (whether in physical or virtual neighborhoods) are comrades in cliquish echo chambers. The principle of clustering around likeness has driven us into ever smaller groups, increasingly isolated from one another, suspicious of those who are different, surrounded by the invisible fencing of fear.

The Fence

In 2014, I happened across a web platform that enables neighbors to share and communicate. My neighborhood has long had a neighborhood association, with officers and a newsletter and a neighborhood directory. Neighborhood concerns would go to a single person who would send information out to everyone on an e-mail list. This model seemed a bit old-school, especially in a neighborhood where increasingly the households include young adults.

So I took the initiative and signed us up for the platform. Part of the process was drawing neighborhood boundaries, so that all the households in the neighborhood would receive invitations to participate. Additionally, I needed e-mail addresses for everyone and had to contact the neighbor who maintained the list.

He has been in the neighborhood a long time and really cares about the place. To my surprise, he was willing to experiment with the platform and happily sent out e-mail requests to everyone to join.

He was concerned, however, about the lines I had drawn marking the neighborhood. He worried that I had included too many households, especially those whose houses were on streets adjacent to the association, making the neighborhood bigger than it technically is. I explained my rationale, wanting all those who considered themselves neighbors to be able to access the platform. He wanted to make sure of its safety and privacy for everyone who participated.

"What," he asked, "should be the appropriate boundaries of the neighborhood?"

We needed to find a balance between inclusion and order, between welcome and security. We finally negotiated a map of neighborhood that best fit with my desire to include and his need to trust.

In a recent book on British politics, Sue Goss argues the future for building meaningful neighborhood is that of "open tribes." Such communities would balance belonging and a sense of shared purpose with openness based in the practice of hospitality, which she calls an "abiding value." Hospitality, she asserts, "enables even closed societies to care for strangers," making even the lives of the poorest people easier with the promise of food and shelter. "We do these things because we know that we may ourselves need that help at some time in the future," calling it the "long swooping reciprocity which works over time through trust and fellow belief."[17]

Someone, however, will surely protest that neighbors must have boundaries: "Good fences make good neighbors." That adage is from Robert Frost's poem "Mending Wall." In the piece, two neighbors come together in the spring to fix a wall between their properties, a task that never seems to end, for the fence is in a constant state of disrepair. One neighbor simply repeats the phrase, "Good fences make good neighbors," throughout. But the other neighbor, the narrator, worries about the whole fence project:

Spring is the mischief in me, and I wonder
If I could put a notion in his head:
"Why do they make good neighbors? Isn't it
Where there are cows? But here there are no cows.
Before I built a wall I'd ask to know
What I was walling in or walling out,
And to whom I was like to give offense.
Something there is that doesn't love a wall,
That wants it down."[18]

So they build the fence. One because that is all he knows—it is what his ancestors did. The other does so unhappily, perhaps understanding that the world does not need another fence.

We will always have fences. But good fences have gates. And that is where hospitality comes in.

The Hospitable Tribe

Most religious traditions originated as tribal stories. Ancient stories from India relate the tales of numerous tribes and their many gods, forming Hindu sacred texts. Israelites tell a story of God's chosen people comprising twelve tribes. Prince Siddhartha Gautama, the Buddha, or the "enlightened one," came from the Kahkya clan, whose origins were thought to be of the sun. Christians proclaim a savior descended from the tribe of Judah and the house of David. Muhammad, from the Banu Hashim clan of the Quraysh tribe, managed to unite warring Arab clans into a religious and political system. And, of more recent vintage, the Book of Mormon relates the story of hostile tribes, the Lamanites and the Nephites, and the appearance of Christ among Native Americans.

Indeed, for much of human history, gods were local. Every village, tribe, or city had at least one divinity from whom the people had descended, typically known by a name and his or her location, such as "Chemosh of Moab" and the like. For ancient clans, it was easy to draw the boundaries. Your god blessed only your tribe. Your god protected only your village. Your god chose only your chief. Your god cured only your faithful tribespeople from disease. The primal pattern was that a god gave birth to a people, made them a home in a particular place, fed them, and kept them safe from outsiders.

But something odd began to occur during the late Iron Age (ca. 1000–200 BCE): some of the local deities transformed into universal gods, most of whom became monotheistic in the process. This development presented a problem. It was easy to conquer or kill neighbors born of a rival god, but harder to do so if one worshipped a God who claimed to be the God of all nations. A universal God called for a universal people in a peaceable kingdom where a world of divinely sanctioned mayhem would no longer suffice. A good number of older faiths were challenged by these new ideas. As a result, the new prophets, storytellers, and philosophers valorized an important ethical and spiritual practice, one that came to form the core of most faith traditions: hospitality.

In the Hebrew Bible, Genesis 18:1–15 records a story of hospitality central to Judaism, Christianity, and Islam. Abraham, of the tribe of Shem, left his home in Ur to go to the land of Canaan. After years of nomadic life, he and his wife, Sarah, his servant Hagar and their son Ishmael, and their household set up their tents by "oaks of Mamre," the location to which God had directed them. Mamre was a Canaanite holy place, complete with a shrine to the sun god that hosted pagan rituals and festivals. This seems a neighborhood unlikely to welcome the father of Western monotheism.

One afternoon, Abraham is outside his tent when three men walk by. Abraham probably assumed that these fellows were heading for the shrine. Abraham, who worships this new God, should avoid them and maintain his tribe's religious purity. Their foreign beliefs might contaminate the worship of the true God; their pagan practices could tempt Abraham's family. Certainly it would be better to let them pass. But the tale is otherwise: "When Abraham saw them, he ran from the tent entrance to meet them, and bowed down to the ground." He begged them to stay, to rest, to be refreshed on their journey. He and Sarah hastily prepared a feast of beef, curds, milk, and bread made of choice flour, giving the entire meal to the guests and eating nothing, even though he was the host.

The lavish act of hospitality has a twist. The strangers are not pagan travelers. Rather, they are messengers of God, perhaps angels, or, as Christians believe, a manifestation of the Trinity. They tell Abraham that Sarah shall bear him a son, through whom many nations will be blessed. This single act of hospitality will multiply into a global community of "righteousness and justice" whereby all the peoples of the earth will know God. The story of Abraham's hospitality is quickly followed by the countertale, the story of Sodom (Gen. 19:1–29). After the strangers leave Mamre, they travel to Sodom, where Abraham's nephew, Lot, offers them hospitality to shelter them from his thieving and violent neighbors (it is worth noting that when Lot's evil neighbors demand to come into his house, he refuses them entry, leading to the conclusion that you do not offer hospitality to those who would hurt other guests). God, angered by the shameless Sodomites who abuse travelers, strangers, and aliens, destroys their city, but rescues Lot and his family from its fate. The point is clear: hospitality is the spiritual practice that saves tribes from tribalism, allowing them to open their gates and widen the boundaries of neighborhood to include those who happen to wander by.

Thus begins a long struggle within religion about neighborhood. Does God bless only our tribe, or does God welcome all people into the tent? Are our neighborhoods like that of Sodom, walled communities of inhospitable self-interest and only a few safe places, or like Abraham's household at Mamre, where shaded tents welcome strangers to feast and rest? For the last couple of millennia, human beings have vacillated between asserting the superiority of their tribe and struggling to practice the hospitality necessary for true neighborliness as commanded by a universal God. The story of that struggle is the narrative drama in many a sacred text, including the Bible, in which the Hebrew people cannot seem to figure out if God is only the God of Israel or the God to whose holy city all nations will stream.

But this is not only ancient drama, confined to old stories, for the tension between hostility and hospitality remains the central conflict underlying the worst episodes of human hatred, oppression, terrorism, and war. To live behind walls of fear, especially those constructed on foundations of divine approval, is to assure a future of global uncertainty and violence. In the 1970s, Catholic priest Henri Nouwen once noted, "Our society seems to be increasingly full of fearful, defensive, aggressive people anxiously clinging to their property and inclined to look at their surrounding world with suspicion, always expecting an enemy to suddenly appear or do harm."[19] It has only gotten worse since then, much worse in the early years of this century. Thus, what Nouwen insisted then remains true today: one of the primary spiritual needs of our world is to "convert" hostility into hospitality, to turn "the enemy into a guest":

When hostility is converted into hospitality, then fearful strangers can become guests . . . [and] guest and host can reveal their most precious gifts and bring new life to others. . . . The term hospitality, therefore, should not be limited to its literal sense of receiving a stranger in our house, but as a fundamental attitude toward our fellow human being, which can be expressed in a great variety of ways.[20]

The world can no longer afford tribes intent on purity who believe God blesses only them; the world is longing for tribes that place hospitality front and center of spiritual practice and work to bless others on their way. We do not need gated neighborhoods, but neighborhoods with open gates.

Practicing Empathy

In December 2014, former Secretary of State Hillary Clinton addressed an audience at Georgetown University regarding women, politics, and conflict resolution. The speech seemed fairly standard Washington fare until she got to one section in which she suggested that having "empathy" for one's enemies is a form of power:

This is what we call smart power—using every possible tool and partner to advance peace and security, leaving no one on the sidelines, showing respect, even for one's enemies, trying to understand and insofar as psychologically possible empathize with their perspective and point of view, helping to define the problems, determine the solutions. That is what we believe in the twenty-first century will change—change the prospects for peace.[21]

I was listening to the speech on the car radio, some Internet station or another, and when Secretary Clinton said, "empathize," I could barely believe what I was hearing. Clinton, a Methodist, was clearly applying the Golden Rule to international affairs and making the case that women have a particular perspective on exercising such "smart power." Reflecting on the speech and the term "smart power," I thought of the *spiritual* power of empathy and the call to love one's neighbor. The world, I thought, could use more such respect.

The speech went unnoticed in most of the media. However, right-wing pundits immediately picked up on her words. They could not believe it either. For more than a week, conservative commentators slammed the speech and raised such a political ruckus that a Republican senator made current Secretary of State John Kerry explain Clinton's "empathy" remark to a Senate hearing. One host interviewed a former soldier who said, "Emphasize with enemies? Our job is to kill them!" Oliver North called her comments "irrational," insisting that her stance amounted to "capitulation."[22]

Empathy is essentially the capacity to see others as you see yourself, the Golden Rule in practice. It is how we love our neighbors, the way to participate in the spiritual revolution. But it is hard to do. It is difficult when your neighbor wakes you up at seven on a fall morning with a leaf blower; it is difficult when someone climbs into your tree and starts hacking away at the branches. And it is a difficult practice to employ on a larger scale—like imagining the planet's ecosystem, members of a rival political party, criminals, or even terrorists as your neighbor. Indeed, the farther the proximity, the easier it is to dehumanize others. The world's not so golden rule might functionally be rendered, "Violate others as they violate you—or even before that if possible," a dictum that has fueled centuries-long cycles of mutual destruction, patterns that now must be broken for the sake of our fragile global neighborhood. Revenge, not reciprocity, has been the story of much of human history.

In the twentieth century, Jewish theologian Martin Buber explained that most arenas of human activity—politics, economics, and education—actually alienate us, because they treat human beings as objects. Modern culture has trained us to distance ourselves from one another, seeing others and the world itself as something to be observed, examined, and critiqued. Essentially, we view everyone and everything as problems to be fixed. When we know others only as objects, what Buber called the "I-it" relationship, it precludes the possibility of community. There is, however, an alternative. If we encounter our neighbors with empathy, remembering that others are subjects, we can enter into an "I-thou" relationship. Seeing others as "thou" opens the possibility of real affection and mutual responsibility. True neighborliness can be described as being mutual subjects, acting toward one another with respect and understanding. Buber said that modern society is an "it" world. But he also claimed that a "thou" world, of connection and compassion, was the only path toward a healthy human future.

Buber's vision easily translates to the possibilities of neighborhood—"thou" is another way of talking about empathy, a connective source for community. If we want good neighborhoods and to be good neighbors, we must be able to treat both places and people as subjects, not objects.

When I first moved to our current neighborhood, I was not entirely happy with the choice. We had moved to Washington, D.C., at a time of rising housing prices. We bought a decent house that we could afford within a reasonable commute to my husband's job. Period. On a modest street that looks like thousands of other

American streets, it was not my dream house. For a time, I referred to it as the "people parking garage," the place we came to and went from—and those living nearby did likewise. I hoped I was a good neighbor, mowing the lawn, being relatively quiet, taking out the trash, but I confess, I thought of my own neighborhood as an "it."

Until a particular day, that is. A cab driver was bringing me home from the airport. He was a nice fellow, a Sikh immigrant, very talkative about his faith and his love for America.

As we turned into my subdivision, he exclaimed, "What a beautiful neighborhood!"

"What?" I asked. I always see the flaws, the siding that needs to be replaced, gardens in need of tending, and houses, like mine, with outdated kitchens, bathrooms too small, and bulging closets.

"Look at these tidy houses!" he exclaimed, "Everyone in the whole world should live on a street like this! I bet you have nice neighbors! This is everyone's dream to grow up in a place like this! You are so lucky!"

The taxicab driver saw my neighborhood more clearly than I saw it, and I became determined to see my world differently. I started to take long walks around the neighborhood, noticing things and praying, for people I knew and people I did not know, and chatting with folks as I walked, not just passing by. As I walked and prayed, I learned that my neighborhood was not just a suburban parking lot. These houses were not objects. They were, instead, the stages of many lives, where families like my own played out of all sorts of joys and sorrows, successes and failures. My walks became a spiritual practice, as I wondered what went on in my neighbors' houses, trying to enter into, through my peripatetic prayers, their lives. The neighborhood itself came alive, became a subject, a "thou."

And that is what empathy is: entering into the lives of others so that the world becomes alive, a real neighborhood that is community.

Local Spirit

On a pleasant summer day, I was buying some lamb at the local farmers' market. Mr. Miller is a livestock farmer, and about half my family's meat comes from him. He is Mennonite of a sort, with a beard and conservatively dressed daughter who covers her head. We often talk theology. But on that particular day, we were talking about how to grill lamb.

"How do you season it?" I asked.

"Their herb mix," he replied, pointing to the farmer in the neighboring booth, who happens to be a Muslim. "Our meat, their herbs. No better combination."

Mennonite and Muslim interfaith cooperation at the farmers' market. The world, I thought, could learn a lot right here. This is a neighborhood place where the walls have come down.

Five years ago, I began shopping at the farmers' market about a mile away from my house. Everything comes from within a hundred-mile (or so) radius and is grown by the sellers. Every week from May to November, I have gone to this same market, buying from the same vendors. As the weeks, months, and years have progressed, I discovered that this was an experience far different from shopping at the chain grocery store. Here, I got to know the farmers—old-time working family farmers from Virginia and Pennsylvania, new immigrants from Mexico, well-off retirees growing organic crops or raising free-range animals. They are a religiously diverse group: Catholics, Protestants, Mennonites, and Muslims, with a few spiritual-but-not-religious folks in the mix. They have taught me about farming practices and managing land, confided their hopes and fears for the future of American farms, and shared their passion for good food. I now know where my food comes from and how rainfall and sunlight and temperature have an impact on the crops.

At the market, I picked up tips from the local gardening club, talked with local politicians, met local clergy, and shadowed a local chef to see what produce he purchased (I bought the same). Regulars recognize me, asking whether shared recipes had worked, if my family had enjoyed vacation, and how my next book was going. Although I might run into someone I know at the grocery store on any random day, the contrast with the farmers' market could not be more obvious: it is a community, and a lively spiritual one at that. It is a model of reciprocity, of mutual exchange, where the typical boundaries that separate suburban dwellers come down.[23] Not surprisingly, a farmers' market is about food. Eating together—or, in this case, shopping together to eat—is an act of hospitality.

A recent book, *The New Parish,* asserts that one of the primary shortcomings of contemporary society is "living above place," which is

> the tendency to develop structures that keep cause-and-effect relationships far apart in space and time where we cannot have firsthand experience of them. For example, you have probably experienced buying groceries without any idea where the food originated or who was involved in the production and delivery process. Living above place describes the process where this type of separation happens so frequently that we become disoriented to reality.

The result is "a cocooned way of life," with people "unaware of how their lives really affect each other and the world."[24] The farmers' market is about living in place, not above it. In a small parking lot next to the public library, people make new connections between the environment and food, family and nutrition, farmers and customers, economy and exchange, learning and teaching. In a real sense, the market serves as the neighborhood table.

The market has become a spiritual practice for me, one that I was actually longing for (although I could not have clearly articulated that in advance). Judging from the number of people who attend on a weekly basis, my neighbors find something meaningful at this gathering as well. Indeed, the farmers' market in my neighborhood reflects a larger shift toward local food. From 1994 to 2014, the number of farmers' markets known to the U.S. Department of Agriculture has risen from seventeen hundred to over eight thousand.[25] More and more congregations have begun to host neighborhood farmers' markets, trying to make overt the relationship between food, neighborhood, hospitality, and spirituality.

One of the most successful is St. Stephen's Market at St. Stephen's Episcopal Church in Richmond, Virginia. Gary Jones, the senior minister at St. Stephen's, refers to the market as the "Saturday congregation." Every week, vendors bring their wares to the market, where the church also invites musicians to play, provides an onsite café, hosts food trucks, and offers activities for children. St. Stephen's opened the market as an act of hospitality. Kate Ruby, the market manager says, "Everyone is welcome, the church, the neighborhood at large. Everyone is welcome at the market. Bring your dog. Bring your kids." The purpose of the market is "connection," a spiritual principle that the organizers trust makes the world better through care for the environment, building community, and teaching people how place and food are related. The market is also connected to larger issues of poverty and social justice: a "gleanings" program asks vendors to donate leftovers to the church's food pantry, and various nonprofit organizations are given space to raise money for community causes.[26]

Farmers' markets are only one indication of a larger trend: the desire for meaningful local community and to locate in a place appears to be an ever growing reality for vast numbers of people. A recent study of American adults showed that three-quarters of the population believe the nation's economic future is dependent on the health and quality of local communities. Both the youngest and oldest American workers would rather choose a *desirable place to live* than a company to work for. Desirable places, however, are of a certain type: good neighborhood schools, public transportation options, creativity and diversity, the presence of family and friends, and the ability to walk to parks, libraries, and stores. According to the findings, "Traditional business recruitment strategies are seen as less important than investing in local amenities and quality of life. Job prospects and economic health are not the overriding factors for choosing where to live." Sixty percent of respondents want to "age in place," while nearly 80 percent seek housing with extra space for roommates or family members to create extended households. Additionally, 58 percent want to be part of communities where people share resources—like bikes, tools, cars, or Internet access—in relationships and business transactions of mutual trust.

As a result, the authors of the study argue that a "new economics of place" has emerged in American life that emphasizes the tie between a "stronger economy and stronger communities" with "quality neighborhoods" driving toward a more optimistic future.[27] Sharing goods, living together, feeding one another, creating an alternate economy—it brings to mind a story in the New Testament where a group of strangers, having experienced a dramatic manifestation of God's Spirit, formed a new community of generosity, hospitality, and mutual care (Acts 2:43–47; 4:32–35). Maybe people are not as selfish as we sometimes imagine. Our shared desires and innovative ideas are surprisingly neighborly.

Neighborhoods are made up of ordinary things. The farmers' market, for example, is a gathering of regular people buying tomatoes or apples. Most of what happens on my street involves leaf blowers, teenage drivers, and dogs. People borrow shovels, swap used baby clothes, hold a yard sale, and surprise others with small gifts. It is about family and friends and acquaintances, about schools and churches and local parks.

When people say what they want in a neighborhood, they say that they want to be able to walk. Indeed, two-thirds of Americans list "walkability" as one of the most important characteristics in a desirable neighborhood.[28] They want to move about in the place where they live, to feel the sun or the rain, to notice things, perhaps to pause and chat with a neighbor, to feel safe and secure on the streets, to wander around or follow a path. You cannot be above a place when you are walking through it. Some historians claim that the car killed American neighborhoods. Maybe walking can help make them anew.

Walking is a way of connecting, of feeling our feet on the ground, a very ordinary and surprisingly spiritual thing. Author Kathleen Norris writes of its power in her small book *The Quotidian Mysteries*. Making the case that God is best known to us in simple, daily activities, she shares that walking is a kind of "poetic meter" that "originates in the bodily rhythm of arms and legs in motion" and "reflects the basic rhythms of creation."[29] Another word for that rhythm, the rhythm of body, poetry, and creation, is prayer.

Praying while walking is an ancient practice. Buddhists have long noted the profound relationship between walking and meditation, emphasizing the harmony that develops between breath, movement, and attentiveness. Some Buddhist teachers point out

that practitioners must keep their eyes open during walking meditation, something that creates an intense awareness of both other
people and the beauty of creation and reminds the walker that
meditation is ultimately for others. Indeed, to understand neighborhood, the deep wisdom that is present when people make a
place together, we must learn to see with new eyes. Our neighborhoods are not as often in decline as they are invisible, taken for
granted and ignored. When I walk around the blocks near my
house, I sometimes think of Buddhist monk Thich Nhat Hanh's
reflection: "Walking with ease and with peace of mind on the earth
is a wonderful miracle."[30] I change the words a bit, however:
"Walking with ease and with peace of mind around the neighborhood is a wonderful miracle." We do not pay as much attention as
we should to these places that we make, communities by happenstance of proximity, where every day we are presented multiple
opportunities to practice the Golden Rule.

"Our neighbors are not the objects of our work or an assign-
ment for getting people into a church building," writes theologian
Alan Roxburgh. "They are God's precious creation. Our calling is
to walk with and beside them in order to call forth the stories and
narratives that are among these people and comprise the wonderful
character of the community."[31]

If we walk away from fear and isolation and choose to walk
together as neighbors, we discover that our various religions and
philosophies make how we treat one another the litmus test of a
meaningful life. Love of God and love of neighbor are of a piece.
When we practice neighborly relations as the locus of divine love,
we encounter the God who dwells nigh. That is a truly spiritual
revolution.

Outside of St. Aidan's, there is a labyrinth. Patterned after the great labyrinth painted on the floor of Chartres Cathedral, it is built under the trees, set back from the main road, and made out of stones and recycled rubber. It is an open place, a gift of the church to the neighborhood for meditation and prayer. There is no fence, no rules for its use, no offering taken. A single path winds toward the center, with a series of circuits and gentle switchbacks, and then leads out again. Labyrinths are a structure for walking prayer, believed to aid in healing and spiritual well-being. Some people think labyrinths create "resonance" between walkers and the world around them and act as mirrors of the soul. Many consider labyrinths sacred. I certainly do.

A week after the prayer service for Hannah, I untied the faded yellow ribbon from the post on our front porch. I walked a few blocks to the neighbor's house where a bin had been placed to collect the bows. A signboard leaned against the overflowing bin: "Holding Hannah in Our Hearts." Around the base, neighbors had placed notes, bouquets, and teddy bears in an impromptu memorial. I said a prayer and reverently laid our ribbon with the others. I looked up and saw the labyrinth across the way. I crossed the street, feeling a call to walk and pray for my neighbors.

I entered, followed the path, and I cried. Approaching the center, I saw that someone had laid a rose at the heart of the labyrinth. I did not know who placed it there, but I knew it was a token for Hannah. As neighbors, we had walked together that autumn through sadness, horror, and loss. Together, we remembered to tell our children how much we love them. We learned the importance of watching over one another, of the need to talk to each other, of the solidarity of yellow ribbons. We had discovered that what is done to one is done to all, for good or for ill. The Golden Rule is so much more than a rule. It is the lifeblood of neighborhood. As Rabbi Hillel said, "What is hateful to you, do not to others. This is the Law: all the rest is commentary."

Someone chose to violate this principle, and the evil he did to our neighbor had created a more powerful pain than most of us had ever known, affecting so many people, those near and far. As I walked the sacred path, I mused that kindness must possess at least the equal power to do so. Hatred of neighbor may be the peril, but love of neighbor was surely the promise. I picked up the rose, fingered its petals, and then remembered that the name "Hannah" means grace.

Commons

Our most basic common link is that we all inhabit this
small planet. We all breathe the same air. We all cherish
our children's future. And we are all mortal.

—*John F. Kennedy*

September 11, 2011, the ten-year anniversary of the terrorist
attacks in the United States, fell on a Sunday. It had been, by
anyone's standards, a horrible decade. War abroad, political
division, financial collapse. When the attacks happened, I was
working in a church where I had watched a congregation react
with fear and a sort of xenophobic patriotism that I never dreamed
possible in a Christian community. I have no taste for mixing
church and state and had no desire to reenact that kind of religious
nationalism again on the anniversary.[1] My best option, I suspected,
would be to stay away from church that weekend.

I no longer attended the church of a decade ago, however, and
I wondered what my new congregation would do to mark the anniversary. Over lunch a few days before, I asked the minister what

was planned for the service. He assured me that the tone would be reflective, not jingoistic.

Perhaps it would be healing to go, I mused. And so, on September 11, 2011, my family and I were sitting together in a pew at St. Paul's Church in Alexandria, Virginia. The service struck the right tone, with somber music and serious prayers. Then a guest preacher mounted the pulpit—not a member of the clergy, but someone who had been working in the White House on the first 9/11. He had been invited to share about the day from his unique perspective.

The sermon began with his memories of the day, what it was like to have been there, how he felt, how some famous people had responded to the events as they unfolded. The preacher, however, kept sneaking in politics and making a subtle apologetic for the war in Iraq. I looked around, wondering if anyone other than me or my husband was uncomfortable, but parishioners sitting nearby did not betray any emotion. If someone had been watching me, that would not have been the case. I was able to restrain myself, but only until he mentioned his sorrow about the four thousand people who have been killed in the past decade as a result of the attacks.

Four thousand? What was he talking about? By the end of the decade, tens of thousands, if not more, people had died in war as a result of what had happened in 2001.[2] Most of those people were civilians, Afghanis or Iraqis, in countries we had invaded. Then I realized that four thousand represented the number of *American soldiers* who had been killed. He was counting only *his* tribe! What about the other people, those invisible to us but loved by their own families and friends? I could only conclude they did not matter.

I gasped audibly. If the church cannot mourn the deaths of all people, Christians and Muslims and Jews, friends and enemies, fellow citizens and strangers, the guilty and the innocent, what good is religion? Had we learned nothing about being human in the last ten years? All the blood spilled, the lives lost, the towns and villages laid waste. Had the decade brought out the worst in us, leading us to believe so starkly in our own righteousness that we still insisted that God blessed only our people?

Hoping not to make a scene, I slipped out of the pew and left the building. I sat down on the stairs outside, trying to let my sorrow and fury subside.

As I attempted to compose myself, I noticed many people walking around the neighborhood, far more than usual, even on a lovely Sunday morning. They were all heading toward King Street, Alexandria's major downtown road. Groups of friends, couples, and families with strollers. It was a beautiful day, not unlike September 11 ten years earlier, with bright blue skies and the first hint of autumn in the air. Without a second thought, I followed the crowd.

Nearing the main street, I realized that it was Art Walk, a yearly festival in Old Town. King Street is closed to traffic and turned into ten blocks of tented galleries. Painters, sculptors, furniture makes, jewelers, crafters, weavers—they are all there. There are musicians too, and food vendors, and nonprofit organizations and political candidates trying to woo donors and voters. As I stood on a corner and looked out on the scene, all my senses were alive, coaxed to full attentiveness by vibrant colors, bright chimes in the wind, the cool sound of a saxophone, the fall breeze carrying delectable evidence of a grill at work nearby. The street was full of people of all sorts, white, black, and brown, young and old, from a wide variety of ethnic backgrounds. Children were laughing and running up and down the street with balloons, gifts from a clown entertaining them at the opposite corner. Neighbors greeted one another. The curious engaged the artists with queries about their crafts. Many people were coming in and out of the surrounding shops and restaurants, others sat in outdoor cafés sipping lattes. The energy, the creativity—how wonderful it was!

As I took in the scene, I thought of a story from the New Testament in which, during a street festival, the Spirit of God descended on a crowd of magnificent diversity (Acts 2:1–13). When the Spirit came, the boundaries of language, nationality, and religion that had separated all those gathered dissolved, and a new community was created, one of a unified humanity. Peter, a friend of Jesus, astonished by what he saw that day, said that it was the fulfillment of an ancient prophesy, the drawing together of humankind as one in the Spirit. Peter recited the prophecy:

> In the last days it will be, God declares,
> That I will pour out my Spirit upon all flesh,
> and your sons and your daughters shall prophesy,
> and your young men shall see visions
> and your old men shall dream dreams.
> Even upon my slaves, both men and women,
> in those days I will pour out my Spirit. (Acts 2:17–18)

My cell phone buzzed. A text message appeared on the screen from my husband. "Are you coming back to church?"

"I don't know," I texted in reply.

It seemed so obvious right then, but I have no idea why I had never noticed before. For years, the church kept me safe inside a building. All the while, the Spirit was out here on the streets.

"Where Is God?" and the Commons

One of the oldest meanings of the word "religion" is "to bind together," that which connects God with us and us with each other. By definition, religion is inherently communal, rituals and relationships that weave a spiritual web of meaning and purpose in the world.

That meaning is largely lost to us. During the last few decades, the word "religion" has fallen on hard times. Contemporary Western people tend to define religion as a structure, organization, or institution. Those who want to speak of lively faith, holy connection, and of finding God in the world or in their lives, often call themselves "spiritual" instead.[3]

Sometimes critics decry spirituality as individualism, but they miss the point. Spirituality is personal, yes. To experience God's spirit, to be lost in wonder, is something profound that we can all know directly and inwardly. That is not a problem. The real problem is that, in the last two centuries, religion has actually allowed itself to become privatized. In the same way that our political and economic concerns contracted from "we" to "me," so has our sense of God and faith. In many quarters, religion abandoned a prophetic and creative vision for humanity's common life in favor of an individual quest to get one's sorry ass to heaven. And, in the process, community became isolated behind the walls of buildings where worship experiences corresponded to members' tastes and preferences and confirmed their political views.

It has been slow but sure, getting to where we are now. But religion has been reduced to "me," a process often aided and abetted by religious institutions themselves. That was a sad mistake, however, for at the very center of every religion, there stands some great communal vision of God, the world, and humanity.

In the Bible, that vision is of a people who know God as an intimate companion, live well with one another, and fulfill God's dream for creation. It is a vision of mutuality, friendship, creativity, conviviality, and generosity. People are to make peace, plant vines and fig trees, treat one another fairly and with compassion, and invite strangers into God's tent. We are either cursed or blessed on the basis of our relationships with others and how we care for the land. People prosper when justice reigns. What is broken is restored, what is amiss is made right. It is a vision of a universal feast, a cosmic table around which all humankind is gathered to eat and drink and dance with God.

Spirituality is about personal experience—the deep realization that dirt is good, water is holy, the sky holds wonder; that we are part of a great web of life, our home is in God, and our moral life is entwined with that of our neighbor. But none of this is for the sake of feeling good, individual prosperity, or guaranteeing a blessed afterlife. It is about tracing the threads of the interconnected universe, about finding God in nature and in community—and, in finding God, discovering that we really are one. The spiritual revolution is a protest movement against forms of religion that have lost the binding vision of peace, wisdom, and equanimity here on earth. But for a spiritual revolution to make any real difference, it must reclaim the primal sense of religion—the "we"—the power that binds us to one another, to God, and to the world. To encounter God here, we must walk out of buildings and discover the life of the commons.

The Commons

Although a neighborhood and a commons are similar, they are not exactly the same. Neighborhood is about whom we live *with,* those next door, whether "next door" is literal or virtual geography. For many centuries, neighborhoods have been defined in terms of proximity—"close dwelling"—and retained an intimate sense of place and relationships. In mere decades, our understanding of neighborhood has broadened in scope and connection, and our nongeographical neighborhoods have widened our circles of acquaintance, friendship, and relationship. However, most neighborhoods are still formed around principles of affinity, people choosing to be near others because of similar background, location, income, tastes, or outlook. At their best, neighborhoods are open tribes that practice hospitality and the Golden Rule. The commons is not that. The commons, sometimes referred to in the singular as the common, is what we live *for,* the public world tribes make together— that serves the good *for* all.

"Commons" is an odd word, almost archaic in many quarters. Indeed, Google Books statistics reveal that the high point of its usage occurred around 1810, and it has been all downhill since then. Indeed, "common," has become somewhat derogatory in contemporary parlance. "Commonplace" means cheap or worthless; common sense has been replaced by expertise. The word "common" is defined at best as ordinary or humdrum, at worst something "showing a lack of taste or refinement, vulgar."

As a positive term, "commons" remained unfamiliar to me until I left home for college. There, the hall where the students ate was referred to as the Dining Commons, or DC, a friendlier acronym. When still a freshman, I remember walking into this strange room, full of long tables and cozy booths, a tray of food in my hands, and not knowing where to sit. The Dining Commons was a bit like a public square, open to all, with people coming and going, scurrying toward multiple destinations, where friendships went far beyond familial bonds or geographical proximity. I remember how lost I felt, standing there in the aisle, looking forlorn while taking in all this frenetic activity, and wondering if I would ever find my way. Could I ever feel at home in the commons?

And then it happened. Someone I had met at orientation waved at me, signaling for me to join her table. I walked up, but there was no space to put my tray. I shook my head. "I'll find another place," I said and almost turned to walk away. She smiled. Pushing the jumble of plates together to make room and pulling a chair up to the table, she insisted, "There's always room for one more."

The people at that table became friends. We were from all over the world (and have wound up living all over the world), yet we formed a community of those who pulled up extra chairs at the table. For the next four years, our mantra was: "There's always room for one more."

I learned many things in college. But that was the most important: the commons is infinitely expandable, a place of hospitality for everyone.

A common is, quite simply, shared space. A place of fluid boundaries, where people come and go, but who come together as one, bound chiefly by the practice of hospitality. When the *s* is added to form "commons," the definition expands to "a self-governing community of people who inhabit or share the use of land; a habitat of mutual interrelationships." And the activity of making a commons is the art of "commoning," "to share, to commune . . . to decide things together . . . a way of life."[4]

After college, I moved to New England. There, commons were still features of the landscape, mostly large open parks, some in a sad state of repair, serving as the geographical reminder of an older world, the original village built around a shared public space. In the center of most New England towns is the commons, a sizable community green space, owned by all, ringed by important public buildings and old homes, where early inhabitants could graze their livestock or plant shared gardens. The commons served as marketplace and community bulletin board, providing for exchange of goods and ideas. The origin of these commons is not entirely certain. However, historians have noticed that what became the town commons was often land that had been deeded to the church, and then these meetinghouse lots were transformed into shared public space. In early New England, the church was the largest building in town and served a multitude of purposes, some religious, some more mundane. The meetinghouse lot extended the sacred into the streets, providing smooth access between the building where the Holy Word was preached and the world where faith would be practiced. Divine worship led directly to diligent work. The church and commons were intimately related, and there was no division between spirit and what was secular. The green was a gift from the godly congregation, thus enabling the whole village to gather and form a congregation outside the walls of the church building.[5]

The commons and hospitality were intertwined, making a space where fluid community could be formed of a variety of people, some in close proximity, some not, with both permanent and temporary structures, all interdependent on each other for emotional, economic, and political flourishing. The commons is a plot of land, but it was also a structured space and a set of practices that embodied the ideals of the inhabitants: sharing goods, learning, faith, governance, sustenance, and shelter. And, unlike the actual meetinghouse—with walls, pews, polity, and membership—the commons was open, its borders permeable. The commons was a visible geography of the inner spiritual reality of the village and the villagers hopes for the world, the very definition of what Christians refer to as a sacrament.

Street festivals, dining halls, green spaces. These are examples of the commons. There are pockets of commons in every locality, places where people from a variety of neighborhoods may meet and mingle. The commons is the geography of hospitality, belonging to none, welcoming all. But the very existence of the commons nearby begs the question: In a world of our many neighborhoods, can we imagine coming together as a global commons?

A World Commons

I went back to St. Paul's, but I could never get that sermon out of my mind. The words that came from the pulpit that day high-lighted a fundamental tension in religion: the tribal tendency to divide humankind into the blessed and the blasphemous versus the sacred possibility that everyone is related in and through creation and God. For far too long, religion has combined with nationalism or ethnicity to claim divine legitimacy for human conquests and crusades, a historical Gordian knot if ever there was one. In the twenty-first century, we can no longer live with this problem, for the knot will surely become a noose for the whole human race. Seeing "our people" as the only ones who count is a little like living in a gated community. You can ignore the world beyond the walls for only so long.

In an essay published shortly before his death, Martin Luther King, Jr., wrote of the dangers of closed tribes as the "great new problem of mankind":

> We have inherited a large house, a great "world house" in which we have to live together—black and white, Easterner and Westerner, Gentile and Jew, Catholic and Protestant, Moslem and Hindu—a family unduly sepa-rated in ideas, culture and interest, who, because we can never again live apart, must learn somehow to live with each other in peace.

He went on to say that all inhabitants of the globe are now neigh-bors; "all men are interdependent" and "all life is interrelated."[6]

King said that the "worldwide neighborhood" was the result of science and technology, reciting a quick history of inventions from the lightbulb to radio and television, to space travel. These developments had transformed the "architectural pattern" of the world house, "shaking" its foundations and enabling men and women around the world to demand a new and better future of equality, freedom, and justice for all. Although King wrote in 1967, the impact of science and technology on remaking the world we inhabit has done nothing but multiply. In the years since his death, widespread air travel, instantaneous news, cell phones, and the Internet have increased the speed and power of human connection. In a very real way, we now see into almost every corner of the world house—sharing joys, fears, arguments, threats, and wonders with dizzying up-to-the-moment access and information.

September 11 was a good example of this. When New York's Twin Towers fell in the terrorist attack, people around the world responded—people who had never set foot in the United States, much less in a neighborhood in New York. Across the planet, there was sympathy, empathy really, for those who had been killed, their families, and the city. Sympathy is extending pity to someone. Empathy is feeling "with others," as if we are them. It was painfully easy to imagine ourselves or our loved ones as the victims of such an attack, in those planes, jumping out of those windows. Although there were some who cheered, most people expressed solidarity. South Americans sang America's national anthem, Europeans paused for a moment of silence, most nations sent condolence letters, and lights dimmed on monuments around the world. What happened on 9/11 was not just an attack on the United States. Citizens of 115 different nations died that day; it was really an attack on the world house. As then UN Secretary-General Kofi Annan said, "We are all traumatized by this terrible tragedy."[7] Had Twitter existed in those days, no doubt there would have been a global-trending hashtag: #WeAreNY.

Empathy, like that poured out on September 11, is the binding ingredient of the world commons. That blinding moment of connection, the unavoidable awareness of relationship, is often visible around tragedy: 9/11, the devastation of an earthquake and the resulting tsunami, the rising waters of Hurricane Katrina, fear of economic collapse, bombs and drones and torture, #bringbackourgirls, an airplane full of passengers falling from the sky, #jesuischarlie, or nine people shot in a church. Through technology, the world lives in an eternal moment of empathetic promise that reveals the possibility of the global commons every time we see a stranger suffering and imagine ourselves or our children in his or her stead. Jeremy Rifkin, an American economist and social theorist, points out that the majority of people in the world's most technologically advanced nations have already developed this sort of global consciousness as part of their functioning worldview, deeply aware that old boundaries have been breached and that humankind shares what Martin Luther King described as the "world house."[8] But, as Rifkin points out, that empathy is more than a moment of connection. The originating event of seeing ourselves in the other and understanding that the "other" is not a stranger but our neighbor can initiate a transformation of awareness—in which each of us "is enlarged and expanded and spills over into broader, more inclusive communities of compassionate engagement."[9] Empathy allows us to imagine the world commons.

Recognizing the world commons calls us to a challenging moral responsibility—dedicating ourselves to participate in what Catholic theology calls the "planetary common good," doing justice for the earth and all of earth's people through compassion and with God.[10]

We Really Are the World

"Think Globally, Act Locally" read the slogan on a worn reusable grocery bag carried by the woman in front of me at the farmers' market. It is most often used to encourage people to think about the world while making decisions, especially regarding environmental issues, and to put one's concerns into action on the local level. Local changes will, in turn, yield big consequences and make a difference to global problems.

Over the last three or four decades, there has been a turn to the local. The farmers' market is a good example of that. As larger systems and institutions have stalled in solving significant social problems, ills ranging from environmental crisis to poverty, people have moved toward more discrete local and regional solutions. As a result, we have local food movements, homeschooling, regional environmental standards, community banks, neighborhood food pantries, special days to celebrate small businesses, and sharing economies. In the larger context of globalization, people are scaling down in order to reconnect with their neighbors and neighborhoods, making life more affordable, trusting, and connected. In the realm of religion, some are calling for new attention to neighborhood churches, synagogues, temples, and mosques as locations for a revitalized commons. Faith communities can strengthen the local practices of the commons by attending to issues of education, immigration, homelessness, and environmentalism in their own neighborhoods and cities.[11] Developing a local consciousness is important work, and the ability to build community relationships to act on issues of education, government, economics, and ecology is key to renewing neighborhoods.

There is, however, a problem with scaling down. Every year, my neighborhood cleans up the creek that runs through our subdivision.

It feels rewarding to gather up all the plastic bottles and strange trash that accumulates on the water's edge. It is, however, a bit of a Sisyphean task. Not only are people careless with garbage, but pesticides from suburban lawns and farms wash into sewers, creeks, and streams, and corporations persist in dumping industrial waste that makes it to the river. Organizing local schoolchildren to pick up trash is worthy and important, but it does not do much good to solve the river's larger problems of pollution and dead zones. All the neighborhoods in a several-hundred-mile stretch have to work together in order to clean up the watershed and keep it clean, not to mention doing the policy and educational work needed to solve the larger problems.

Local is not nearly enough. The global commons involves the multiplication of local concerns into larger connected communities in coordinated action for the sake of the world. Philosopher Slavoj Žižek, a noted thinker on issues of community, argues that the local is too often a matter of lifestyle choice—individual people in a particular community choose to recycle, buy green, or support a local farmers' market motivated by kindness, obligation, or guilt. Although many people choose well, such actions are limited in their ability to transform large-scale problems. Global problems call for the action of a global commons. Žižek claims that the big ideologies of the twentieth century—capitalism and Communism—tried to address worldwide issues, but both failed. Indeed, capitalism and Communism contributed to making the very things that now threaten to undermine the human future. What kind of community can rise to engage these concerns? The commons must be enlarged to a global commons where everyone can participate in addressing environmental, economic, and technological concerns.[12] We must not only think globally and act locally, but we must *think and act globally and locally simultaneously*. We live in a layered commons: our streets, neighborhoods, cities, regions, nation, and globe. The work of the commons needs to harmonize on all levels in order to develop effective strategies for social and political change.

Decades before philosophers and political theorists like Žižek pointed out the limits of the local commons, Martin Luther King ruminated on the same, detecting the hypocrisy of self-interest that undermines global well-being: "The heads of all the nations issue clarion calls for peace, yet they come to the peace table accompanied by bands of brigands each bearing unsheathed swords." He pointed out: "We have ancient problems to deal with, vast structures of power, indescribably complicated problems to solve." He foresaw a day when both capitalism and Communism would fail and need to be replaced by a "revolution of values":

> A genuine revolution of values means in the final analysis that our loyalties must become ecumenical rather than sectional. Every nation must now develop an overriding loyalty to mankind as a whole in order to preserve the best in their individual societies.
>
> This call for a worldwide fellowship that lifts neighborly concern beyond one's tribe, race, class and nation is in reality a call for an all-embracing and unconditional love for all men. . . . When I speak of love, I am speaking of that force which all the great religions have seen as the supreme unifying principle of life.[13]

As King saw it, the human future was a choice between a global beloved community, a commons based on spiritual and moral revolution, and a planet in chaos.

The world commons is already growing among us, mostly through economic globalization and shared technologies. But will the global commons have heart, incarnating our best shared aspirations? Or will it just be another manifestation of oppression and death? Much depends on whether it will comprehend the spiritual elements of community: *communitas,* communion, and compassion.

Communitas:
The Spirit of Unity

On a late summer night in 2012, my family went to a Washington Nationals baseball game. It had been a great baseball season for our team. The Nationals were in first place, and speculation about playoffs was rife. On that Friday night, the Nats played the St. Louis Cardinals. Our pitcher was Gio Gonzalez. The Nationals came on strong, scoring ten runs. And the Cardinals? Well, they did not score at all.

That might seem kind of boring, a 10–0 rout. But something happened that night at Nationals Park. As the innings went by, we realized that Gio was pitching a great game, every ball thrown with more passion than the last. Instead of looking tired, the pitcher appeared determined, even electric. The opposing team still had not scored a run. Maybe it would be a shutout. From somewhere in the crowd, a rhythmic chant arose, invented by an unknown fan in the upper deck: "Let's go, Gio!" With each pitch throughout the final innings, the chant got louder and more deliberate; thirty thousand voices joined in creating an ecstatic chorus of crowd and players. People stood together, practically breathed together, and chanted, gasping at each close call and cheering wildly when a batter was out.

And then, in the ninth inning, it happened: Gio seemed to falter. Two Cardinals players reached base, but no runs had yet been scored. With two outs, another batter stepped to the plate. We jumped to our feet, chanting as one, "Let's go, Gio!" clapping and stomping our feet as if our incantation would raise the baseball gods from their slumber. The first pitch—a strike. "Let's go, Gio!" Surely we could be heard in Philadelphia. The second pitch. He hit it! A long, high arching ball toward center. Caught! The game was over. The crowd went wild. It was like New Year's at Times Square and winning the World Series all rolled into one.

That night, spectators became participants. And Washington, D.C., became a baseball town.

Communitas is a Latin noun for the spirit of community, typically those groups that form beyond regular institutions and organizations and create a profound sense of equality and togetherness. It is the opposite of the feeling of alienation and isolation. Instead, it is the movement of some sort of spirit in which people discover that solidarity is possible. Some sociologists have noted that *communitas* has spiritual or sacred dimensions through which people overcome division and achieve a new sense of identity and purpose. Author Barbara Ehrenreich puts it more bluntly: "*Communitas* and *collective effervescence* describe aspects or moments of communal excitement; there is no word for the love—or force or need—that leads individuals to seek ecstatic merger with the group."[14]

What happened at Nationals Park that night was an example of *communitas*. "Normal" Washington was only weeks away from the next presidential election. The country was fractious, divided between red and blue, as was the city itself. But at the ballpark everyone moved into a different space, wearing team colors, not political ones, and through sharing a thrilling sports event together we became something much different in community than we were when we arrived that night. We became one. Through late summer and early autumn, baseball solidarity gripped Washington. It was easy to ignore a divided Congress and political campaigns, especially when both sides were cheering for the same team. Weeks later, when the Nationals lost in the playoffs to that same Cardinals team, I heard one sportscaster moan, "Well, I guess it will be back to usual in Washington."

Sports are a focal point for *communitas*. "For most people in the world today," writes Barbara Ehrenreich, "the experience of collective ecstasy is likely to be found, if it is found at all, not in a church or at a concert or rally but at a sports event."[15] Sports bind people together in a nearly transcendent experience, revealing the deep spirit of connection that humans share in play, teamwork, achievement, and excellence.

I have often heard religious leaders bemoan sports as competition with church, blaming shrinking church attendance on Sunday sports leagues. The criticism misses the point. Sports do not compete with church because of bad scheduling. Instead, sports offer an alternative way to access communal spiritual awareness. Regular participation in religious services may or may not create *communitas,* but a heightened sense of communal oneness is a frequent occurrence in sporting events.

Throughout history, religious authorities have understood that sports can produce this strong response, that there is a relationship between communal sporting events and spiritual experience. In an attempt to minimize any confusion, many religions have placed strictures and prohibitions around sports by outlawing particular ones, setting theological standards to prevent sports from becoming an object of worship, determining who may or who may not attend sporting events, or relegating sports to certain days and times. Indeed, in medieval England, one could be thrown in prison for playing football. And in early New England sports were completely illegal, which perhaps explains why now their fanatically adored team is called the Patriots and not the New England Puritans. It is safe to say that, when it comes to sports, such attempts have failed.

In other arenas, however, the drive by authorities to control or contain *communitas* is far more successful. Throughout Western countries, the practices and expression of communal spirit have declined in the last few centuries, increasingly limited by decorous middle-class mores or turned into staged consumer extravaganzas or military shows of arms. Indeed, many anthropologists believe *communitas* is not compatible with "industrialization, market economies, and a complex division of labor," that festivity and spontaneity are throwbacks to earlier human communities, perhaps even psychologically dangerous anachronisms.[16] Play and sorrow too often have become personal affairs in contemporary society: lonely workouts at a gym, a child sitting at a computer console, a single mourner spreading the ashes of a loved one at the ocean's edge. When we do gather in large groups, it is often in the form of attending a commercial spectacle, entertainment that distracts us from the problems of our communities rather than empowering the human spirit to achieve new levels of creativity, compassion, and justice. All of these things have replaced the crowds of carnivals or mobs of mourners in the streets, the communal emotional outpourings that make us both different and more than we are as individuals.

Communitas, however, cannot be ultimately constrained. I suspect it is always hovering at the edges of most human gatherings. Like the wind, it comes of its own accord, a deep need for common spirit that finds unexpected expression in a chant that originates in the bleachers or by candlelight in vigils of hope and unity. *Communitas,* this ecstatic solidarity, might best be experienced now in sports, but it arises in other mass gatherings as well: street fairs, carnivals, concerts, political movements or protests, viewings of film or theater, or even special religious events (such as a revival meeting, summer camp, the Hajj, or the Kumbh Mela). At festivals like Burning Man, Greenbelt, Wild Goose Festival, SXSW, and the Fringe Festival, people take over the street, camp, or make their own cities at rivers or in the desert to dance, create, dream, sing, imagine, worship, and revel. Some of these festivals have commercial or corporate sponsors, but all of them somehow manage to escape the restraints of decorum and consumerism to achieve genuine spirit. These sorts of gatherings are necessary for the world's soul, mostly because they are egalitarian and playful, filled with collective joy. Perhaps the loss of *communitas* is one reason why we feel our societies have declined and the commons feels empty. We have forgotten to dance in the streets with strangers.

Communion:
The Spirit of Relationship

Early on a Sunday morning, my friends and I walked down to the beach. We were on a young adult retreat with our church and had decided to hold Communion on the sand. There were no more than twenty-five of us, all dressed in beach clothes or swimsuits. The priest had dressed up his T-shirt and shorts with a seasonally appropriate stole. He held a prayer book, but the rest of us had single-page bulletins or recited the liturgy from memory. Someone had a guitar. There were no pews in rows, only friends, most barefoot, standing together on the beach. A few people nearby, not part of our group, either curious or not wanting to disturb us, moved closer or farther away. There, with our toes in the sand, sun shining down, and the sound of waves to accompany prayers, the priest bid us to worship: "Blessed be God: Father, Son, and Holy Spirit." We responded, "And blessed be his kingdom, now and forever. Amen."

An ancient liturgy unfolded on the beach, complete with grains of sand along with the bread and wine that we fed to one another.

"Communion" is the word Christians use to describe this service, the giving of bread and wine in memory of Jesus. It is also called the Last Supper, Eucharist, or the Mass. It seems so distinctly theological and exclusive that the word "Communion" might not appear appropriate as part of a discussion about the world commons. The world, with its multitude of faiths, does not share in this particular meal. Indeed, there are limits as to who may partake. Some Christian communities refuse admission to the table to all but members of their church or closely related churches, those with appropriate baptisms, or the baptized. Communion does not seem to be about the commons; rather, it is only for those who belong to certain faith communities. The seats at the table can be guarded, reserved for those who are saved, especially when the sacred meal is celebrated within the confines of a church building.

But on this particular Sunday, with the sun and wind and water and sand, with other beachgoers and noisy children nearby, I intuited that Communion was about more than a priest serving a meal to church members. There were no dressy clothes marking social class, no kneeling before a religious authority, no sense of pleading with a distant God to forgive our sins. We were not taking Communion as much as we were *communing*—experiencing a deep spiritual connection with nature, our friends, and God. And this holy meal was not so much for the church as it seemed a sacred feast both in and for the world. Too often I had closed my eyes while kneeling at a railing in a darkened church to receive bread and wine. But the point of Communion was exactly the opposite: to open our eyes to "live in the world, seeing everything in it as a revelation of God."[17] As a ritual, Christian Communion is a path of spiritual connection with God and creation.

Although Christians commune in a particular way, the practice of communing is present in other traditions as well. Jews set aside a day a week to commune, Shabbat, a time for rest, prayer, and family, to recall God's blessings and presence in life. The prayer over the bread at Shabbat, "Our praise to You, Eternal our God, Sovereign of the universe, Who brings forth bread from the earth," is a reminder of the spiritual connection between God, the ground, and human life. Buddhist meditation is a practice of right communing, of moving away from distraction toward the goals of enlightenment, insight, wisdom, and love. The Sufi mystic tradition in Islam suggests that communing, creating intimacy with God, comes through the "two eyes" of reason and imagination in practices of faithful service and prayerful awe. In many native traditions people commune with God, gods, ancestors, or spirits through dance, feasting, or specific rituals designed to thin the boundaries between this world and worlds beyond. In all these cases, communion is about creating a relationship, a reciprocal exchange, between nature and God and human beings. Communion is not something given to passive recipients. Rather, to commune means to accept a gift from another and then to do something in return; it is about participation in what is sacred. It is about sharing with one another and with the world.

Meals often serve as the setting for communion. We commune with friends and family over dinner or feasts, while drinking coffee or hanging out at the pub. But communing happens other ways as well. I will never forget a sunset about twenty years ago in Santa Barbara. The sky was so vivid, the clouds so magnificent, that commuters pulled their cars over to take in the moment. I was with my husband, and a small crowd of people gathered where we were standing on a cliff at a park overlooking the ocean. As the sun set, this group of strangers received a gift of nature. Our fellow sun worshippers gasped and sighed, commenting to others in the improvised congregation about the vibrant shades of purple and orange, sharing a communal sense of amazement and gratitude. It was obvious that all who gathered felt a spiritual connection to creation in this dazzling act of communing.

We commune with animals when we pay attention to their barks and chirps, observing their wants and needs. We commune with the human spirit when gazing at a great painting as it "talks" to us in a museum or listen to a symphony as it "speaks" to our soul. We commune with our ancestors when we search their faces in faded pictures for emotions we recognize or read the diaries of those who have passed away. Communing is sharing with someone or something in a relational way. And all around us, at all times, the world is open for communion.

Thus, being in communion or communing is a powerful aspect of the commons. While *communitas* is the spirit of community, *communion* reminds us that the commons is also a mutual sharing of gifts and interdependence. Communing implies empathy, listening, developing a reciprocal sense of the other, whether God or nature or a neighbor. Practicing communion holds *communitas* to moral engagement; the "spirit" we experience together must be invested in feeding one another, serving with kindness and mercy, using our minds and hearts on behalf of others, and caring for creation.

To be in communion is to recognize what Martin Luther King referred to as "our inescapable network of mutuality," the "interrelated structure of reality" in which we all live.[18] That structure is not a theory. It is the nature of this planet, made plain when we take time to commune, to engage in deep sharing with one another. We are not alone.

Compassion:
The Spirit of Action

Communitas emerges when human beings gather, a collective sense of unity. Communion is the sort of sharing that results in a more profound sense of our relationships to each other and the world. And compassion insists that we have a moral responsibility for each other.

"The plane has not landed yet," announced the gate agent at the Albany airport. "We expect it in about forty minutes." People awaiting the late afternoon flight from Albany to Washington, D.C., groaned. June thunderstorms can make travel so difficult.

Most of my fellow travelers left to get coffee or a quick lunch. I stayed in my seat in the gate area. Only one other person remained—a middle-aged man sitting at the far edge. I had not noticed him before. He looked distraught, perhaps ill. Maybe he needed help.

I crossed over to him and asked, "May I get you something? A drink, perhaps?"

He let out a primal-sounding sob.

I sat down. "I'm so sorry. Are you okay? Is there anything I can do?"

"I buried my wife this morning," he managed to say. "And now I'm going home. To nothing."

His entire countenance was that of sorrow, mourning had bowed him, and he slumped in the chair as if falling toward the floor. I glanced about. He was alone.

Perhaps I should have left him to his grief. Instead, I asked, "What was her name? Tell me about her."

For the next half hour, he told me about his wife, her illness, and her untimely death. They had no children; she had been his best friend since high school. Their parents had all passed away. He had taken her to be buried where they had grown up in New York, a place they both loved. Most of their childhood friends had moved away. There had been no funeral, just him and a priest at a graveside to say a few prayers and good-bye. Now he was going home, back to work. Other than a few friends, he was alone.

As he shared, he unconsciously had taken my hand and was gripping it tightly. When he paused, I said how wonderful it was to love so deeply. I squeezed his hand. "I'll get you some water. Be right back."

He nodded, a slight gesture of gratefulness.

On my way back with the water and before reaching him, I found the flight attendant who was waiting for our plane. I told her about the man and his wife, how he had buried her that day. She looked concerned and thanked me, saying, "We'll take care of him."

I sat back down and gave him the water. The gate agent announced that our plane had landed.

There were only about fifteen people on the flight that day, and I do not know exactly how it happened, but everyone found out about their fellow passenger in mourning. Perhaps the flight attendant told the gate agent, and another person overheard. By the time we boarded, people were going out of their way to be kind to the sorrowful man. A crewmember escorted him aboard, tending to his needs, and other passengers treated him with great courtesy. They seated him in the back of the plane to be alone with his thoughts and whatever tears might come.

When we landed, some silent agreement formed between us to let him exit first. Instead of the usual rush and urgent calls on cell phones, everyone stood quietly, forming two lines of respect, as he walked down the aisle toward the cabin door; some nodded gravely as he passed. One woman reached out and touched his shoulder. When he reached the front of the plane, he turned back and looked at us, an acknowledgment of the sympathy offered by our impromptu party of mourners. The pilot came out of the cockpit and took the man's hand, and together they descended the steps. The rest of us followed in silence. On the tarmac was a private car, dispatched by the airline to deliver him home.

"Compassion" comes from the Latin word *compassio,* meaning "to pity, sympathize with, or suffer with," and is related to the Greek word *sympatheia,* denoting "fellow feeling, community of feeling." Quite literally, "compassion" means to endure *with* another person, to experience another's grief or suffering or need. A community of those who suffered *with* a mourning stranger—that is what formed among a small band of compassionate travelers one summer day on a delayed flight from Albany to Washington.

All of the world's great faiths place compassion as the central virtue of human life, an ideal that comes from the very being and character of truth, wisdom, or God. The Buddha taught that nirvana could be achieved by meditating on loving-kindness, compassion, sympathetic joy, and fair-mindedness, the four qualities of unconditional love. In the Hebrew Bible, God is both gracious and compassionate, willing to both forgive and stand with wayward humankind. The biblical word for "compassion" is derived from the Hebrew *rechem,* which means "womb," clearly likening the practice of feeling with others to the relationship between mother and child, while implying that all human relationships should be governed by the warmth of kinship.[19]

It should be no surprise, therefore, that when Christians speak of Jesus being born of a woman, it is not only a statement of his humanity, but an allusion to his compassion, a characteristic observed by his friends and followers throughout his ministry. He summed up his own teaching on compassion, the practice of "withness," by proclaiming that whatever was done to the poor, marginal, or outcast was, in reality, done to him (Matt. 25:40). Paul lists "compassionate hearts" (notice the plural) as a primary quality of the beloved community (Col. 3:12–13, ESV). The Qur'an follows in like manner, beginning each chapter with, "In the Name of Allah, the Compassionate, the Merciful." The whole point of Islam is the surrender of the self to God's compassion in a struggle against spiritual laxness and hypocrisy.

Although it is de rigueur to speak of religion as corrupt, controlling, and violent, the root of all human evil, one does not need a doctorate in history to recognize that the vast majority of the world's greatest saints and heroes, those who served the human race with dignity and grace, were motivated by their faith's call to compassion. It is impossible to calculate the number of lives saved in crisis, hungry people fed, widows and orphans cared for, battles ended, prisoners freed, movements of justice fashioned, tyrants overthrown, and simple acts of kindness done in the practice of compassion. Oddly enough, we generally do not judge economic or political systems on the basis of compassion withheld or inspired—although perhaps we should. We do judge religion this way, because religion insists that compassion is the whole purpose of any sort of spirituality or morality or ethics. When religion fails at compassion, it fails at its own test. To neglect loving your neighbor—to lack compassion—that is *the* problem underlying all other human problems.

Jesus made this point in his parable of the Good Samaritan. Indeed, as my fellow passengers learned on the Albany flight, it takes some courage, but ultimately it is not difficult to assist a wounded traveler. We put ourselves in his place, felt the hurt of having lost a beloved spouse, of being sad and lonely. He was right there with us;

it was relatively simple to be with him. He was our immediate neighbor. It is far more difficult when we realize that, as my friend Jim Wallis says, "There are no 'nonneighbors' in this world." That raises the bigger question: "What does it mean for the Good Samaritan to go global?"[20] That nags at me. Is global compassion possible?

In 2008, Karen Armstrong won the TED Prize based on her wish to create a global community of compassion. Religion, she insists, must drive us toward the largest possible expression of compassion. "We cannot confine our compassion to our own group," she states. "We must reach out in some way to the stranger and the foreigner—even the enemy." Compassion must stretch out to the "wider global community" as "concern for everybody."[21]

The *Charter for Compassion* is a call created by religious leaders from around the world as a result of Armstrong's dream. Stating that "the principle of compassion lies at the heart of all religious, ethical and spiritual traditions," the charter outlines practices of nonviolence, respect, and appreciation that "cultivate an informed empathy with the suffering of all human beings—even those regarded as enemies."[22] More than a hundred thousand individuals and hundreds of communities around the world have signed the charter or are making "compassion plans" for their towns or cities, and many more have read and shared Armstrong's guide to a "compassionate life." It is hard to imagine that a document on compassion might make a difference in a world mired in division and conflict.

Compassion is a building block of the world commons. And the stakes are high, as Armstrong notes: "If we don't manage to implement the Golden Rule globally so we treat all people as though they are as important as ourselves, I doubt we'll have a viable world to hand on to the next generation."[23]

The Problem of Fear

Yet, sadly, a very powerful adversary threatens compassion's advance: fear. New forms of religious fundamentalism and exclusion are nurturing fear across the planet, movements to build boundaries between nations and religions, to reinforce walls that divide, claiming that foreigners and strangers must be contained, exiled, or eliminated. Every night on every news station and from the Internet around the world, we hear, see, and read evidence of those who advocate purity over empathy and revenge over compassion, all to terrifying effect.

The future hangs in the balance of the choice between purity and revenge, on one hand, and empathy and compassion, on the other. A recent example proves instructive. When elected in 2000, President George W. Bush outlined a platform of "compassionate conservatism," using the language of communal care and the common good. I am not a conservative, and I did not vote for him. I was, however, intrigued by the possibility of compassion as the measure of a presidency, and I sincerely hoped that he was committed to the idea.[24]

September 11, 2001, however, changed all that. In the wake of the terrorist attacks, the president who had emphasized compassion certainly exhibited it—but only toward those he deemed neighbors or friends. In his "Bullhorn Speech," remarks made while standing on the rubble of the Twin Towers, President Bush demarcated the boundaries of compassion:

President Bush: Thank you all. I want you all to know—it [the bullhorn] can't go any louder—I want you all to know that America today, America today is on bended knee, in prayer for the people

whose lives were lost here, for the workers
who work here, for the families who mourn.
The nation stands with the good people of
New York City and New Jersey and
Connecticut as we mourn the loss of thousands
of our citizens.

Rescue Worker: I can't hear you!

President Bush: I can hear you! I can hear you! The rest of the
world hears you! And the people—and the
people who knocked these buildings down
will hear all of us soon!

Rescue Workers: [Chanting] U.S.A.! U.S.A.! U.S.A.! U.S.A.!
U.S.A.![25]

Compassion was only for us. We failed to see how the world was
suffering with us, how compassionate others were toward our loss.
Fear blinded us, and we did not understand that we were the
wounded traveler, and many, many people were reaching out their
hands to help. The world commons extended its compassion to
New York.

But somehow, our leaders did not grasp the idea of reciprocity.
Instead, they seized a political opportunity. Fear mutated *communitas* into a sort of morbid xenophobia, bringing forth a desire for
revenge. Revenge brought forth war. And war destroyed the possibility of communion—it divided the nation, demonized foreigners,
and wrecked relationships across the world. We are left to wonder:
What if global compassion had ruled? No shock and awe? No Guantanamo Bay or Abu Ghraib? What if we had launched a campaign
of international and interreligious cooperation instead of missiles

and drones? What path was forever lost by the Bullhorn Speech? "We should ask ourselves," suggests Karen Armstrong, "whether our own nation has contributed to the problems of a particular region and realize that, in our global world, if we ignore the pain of a people, it is likely that at some point this negligence will rebound on us."[26] At some point? How about now?

I can only remember one thing clearly from those days about compassion, at least the sort of compassion that is at the core of the world commons, perhaps the clearest statement of such I have ever read. It showed up on a bumper sticker on a car in the parking lot at Virginia Theological Seminary, where I was then teaching:

WHEN JESUS SAID, "LOVE YOUR ENEMIES,"
HE PROBABLY DIDN'T MEAN "KILL THEM."

We lost so much more than those who died on 9/11, so much more than the four thousand American soldiers who were killed in the decade since, even more than the numberless thousands known only to God. The world lost a moment when the compassionate promise that opened on that September day passed by, when we chose the wrong path. And the global commons suffered because of it. We are still suffering.

But that need not be the last word on the commons. To lose one moment does not mean we have lost all such moments. The commons belong to us—we can make of it what we will. We have often violated the trust of the commons, but the commons has also been the stage for great good. For every crusade summoned, there have been countless calls from others who have proclaimed a vision of a just commons on the basis of *communitas,* communion, and compassion. And when the common good comes to the fore, it is not a miracle. By playing together, we create *communitas;* by eating together, we experience communion with one another and God; by acting on behalf of others, we practice compassion. These are things we human beings do when we are at our best and our most courageous, especially when we recognize that God is right here with us, our partner in renewing the planetary commons.

A Common Life, a Common Journey

On Christmas Eve 2014, my family was at St. Paul's for the midnight liturgy, the candlelight service to welcome the birth of the Holy Child, Jesus. The rector, the Reverend Oran Warder, began to preach. In the sermon, he told a story about World War I, the Christmas truce of 1914:

> It was one hundred years ago this very night, perhaps at this very hour—December 24, 1914—that something amazing happened. The Great War—the First World War—the War to End all Wars—had raged on for five months and had already claimed nearly one million lives. This was the first mechanized war in human history, and it brought with it a level of devastation and brutality that the world had never seen before. . . . On that day two great armies faced each other across a front that extended along the French-Belgian border. Troops were crouched in cold muddy trenches. Between the trenches was fifty to a hundred yards of no-man's-land. The snipers who were posted on either side had standing orders to shoot anything that moved.
>
> On this night, Christmas Eve, one hundred years ago, perhaps at this very hour, mysteriously and without orders, the fighting stopped—the fighting stopped. From diaries and letters sent home afterward, we learn that the

British soldiers were startled to see Christmas trees with lighted candles on the parapets of the German trenches. In one spot a German soldier shouted across no-man's-land, "A gift is coming," and the British soldiers took cover and braced for a barrage of artillery. Instead, what came across the enemy line was a boot filled with sausages. The boot was then returned full of plum pudding. Spontaneous singing started on one side, which was greeted with applause from the other. Then, after one long eerie silence, German soldiers began to quietly sing "*Stille Nacht*"—and the British soldiers joined their voices—singing in English—"Silent night, holy night, all is calm, all is bright . . . sleep in heavenly peace."

On Christmas morning—along this tiny section of a very long enemy line—opposing troops dared to venture out of the trenches. There they extended greetings, awkward handshakes, and small gifts. It is recorded that in several places soccer games were played.[27]

This was a holy moment, the spirit of human solidarity, of true communion, of compassion. The no-man's-land became shared space, and a zone of death was transformed into a hospitable place, where enemies were, for a time, friends. It was a glimpse toward a global commons. "For a few short hours," writes social critic Jeremy Rifkin of the same incident, "no more than that day, tens of thousands of human beings broke ranks, not only from their commands but from their allegiances to country, to show their common humanity. Thrown together to maim and kill, they courageously stepped outside of the institutional duties to commiserate with one another and to celebrate each other's lives."[28] Peace did not last. But the memory of it suggests a different way is possible.

Oran put it in more distinctly spiritual terms: "That it is precisely when we recognize our common humanity—when we recognize our own humanity in the face of the other—it is then that we also recognize the face of God." This is salvation, this seeing God in all other faces, the very meaning and purpose of Jesus, whose birth we gathered to celebrate: "In him we are forever connected to God and forever connected to one another. We are not another race of creatures bound on other journeys. We share a common life—we share a common journey—and we are forever bound together by God's divine love."

Three years had passed since the anniversary of 9/11, when a sermon of exclusion chased me out of the church and onto the street. Since then, I have walked about in the world, finding the spirit of the commons, hearing the call toward the common good, and embracing the joy of our common humanity. I thought not only of Jesus, born that night, but Moses, Buddha, Muhammad, and all the great teachers who have proclaimed the oneness of humankind, fashioned from the mud of the same primal garden, on a journey toward a world commons of hospitality, justice, and peace. It is pretty simple, really. Unity, relationship, action. Maybe moments that hold compassionate promise happen more often than we notice. All it takes is for courageous souls to break ranks and walk into no-person's-land.

That night, as we lit the candles and sang "Silent Night," I felt glad to have come in from the streets, braver and more hopeful, warmed by the God who is with us. The ancient promise of God fulfilled.

Revelation

Our task is enormous. . . . To look at all that
has gone before us, and to recognize that each
one of us, however small, has a unique task
in co-creation—a unique contribution to make
in the world and to humanity.

—*Edwina Gateley*

On September 12, 2001, I drove my daughter to preschool. It was like any early autumn day in Washington, D.C., warm, sunny with brilliant blue skies. Except that it was not normal. It was the day after 9/11. Officials told us to go on. Go to work or school. Get up and go on.[1]

As we drove north on the George Washington Parkway along the banks of the Potomac River, a song came on the radio:

I see trees of green, red roses too,
I see them bloom, for me and you,
And I think to myself
What a wonderful world.

I see skies of blue, and clouds of white,
The bright blessed day, the dark sacred night,
And I think to myself
What a wonderful world.

With Louis Armstrong's gravelly voice singing "What a Won-derful World," I pulled into a parking lot, the same place where a dozen years later I would sit and reflect on the water, and sobbed. It was as if the universe had ripped in two, revealing a vast emptiness at its core. The world was fractured, broken, covered in the dust of pain, oppression, violence, and death. Was the world ever really wonderful? Wasn't it always sinful? Didn't 9/11 just confirm the story of the fall, of this brutal place where brother has always turned against brother and neighbor killed neighbor?

A wonderful world? Really? I turned the radio off and drove on in silence.

Where was God in the midst of all this? On that day, I had no idea.

But I knew that nothing would ever be the same.

The Last Days

Not surprisingly, in the wake of 9/11 certain Christians proclaimed that the attacks were part of biblical prophecy. God was warning America to prepare for Christ's return, and this signaled the end times. One might expect such a message in fundamentalist churches. American religion, however, turned apocalyptic on a larger scale. The end of the West! The end of Christianity! The end of the world! It was an orgy of cataclysm, the last days unfolding on the nightly news.

The book of Revelation, the last book of the New Testament, is an oddly influential text in Western history, and most especially in American history. Written by an unknown Christian to encourage a persecuted church, the book has always been controversial. Many theologians—including Martin Luther—argued that it should not be in the Bible. Critics have often pointed out that the book's bizarre tales foster ambivalence toward the world, violence toward nonbelievers, and an escapist mentality toward faith.[2] God will destroy everything in the end, and believers will be taken up to heaven (and nonbelievers thrown into an eternal lake of fire). Except for the fact that the world is where we must decide to follow Christ, the earth does not really matter. Such disregard for the world has had profound consequences in history—and not just during the years since 9/11.

But the book of Revelation is not a heavenly escape story. Instead, it tells the opposite tale. We do not go to heaven. Heaven comes to us. The end of history is not destruction; rather, its end is sacred restoration. When sin and evil pass away, a holy city descends to us:

> See the home of God is among mortals.
> He will dwell with them;
> They will be his peoples,
> And God himself will be with them. (21:3)

The Christian scriptures end with a vision of a beautiful world. Water, trees, and sparkling streets: "Jerusalem coming down out of heaven from God. It has the glory of God and a radiance like a very rare jewel" (21:11). The land is healed and bears fruit. The Bible does not end in heaven. It ends here. On earth. "And the one who was seated on the throne said, 'See, I am making all things new'" (21:5).

The Bible begins in a perfect garden and ends with a sacred city. And that sacred city draws together nature and human community into an intimate relationship with God, the One who dwells in the midst of it all. Here on earth.

Sacred Cosmopolitanism

We do, of course, live on earth—but we dwell between the paradisial garden and the holy city. We live in the world as it is. And earth is, of course, not as it used to be. More than seven billion people inhabit the planet, many of them in huge urban areas, now connected to one another through economics and technology. Neither nature nor humanity has ever been in this particular situation before. Philosophers, historians, and social scientists have begun to describe the twenty-first-century world as "cosmopolitan," meaning that all human beings are citizens of the world, that is, "citizens of the cosmos." Boundaries have thinned between nations and cultures, and we participate in multiple worlds and our lives are simultaneously local and global. Although the idea of being world citizens has a long and noble history, a history that began with Greece and Rome, it has taken on a particular meaning in our time. Today we are interdependent global tribes, people with different governments and faiths, yet who depend on one another in the same web of politics, economics, and technology. And religion.[3]

Some call this globalization, but that is not quite the right word. Globalization flattens the world and makes us all the same. In many ways, globalization is an economic system and political vision imposed from outside any particular culture. And there are plenty of "outside" interests who would like to force this agenda on the planet. But cosmopolitanism is not that. It is, rather, a disposition and an inner awareness that our individual lives and national identities are playing out on a vast global stage. This implies recognition and a shift of perspective—of seeing and experiencing the web in which we live. Recognition, in turn, gives birth to empathy and the profound realization that we really, truly are in this together.

Throughout this book, I have been trying to demonstrate that a sort of sacred cosmopolitanism—an awareness of the connections we share with God and others here on earth—has been born, something that is visible in religious attitudes, membership, and practices and revealed in stories, experiences, and data. In certain ways, this awareness has always been with us. In the past, this understanding has embodied humankind's greatest aspirations, and it has guided artists, prophets, gurus, mystics, and saints through the ages. But what was once the vision of only a few has now become a theological revolution of many. It is an understanding and experience of God that goes over boundaries: the boundary that once divided Creator from creation, the boundary that divided nature from the human community, the boundaries that divided human communities, and finally the boundary that divided God from humankind. Instead of living inside of tight religious boxes, many people are experiencing a borderless kind of spiritual awareness that has enabled them to find God in the world of nature and in the geography of human life. Although I have written about this from a largely Christian perspective, it is not distinctly Christian. Part of the boundary crossing involves going beyond religious boundaries as well as ethnic and national ones. And the recognition of the sacred cosmopolitan—that we are citizens with God and one another in a holy cosmos together—is found among people in all faith traditions.

This does not mean, however, that all religions are alike or that we shall be happily forming a single world "church" anytime soon. Indeed, the sacred cosmopolitanism of nature and neighborliness in these pages might be also described as *humane localism,* a way of life in our worldwide web that cherishes the distinctiveness of our particular traditions and cultures while embracing the universal aspects of human community and the larger quest for God and meaning.[4] Even the book of Revelation describes a vision of diversity, of people from every tongue, tribe, and nation, who gather in the New Jerusalem. In the holy city, we maintain our uniqueness while God dwells in our midst. Unity is experienced in love and friendship, not doctrine or dogma. There is no coercion of faith.

In the book of Revelation, a throne is at the center of the sacred city. In a hierarchical world, thrones are elevated chairs, the special places where kings or queens sit. But a throne is just a fancy chair. If asked to think of a room where there are chairs, most of us do not say, "throne room." Most of us say, "dining room." Instead of thinking of Revelation's sacred city as a sort of imperial throne room, perhaps we should see it as a dining room. And around the table are many chairs. The places are marked with cards: "Christian," "Jew," "Muslim," "Buddhist," "American," "Arab," "Chinese," "African," "Human," "Animal," "Fish," "Tree," and so on. No one owns the table. No one gets to take it over. We receive this table; it is the gift of heaven to earth. Our job is to pull up more chairs. And to make sure all are fed.

Where is God? God hosts the table at the center of the world. The sacred cosmos is a feast, a party of host and guests, seated around the table that practices hospitality for all. The only requirement for joining in is that you want to be there.

Co-creation

Critics often worry that spirituality and mysticism seem passive and promote individualism. Two professors at the University of California at Berkeley, however, have concluded that experiences of awe have actually led to greater acts of compassion for others.[5] Their research demonstrates a connection between spirituality and justice, between encountering God and acting on behalf of others. Experiencing the divine or the sacred in the world results in people doing things to make the world better.

"Co-creation" is a concept in business circles that emphasizes partnership as the source of creativity. According to the theory, co-creation involves a variety of people (typically a business and its customers) coming together to create something no one could on one's own.[6] In business, co-creation emphasizes the shift in the role of the customer from passive recipient of a company's goods to participant in innovation, productivity, and value. It replaces top-down models of work with a structure of business that theorists have identified as "constellation" or "web."

I was a bit surprised when I learned that "co-creation" had become a management theory, for I first heard the term in the 1980s. In his 1983 book, *Original Blessing,* Matthew Fox, then a Roman Catholic priest, argues that we are "co-creators with God." He calls the path of life-giving faith the "*via creativa*" that "invites us to trust our vocation as artists, as new imagers and new birthers" and participate with God in a process of ongoing creation.[7] I remember how radical these ideas seemed, bordering on what I then considered heresy. But the brilliance of Fox's book is that he presented co-creation as the unnoticed story of faith and traced its development through Jewish theology, Eastern Orthodoxy, medieval Catholic mysticism, and contemporary spirituality. Creating the world with God, an active and ever-present partner, is the primary human vocation. In the years since, the idea of co-creation has become widespread in many faith communities, taught in seminaries, proclaimed by preachers, and shared in popular spiritual works.[8] From a faith perspective, the link between awe and action is at the heart of co-creation.

Both Genesis and Revelation are creation stories. But they are not stories of a static creation, where God makes the world, gives it to us to have dominion over, and then goes away. Instead, they invite us to make the world *with* God. Genesis invites us into a world of agrarian creativity—to plant, produce, and procreate. Revelation invites us into a world of urban creativity—to be people who live by God's light, continue to bring forth fruit, and govern with God forever. From beginning to end, the biblical story is one in which we make a peaceable world with God.

If we understand that we are dirt, that God is the ground of all that is, well, then, we might think twice about how we treat soil. If water is the river of spiritual and physical life, we will care about what we are doing to watersheds. If air sustains us and we are made of stardust, then the sky and what happens to it matters. Knowing our own roots is the first step in knowing ourselves and recognizing our common humanity. Making a home is a radical act of claiming a place in the world. Being neighborly is the path to empathy, of enacting the Golden Rule. Building the commons, the "we" of our world house, is to pull the vision of heaven out of the clouds to earth here and now. We are constantly creating a sacred architecture of dwelling—of God's dwelling and ours—as we weave nature and the built environment into a web of meaning. Awe and action are of a piece.

We do this. God did not leave humankind a garden and say, "Don't touch it." Instead, God asked us to watch over and care for the garden, to "till and keep" the soil. God did not bring down the New Jerusalem and say, "Show's over." Instead, God welcomes the beloved into a life free from pain, suffering, and oppression and opens the city gates to an unlimited human future. The book of Revelation does not end with God judging a sinful world. It ends with an invitation: "The Spirit and the bride say, 'Come!'" (22:17).

Spirituality is not just about sitting in a room encountering a mystical god in meditation or about seeing God in a sunset. Awe is the gateway to compassion. It is a deep awareness that we are creators, creators who work with the Creator, in an ongoing project of crafting a world. If we do not like the world or are afraid of it, we have had a hand in that. And if we made a mess, we can clean it up and do better. We are what we make.

The Last Days of Religion

September 11, 2001, shocked nearly everyone. In the days immediately afterward, people streamed into churches, synagogues, temples, and mosques for comfort and solace. They asked why it had happened. They asked where God was.

Some preachers thought it was the beginning of a great revival and that millions of the lax would return to faith. They were wrong. The exact opposite happened.

September 11 and the events following did not bring millions back to conventional religion. Instead, it prompted profound questions about ethics, faith, and God that most religious communities were neither ready for nor able to answer. There were some incredibly brave clergy who preached about a God of love who was with us, a God of peace who abhors revenge and violence, a God who knows no religious or theological boundaries, a God who dwells in compassion. But the vast number of people who went searching for meaning found in church a God that strangely resembled the God of their grandparents: an all-powerful deity sitting on a throne in heaven, draped in an American flag, who was concerned primarily about winning the war, keeping gay people out of church, what kind of hymns were sung in worship, whether or not to move the pews, and individual salvation.[9]

There was a brief bump in religious attendance. After a couple of months of fuller pews, however, things pretty much went back to normal for most congregations and most religious institutions. People came and then they left again. Yet the quest to find God went on—in some renegade congregations, at the edges of institutional religion, or outside the boundaries of conventional faith.

September 11 did not cause the changes about which I write in this book. They began some fifty or more years ago. September 11 hastened them. Before anyone imagined planes would crash into the World Trade Center towers in New York, signs of religious decline had been evident in many quarters—for decades. Europe has been largely postreligious and secular, with Canada and Australia not far behind, and across Asia, large numbers of people profess no religious identity. Americans always thought their country was an exception to the forces of secularism and religious decline. But, as sociologist Mark Chaves points out, conventional religious identity in the United States (that includes Protestants, Catholics, and Jews) has been declining since 1972, first slowly, and with increasing rapidity since 1992, with the percentage of "nones" increasing throughout the same period. Trends already in place gained increasing momentum after 2002. According to Chaves, the United States has been in a five-decade religious decline, accompanied by greater religious decentralization, non-Christian religious diversity, and religious disaffiliation.[10]

In May 2015, Pew Research Center released the latest installment of its work on the changing landscape of American religion. In just seven years, the percentage of Americans who are Christians has dropped sharply, from 78.4 percent of the population to 70.6 percent, while the number of religiously unaffiliated people has grown from 16.1 percent to 22.8 percent. Following the new report, church leaders, scholars, and bloggers all offered up opinions

on the cause of the decline and what it all means for American religion, society, and politics. There was talk about demographics
(especially birth rate and immigration), changing patterns of religious practice, arguments about conservative versus liberal churches
and theology, and jeremiads against American individualism. About
a thousand blogs appeared on how to attract young adults and the
"spiritual-but-not-religious" to church. No one, to my knowledge,
in any major media outlet suggested that the report signaled a spiritual revolution regarding God.

The old God, the one believed in, preached, celebrated, and
served in conventional religious institutions, is fading from view.
And a new God, one of intimate longing and infinite love, experienced and proclaimed by seers and prophets through the ages, has
risen just over the horizon. It is a new spiritual day.

Where Is God?

I have had three conversions in my life, each time seeking a deeper
awareness of God. The first was in the summer of 1975, when I left
my childhood faith, which I had inherited from my parents, and
embraced evangelical Protestantism, a form of faith that seemed
empowering and meaningful. The second was in the early 1990s,
when I left evangelicalism (which proved more constraining than I
had thought) and embraced liberal Christianity as embodied in the
Episcopal Church.

The third conversion began on September 12, 2001, when the
radio was playing "What a Wonderful World" and I realized that I
did not think the world was wonderful. Indeed, I thought the world
was frightening, a place to be endured. Although it took me some
time to understand, I had largely wanted church to protect me from
the world, a community offering the comforting arms of a benevolent

Father in Heaven, familiar rituals, a strengthening meal, and that promised eternal reward for being good. I had experienced both conservative and liberal forms of this church, but came to realize that they were different forms of a very similar thing, two versions of faith in the same vertical God.

My third conversion was not about rejecting church (as the living expression of Jesus in the world), Christianity, or faith. Rather, my third conversion was about leaving behind the vertical God and elevator church. The third conversion is a turning toward God-with-us and a hope for faith community that risks stepping off the elevator. This conversion loves the world, seeks God with the world in all its beauty and pain. It is a quest to find others who have experienced the same—and a dream that together we can build a spiritual architecture of loving God and neighbor, the God who dwells with us in grace. Once I believed in a God who was both here and up there (as in "up" in heaven); now I experience God as the one who is both here and out there (as on the "edge" of the horizon). Once I encountered awe when considering a majestic and holy divinity, singing praises to the God who would save me from this sinful earth. Now, I am moved by the love that enlivens the earth and the mystery that hovers just beyond sight. My orientation shifted. And the change of perspective from vertical to horizontal amounts to a personal spiritual revolution. On September 12, I converted to the world, the dwelling place of the divine.

I know I am not alone. All those statistics—the ones about decline—point toward massive theological discontent. People still believe in God. They just do not believe in the God proclaimed and worshipped by conventional religious organizations. Some of the discontented—and there are many of them—do not know what to call themselves. So they check the "unaffiliated" box on religion surveys. They have become secular humanists, agnostics, posttheists, and atheists and have rejected the conventional God. Others say they are spiritual but not religious. They still believe in God but have abandoned conventional forms of congregating. Still others declare themselves "done" with religion. They slink away from religious communities, traditions that once gave them life, and go hiking on Sunday morning. Some still go to church, but are hanging on for dear life, hoping against hope that something in their churches will change. They pray prayers about heaven that no longer make sense and sing hymns about an eternal life they do not believe in. They want to be in the world, because they know they are made of the same stuff as the world and that the world is what really matters, but some nonsense someone taught them once about the world being bad or warning of hell still echoes in their heads. They are afraid to say what they really think or feel for fear that no one will listen or care or even understand. They think they might be crazy. All these people are turning toward the world because they intuit that is where they will find meaning and awe, that which those who are still theists call God.

They are not crazy. They are part of this spiritual revolution—people discovering God in the world and a world that is holy, a reality that enfolds what we used to call heaven and earth into one. These people are not secular, even though their main concern is the world; they are not particularly religious (in the old-fashioned understanding of the term), even though they are deeply aware of God. They are fashioning a way of faith between conventional theism and any kind of secularism devoid of the divine.[11] In our time, people are turning toward the numinous presence that animates the world, what theologian Rudolf Otto called "the Holy." They are those who are discovering a deeply worldly faith. Decades ago Catholic theologian Karl Rahner made a prediction about devout people of the future. He said they would either be "mystics," those who have "experienced something," or "cease to be anything at all"; and if they are mystical believers, they will be those whose faith "is profoundly present and committed to the world."[12] The future of faith would be an earthy spirituality, a brilliant awareness of the spirit that vivifies the world.

Conversions are always experiences of God. The odd thing about my third conversion, however, is that it never ends. Every time I think I love the world enough, every time I think I experience God's presence with the earth enough, there is more. Every time I think I can answer the question "Where is God?" the question sounds anew. What a relief to remember the biblical promise: "Seek and you shall find." Perhaps it is less a conversion than an evolution—an ongoing spiritual evolution that amounts to a revolution of faith.

God is with us. Here.

A Note to the Church

Faith itself sometimes needs to be stripped of its social and historical encrustations and returned to its first, churchless incarnation in the human heart.

—*Christian Wiman*

When I walked into the hundred-year-old neo-Gothic sanctuary of St. Stephen's Episcopal Church, I was grateful to come in from the blistering heat. The cool, dark medieval space provided welcome relief from the humid, hazy sunlight of this Richmond, Virginia, late afternoon. I took off my sunglasses, and my eyes slowly adjusted to the interior, a nave lit only by hundreds of burning candles and the natural light streaming in through the stained-glass windows. There were few seats left for evening worship, known as the Celtic service, an alternative to the conventional Sunday morning Episcopal liturgy.

"There must be 600 people here," I whispered to my husband. "And it is the Fourth of July weekend!" He nodded in agreement.

(We would later find out that the number was closer to 850.) We found seats in the middle of a row far in the back.

Haunting music filled the building as a small group played folk tunes on traditional Celtic instruments. The priest and worship leaders entered the sanctuary, and the liturgy began with a poem about trees by Mary Oliver.

It was followed with readings from scripture, contemplative music, and healing prayer. There was no sermon. Rather, a guest speaker reflected on why Christians needed to be on a journey with Jews, Muslims, Buddhists, and Hindus and what we might learn of God from one another. The priest invited everyone to participate in Communion.

For more than thirty years, I have worshipped in Episcopal churches, and I am intimately familiar with their prayers and liturgies. Despite having changed the specific form, St. Stephen's retained the structure and flow of the Episcopal service, but it had reoriented the direction of worship and contemplation. Instead of lifting our attention toward heaven, we were invited to see the world around us more deeply, to consider both nature and human community in new ways. The distant patriarchal God was gone, replaced by the presence of the Spirit who dwells with creation and in us. We were invited to encounter the sacred unity at the heart of all things, enlarging our field of vision to experience ourselves, our neighbors, and God as an interrelated ecology of faith.

After the service, we walked out the great doors at the back of the church and were immediately in line for a meal to be shared together. This week it was an American-style picnic on the lawn, with food from the church's farmers' market. We literally went from the Communion table to the picnic table without missing a beat. I laughed—it was actually impossible to leave the property without being fed. People practiced hospitality as if they were welcoming you into their own home. Everyone was talking to everyone else, greeting friends and strangers alike. At least a dozen people told me how they had given up on church until they found the Celtic evening service. Some shared with me that this was their first experience of church—that they had never before been part of any faith community.

This was not a program to bring people into church. It was not that worship was in the evening instead of the morning to raise attendance or that there was good music and candlelight to make church more appealing. And this was not designed to reach any particular demographic or interest group in order to attract new members. Rather, the Celtic evening service is a sacred experiment in creating community on the horizon of faith. Is it possible to be a different sort of church, one not on the mountain of privilege but one that celebrates the living web of God and the world?

The answer at St. Stephen's is a resounding yes. The power of the Celtic service is not in its programmatic pieces. Rather, its power comes from the simple fact that it addresses the question "Where is God?" This vibrant gathering centers on theological transformation—an encounter with the God who dwells here. And its particular liturgical experience enables people to touch the reality of the Spirit, to know that they are not alone in the journey to find God in the world, and to be strengthened to make the earth more habitable for the holy. As a community, they are living the spiritual revolution.

Some congregations (and not just Christian congregations) are following the same path. But, if survey data is any indication, churches like St. Stephen's are the exception, not the rule, as the gap between the spiritual revolution and religious institutions both persists and widens. For the most part, the spiritual revolution challenges the church. It challenges the vision of a distant God that has been the basis of much of religious life for the last thousand years or so. The good news is that God is closer than ever before, and many people are making new connections with the spirit of love and life to heal the broken places of the world. The spiritual revolution does not destroy the church—unless, of course, the church ignores it, denies it, dismisses it, or pushes it away.

It is surprisingly easy to join in: get off the elevator, feel your feet on the ground, take a walk or hike, plant a garden, clean up a watershed, act on behalf of the earth, find your roots, honor your family and home, love your neighbor as yourself, and live the Golden Rule as you engage the commons. Pay attention. Play. Sing new songs, recite poetry, write new prayers and liturgies, learn sacred texts, make friends with those of other faiths, celebrate the cycles of the seasons, and embrace ancient wisdom. Weep with those who mourn. Listen for the whisper of God everywhere. Work for justice. Know that your life is in communion with all life.

The spiritual revolution, finding God in the world, is an invitation to new birth, most especially for religion. There is no better place to start than in your synagogue, mosque, temple, or church.

And that new birth is happening. You can hear it as the earth groans for salvation, as poets and philosophers tell its stories, as scientists search the soil and the cosmos for life, as the oppressed, poor, and marginalized push for dignity and economic justice. It is time for the church to wake up. There is nothing worse than sleeping through a revolution.

ACKNOWLEDGMENTS

I have two best friends. Teresa, a missionary pastor in Japan, and Julie, a secular professor of religious studies in Florida. They have never met. They live worlds apart and have nothing in common. Except, of course, me.

For more than three decades, I have learned from both of them. One is convinced of more faith than I could ever summon; the other, convinced of more doubt than I could ever embrace. Faithful Christian and committed secularist, they have been my spiritual and intellectual pushmi-pullyus, neither one ever afraid to ask the most pointed question at the most inconvenient times. This book is, in part, my attempt to craft a middle way through their worlds, describing the possibility of being in God, but not overly certain, and being in the world, but not completely secular. Finding the spirit of God with the spirit of the world is the direction they both pointed me in from their very different paths.

Questions are my classroom. And over the years each book I have written prompts new questions from faithful readers, mostly those in mainline and progressive faith communities in the United States and Canada. So many churches, seminaries, and colleges have invited me to speak and preach to their congregants, students, and guests, who, in response, asked me thousands of good questions. In the last five years, most of those questions have centered on the tension between their faith traditions and the increasing number of people leaving religion and what this might mean for the future of faith. I have realized that many people have their own Teresa on one side and their own Julie on the other and find it difficult to maintain spiritual equilibrium between the two. I cannot claim to have answered their questions perfectly, but I can promise that I took them seriously and wrestled with them in my own life. Herein I have answered them to the best of my ability. Thank you for your hospitality, and thank you for your questions. I hope for many more years of both.

Other writers, many of whom are collegial friends and some known to me only through their books, have influenced this project through conversations, interviews, or their own writing. They include Brian McLaren, Larry Rasmussen, John Philip Newell, Forrest Pritchard, Mallory McDuff, Norman Wirzba, Barbara Brown Taylor, Willis Jenkins, Sam Hamilton-Poore, Philip Clayton, Walter Brueggemann, Bill McKibben, Jim Wallis, Phyllis Tickle, Richard Rohr, Harvey Cox, Bron Taylor, Sallie McFague, John Dominic Crossan, and the late Marcus Borg. In recent years, I have been inspired and challenged by a host of contemporary poets and their prophetic vision, especially Wendell Berry, Mary Oliver, Naomi Shihab Nye, Marge Piercy, Mark Nepo, and David Whyte.

Several people played key roles in helping me both think through and experience the issues explored in this book, most especially Robert Jones, Jim Antal, Gary Jones, Julie Ingersoll, Anne Howard, Marianne Borg, Joe Stewart-Sicking, Doug Gay, Erin Dunigan, Donna McNeil, Mark Sandlin, Danny Zemel, Jessica Tate and the NEXT Church Presbyterians, Anna Woofenden, Phil

Zuckerman, Mary Ray, Angela Cannon, friends in my closed Facebook community, and my Ring Lake Ranch companions.

While writing this book, my longtime editor and friend, Roger Freet, left HarperOne and became my agent. Katy Hamilton and Michael Maudlin assumed the task of editing a half-finished book, making the midstream transition as painless as possible. Anne Moru was a wonderful copyeditor, as she has been for me in the past. Every religion writer deserves a copyeditor who is familiar with the Qu'ran and classical Latin. The art department created the book cover of my dreams, and Janet M. Evans designed a beautiful book. Suzanne Quist and Suzanne Wickham brought their expertise and enthusiasm to this project and helped clarify its voice. Thank you so much. As always, I appreciate the vision, passion, and support of Mark Tauber and Claudia Boutote (now leading HarperElixir), who have always cared about and believed in my work.

Finally, my family served as the main influence for this book. My daughter, Emma, and my stepson, Jonah, both sharp and insightful millennial Christians, ask questions about God and the world that constantly challenge me—and have changed me. My main theological coconspirator, however, is my husband and best friend, Richard Bass, who embodies the twinned spirits of liberal Protestantism and American Transcendentalism and has spent almost two decades pulling me down to earth. Thank you for grounding me.

NOTES

INTRODUCTION

1. David Buchdahl, quoted in William McLoughlin, *Revivals, Awakenings, and Reform* (Chicago: Univ. of Chicago Press, 1978), p. 215.

2. For data on religious experience, see "Mystical Experiences," Pew Research, December 29, 2009, http://www.pewresearch.org/daily-number/mystical-experiences. See also Barbara Ehrenreich, *Living with a Wild God: A Nonbeliever's Search for the Truth About Everything* (New York: Twelve, 2014).

3. For an exploration of divine nearness throughout church history, see Diana Butler Bass, *A People's History of Christianity* (San Francisco: HarperOne, 2009).

4. H. Richard Niebuhr, *Christ and Culture* (New York: Harper, 1951).

5. See also John Philip Newell, *The Rebirthing of God: Christianity's Struggle for New Beginnings* (Woodstock, VT: SkyLight Paths, 2014).

6. Wilhelm and Marion Pauck, *Paul Tillich: His Life and Thought,* vol. 1, *Life* (New York: Harper & Row, 1976), p. 51.

7. Charles P. Henderson, Jr., "Paul Tillich: Theism Rewritten for an Age of Science," chap. 6 in *God and Science: The Death and Rebirth of Theism* (Atlanta: John Knox, 1986); online version at GodWeb, http://www.godweb.org/Tillich.htm.

8. D. Mackenzie Brown, *Ultimate Concern: Tillich in Dialogue* (New York: Harper & Row, 1965); online version at Religion Online, http://www.religion-online.org/showchapter.asp?title=538&C =598.

9. Benjamin Sommer, *The Bodies of God and the World of Ancient Israel* (Cambridge: Cambridge Univ. Press, 2009).

10. Sallie McFague, "God and the World," in David B. Lott, ed., *Sallie McFague: Collected Readings* (Minneapolis, MN: Fortress, 2013), p. 222. This essay comes from McFague's *The Body of God: An Ecological Theology* (Minneapolis, MN: Augsburg Fortress, 1993), chap. 5.

11. For the trends and an "on the ground" view of postreligious culture in America, see Phil Zuckerman, *Living the Secular Life* (New York: Penguin, 2014); the per-year data is found on p. 60.

12. Mark Sandlin, "The Rise of the Dones," *Patheos,* November 21, 2014; http://www.patheos.com/blogs/thegodarticle/2014/11/ the-rise-of-the-dones-as-the-church-kills-spiritual-community/. See also Josh Packard and A. Hope, *Church Refugees: Sociologists Reveal Why People Are Done with Church* (Loveland, CO: Group, 2015).

13. Data in this paragraph are drawn from the work of Public Religion Research, especially its work on religious disaffiliation, http://www.pewforum.org/2012/10/09/nones-on-the-rise/ http://publicreligion.org, and Pew Forum on Religion. A quick glance of the trends may be seen at Tobin Grant, "Graphs: 5 Signs of the 'Great Decline' of Religion in America," Religion News Service, Aug. 1, 2014, http://tobingrant.religionnews.com/2014/08/01/

five-signs-great-decline-religion-america-gallup-graphs-church/. For Canadian statistics, see "Religion and Faith in Canada Today," http://angusreid.org/faith-in-canada/.

14. Michael Hout, Claude Fischer, and Mark Chaves, "More Americans Have No Religious Preference: Key Finding from the 2012 General Social Survey," March 7, 2013, http://issi.berkeley .edu/sites/default/files/shared/docs/Hout%20et%20al_No%20 Relig%20Pref%202012_Release%20Mar%202013.pdf.

15. Sam Harris, *Waking Up: A Guide to Spirituality Without Religion* (New York: Simon & Schuster, 2014).

16. See Zuckerman, *Living the Secular Life,* especially chap. 3, "Irreligion Rising," pp. 55–77.

17. Diana Butler Bass, *Strength for the Journey: A Pilgrimage of Faith in Community* (San Francisco: Jossey-Bass, 2002).

18. The phrase is from Elizabeth Johnson, *Quest for the Living God: Mapping Frontiers in the Theology of God* (New York: Continuum, 2008), pp. 25ff.

CHAPTER 1: DIRT

1. On the impact of the Industrial Revolution on our understanding of land and spirituality, see Wendell Berry, "Our Deserted Country," in *Our Only World: Ten Essays* (Berkeley, CA: Counterpoint, 2015), pp. 105–57.

2. Forrest Pritchard, *Gaining Ground: A Story of Farmers' Markets, Local Food, and Saving the Family Farm* (Guildford, CT: Lyon, 2013), p. 315.

3. Sallie McFague, "God and the World," in David B. Lott, ed., *Sallie McFague: Collected Readings* (Minneapolis, MN: Fortress, 2013), pp. 215–16. This essay comes from McFague's *The Body of God: An Ecological Theology* (Minneapolis, MN: Augsburg Fortress, 1993), chap. 5.

4. Walter Brueggemann, *Genesis* (Atlanta: John Knox, 1982), p. 30.

5. Ellen F. Davis, professor of Hebrew Bible at Duke University, suggests that the idea of "dominion over" is better understood as "mastery among" or "working on behalf of," not a sort of ruling over, as the directive is placed within created community: "The basic meaning of the verb is not to rule; the word actually denotes the traveling around of the shepherd with his flock" (*Scripture, Culture, and Agriculture: An Agrarian Reading of the Bible* [Cambridge: Cambridge Univ. Press, 2009], pp. 29, 55).

6. Fred Bahnson and Norman Wirzba, *Making Peace with the Land: God's Call to Reconcile with Creation* (Downers Grove, IL: IVP, 2012), p. 16.

7. Larry L. Rasmussen, *Earth-honoring Faith: Religious Ethics in a New Key* (New York: Oxford Univ. Press, 2013), pp. 197–98.

8. Davis, *Scripture, Culture, and Agriculture,* pp. 8–9.

9. Wes Jackson, "The Agrarian Mind: Mere Nostalgia or Practical Necessity?" in Norman Wirzba, ed., *The Essential Agrarian Reader* (Berkeley, CA: Counterpoint, 2004), pp. 140–53.

10. Susan S. Lang, " 'Slow, Insidious' Soil Erosion Threatens Human Health and Welfare as Well as the Environment, a Cornell Study Asserts," *Cornell Chronicle,* March 20, 2006, http://www .news.cornell.edu/stories/2006/03/slow-insidious-soil-erosion -threatens-human-health-and-welfare.

11. Elizabeth DeRuff, *Stories of Food and Farm Ministries,* https:// farmtoaltartable.files.wordpress.com/2013/08/stories-of-food-and -farm-v–2.pdf.

12. See, for example, Mallory McDuff, *Natural Saints: How People of Faith Are Working to Save God's Earth* (New York: Oxford Univ. Press, 2010), and Fred Bahnson, *Soil and Sacrament: A Spiritual Memoir of Food and Faith* (New York: Simon & Schuster, 2013).

13. The Garden Church, http://gardenchurchsp.org.

14. National Gardening Association Special Report: *Garden to Table, A 5-Year Look at Food Gardening in America,* 2014, www .garden.org/articles/articles.php?q=show&id=3819.

15. Waterloo Region Food Charter, http://www.wrfoodsystem .ca/food-charter.

16. Amanda Lewan, "The Business of Urban Farming Takes Root in Detroit," *Entrepreneur,* December 2, 2014, http://www .entrepreneur.com/article/239844.

17. Around 350 million years ago, when massive plants, insects, and animals died, they decomposed and compressed, leaving behind huge geological deposits of their remains that eventually formed carbonate rocks, coal, oil, and natural gas. Some of that matter was broken down by acidic rains, creating the rich soils from which the human race would benefit. Plants grew out of the carbon-rich soil, pulling excess carbon dioxide from air, and separated the carbon from the oxygen. The plants then deposited carbon compounds back into the ground, further enriching the soil in which they grew. At the same time, plants released oxygen into the air for other creatures to breathe. This extended carbon cycle took about 300 million years, and it formed the planet that sustains us. We harvest both energy (in the form of coal, gas, and oil from it) and food from the ground as a result of it.

18. Three good books on the topic of soil farming and climate change are Kristin Ohlson, *The Soil Will Save Us* (New York: Rodale, 2014); Judith D. Schwartz, *Cows Save the Planet and Other Improbable Ways of Restoring Soil to Heal the Earth* (White River Junction, VT: Chelsea Green, 2013); and Courtney White, *Grass, Soil, Hope: A Journey Through Carbon Country* (White River Junction, VT: Chelsea Green, 2014).

19. Bahnson, *Soil and Sacrament,* pp. 2–3, 13.

20. USDA, "Under Cover Farmers," https://www.youtube.com/watch?v=nWXCLVCJWTU&list=TLsE9MAyLxRnP6v5rPy4Brwu453ENSUDv8.

21. Ohlson, *The Soil Will Save Us,* p. xii.

22. John O'Donohue, *The Four Elements* (New York: Harmony, 2010), pp. 129–59.

23. McFague, *Body of God,* pp. 102–3.

24. About one in four Americans hold to the idea of God as a loving presence active in the world. See Paul Froese and Christopher Bader, *America's Four Gods* (New York: Oxford Univ. Press, 2010). The sociological data presented in this book probably come the closest to getting at the theological revolution of a radically present God that I describe here. And I suspect that in the last five years, that percentage has increased.

25. McFague, *Body of God,* p. 144.

26. Wendell Berry, remarks to the American Academy of Religion, interview with Norman Wirzba, from my own notes, Baltimore, November 2013.

27. W. C. Lowdermilk, "Conquest of the Land Through Seven Thousand Years," www.wasco.oacd.org/linked/conquest.pdf.

28. Laura Parker, "Parched: A New Dust Bowl Forms in the Heartland," *National Geographic,* May 17, 2014, http://news.nationalgeographic.com/news/2014/05/140516-dust-bowl-drought-oklahoma-panhandle-food/.

29. David Henson, "Dirt Is Resurrection and God Is a Bad Farmer (Homily for the Parable of the Sower)," *Patheos,* July 5, 2014.

30. Mary Oliver, from "One or Two Things," in *New and Selected Poems: Volume One* (Boston: Beacon, 1992).

31. Quoted in McFague, *Body of God,* p. 111.

CHAPTER 2: WATER

1. The Chesapeake Bay Program has a good page with links to Smith's early description of the bay—one of the treasures of early American nature literature—on its website: http://www.chesa peakebay.net/discover/bayhistory/johnsmith.

2. Quoted in Wallace J. Nichols, *Blue Mind: The Surprising Science That Shows How Being Near, In, On or Under Water Can Make You Happier, Healthier, More Connected, and Better at What You Do* (New York: Little, Brown, 2014), p. 9.

3. Nichols, *Blue Mind*, p. xviii.

4. The story is found in Adamnan's *Life of St. Columba of Iona*.

5. The best discussion of water in world religions is Ian Bradley, *Water: A Spiritual History* (London: Bloomsbury, 2012), chap. 1. Some of the material in this section follows his excellent analysis.

6. Bradley, *Water*, pp. 10–28.

7. These aquifers are a considerable point of tension in the contemporary politics and ongoing crises between the Palestinians and the Israelis, especially surrounding issues of West Bank settlement and occupation.

8. Nichols, *Blue Mind*, p. 61.

9. Nichols, *Blue Mind*, p. 89.

10. Nichols, *Blue Mind*, esp. pp. 24–78.

11. An introduction to this emerging field of study, "Neuro-conservation: Your Brain on Nature: Wallace J. Nichols at TEDxSantaCruz," can be found at https://www.youtube.com/watch?v=r2_X7mTUirk.

12. International Spa Association, "Growth in Spa Industry Generates Record-Setting Number of Spa Visits," August 14, 2014, http://www.experienceispa.com/articles/index.cfm?action=view &articleID=796&menuID=75.

13. Richard Schiffman, "Why People Who Pray Are Healthier Than Those Who Don't," *Huffington Post,* January 18, 2012, http://www.huffingtonpost.com/richard-schiffman/why-people-who-pray-are-heathier_b_1197313.html.

14. Nichols, *Blue Mind,* p. 6.

15. Aldo Leopold, *A Sand County Almanac* (New York: Oxford Univ. Press, 1989), p. 214.

16. Brian Clark Howard, "Worst Drought in 1,000 Years Predicted for American West," *National Geographic,* February 12, 2015, http://news.nationalgeographic.com/news/2015/02/150212-megadrought-southwest-water-climate-environment/.

17. Dennis Dimick, "If You Think the Water Crisis Can't Get Worse, Wait Until the Aquifers Are Drained," *National Geographic,* August 21, 2014, http://news.nationalgeographic.com/news/2014/08/140819-groundwater-california-drought-aquifers-hidden-crisis/.

18. Mark Koba, "California Drought: 'May Have to Migrate People,'" CNBC, July 31, 2014, http://www.cnbc.com/id/101884085#.

19. Elaine S. Povich, "California's Drought Grabs Headlines, but Other States Face Water Woes Too," April 16, 2015, *Huffington Post,* http://www.huffingtonpost.com/2015/04/16/california-drought_n_7078820.html?ncid=tweetlnkushpmg00000016.

20. For a full history of how the world's rivers became threatened and the corresponding threat to us, read Alice Outwater, *Water: A Natural History* (New York: Basic, 1996).

21. Fred Pearce, *When the Rivers Run Dry: Waters—The Defining Crisis of the Twenty-First Century* (Boston: Beacon, 2006), p. 25.

22. T. S. Eliot, from *Four Quartets,* "The Dry Salvages," ll. 1–10, 15.

23. Hildegard of Bingen, *Liber Divinorum Operum* (LDO) VII,

2. I used these words of Hildegard's in my *A People's History of Christianity* (San Francisco: HarperOne, 2009, p. 291) in connection with "river" as the best metaphor to describe contemporary Christianity. At the time I wrote that book, I do not think that I realized the full power of the metaphor, especially in light of the crisis of watersheds and water all over the world.

24. The Water Project, http://thewaterproject.org/about_us.

25. Benjamin M. Stewart, *A Watered Garden: Christian Worship and Earth's Ecology* (Minneapolis: Augsburg Fortress, 2011), pp. 23–25.

26. Ched Meyers, "Watershed Moment," *Sojourners,* May 2014, http://www.chedmyers.org/awatershedmoment. For more on the practice of watershed discipleship, see http://watersheddiscipleship .org.

27. "Religious Leaders Highlight Significance of Water at WCC Assembly," https://www.oikoumene.org/en/press-centre/news/religious-leaders-highlight-significance-of-water-at-wcc -assembly.

28. The social justice history of British Christianity can be found in Bradley, *Water,* pp. 155–80.

29. Ibrahim Abdul-Matin, *Green Deen: What Islam Teaches About Protecting the Planet* (San Francisco: Berrett-Koehler, 2010), pp. 119–23.

30. Imam Ja'far al-Sadiq, *Bihaar al-Anwaar,* vol. 75, p. 234.

31. GreenFaith Water Shield, http://www.greenfaith.org/programs/greenfaith-shield/greenfaith-water-shield.

32. Adelle M. Banks, "Water Initiatives Get Congregations to Pledge to Conserve," Religion News Service, October 8, 2013. http://www.greenfaith.org/media/press-clips/water-initiatives-get -congregations-to-pledge-to-conserve.

33. Ted Hughes, quoted in Bradley, *Water,* p. 223.

CHAPTER 3: SKY

1. I have lived in Arizona, as I noted, a place of sky. But light pollution inhibits stargazing in Phoenix and its environs. Even far out into the desert, city lights have an impact on the night sky. On the East Coast, there are some good places to see stars, like the West Virginia mountains. Yet even there the glow of big cities takes some of the splendor away from the skies. The clarity of the skies in more remote places in Wyoming and Montana are, in a word, extraordinary. There, one gets a sense of the primal human reaction to the night sky.

2. An intelligent and interesting book that covers some of the same themes discussed here, but from the perspective of science and posttheism, is Nancy Ellen Abrams's *A God That Could Be Real: Spirituality, Science, and the Future of Our Planet* (Boston: Beacon Press, 2015). Some of our conclusions about God are startlingly similar, even though we approach the topic from such different angles.

3. P. Nash Jenkins, "After One Brief Season, *Cosmos* Makes Its Final Voyage," *Time,* June 9, 2014, http://time.com/2846928/cosmos-season-finale/.

4. Jeffrey Kluger, "The Science of Stupid: Galileo Is Rolling Over in His Grave," *Time,* February 17, 2014, http://time.com/7859/the-science-of-stupid-galileo-is-rolling-over-in-his-grave/. It is worth noting that, in the same National Science Foundation study, 36 percent of Europeans got this wrong too.

5. Judy Cannato, *Field of Compassion: How the New Cosmology Is Transforming Spiritual Life* (Notre Dame, IN: Sorin, 2010).

6. At the time of writing, the argument between these two theories was revived in a paper by scientists from the University of Lethbridge in Canada. Lisa Zyga, "No Big Bang?" February 9, 2015, http://phys.org/news/2015–02-big-quantum-equation-universe.html.

7. Other physicists, such as Tulane University's Frank Tipler, define the cosmological Omega Point specifically as heaven.

8. John L. Allen Jr., "Pope Cites Teilhardian Vision of the Cosmos as a 'Living Host,'" *National Catholic Reporter,* July 28, 2009, http://ncronline.org/news/pope-cites-teilhardian-vision-cosmos -living-host.

9. Pope Francis, Encyclical Letter, *Laudato Sí,* 2015). http:// w2.vatican.va/content/francesco/en/encyclicals/documents/papa -francesco_20150524_enciclica-laudato-si.html. David Gibson, "U.S. Nuns Haunted by Dead Jesuit: The Ghost of Pierre Teilhard de Chardin," Religion News Service, May 22, 2014, http://www.religionnews .com/2014/05/22/nuns-jesuit-vatican-teilhard-de-chardin/.

10. Elizabeth Johnson, "For God So Loved the Cosmos," *U.S. Catholic,* April 2010 (emphasis mine), http://www.uscatholic.org/ culture/environment/2010/07/god-so-loved-world-jesus-and -environment.

11. Allison Eck, "In the Past 24 Hours, 60 Tons of Cosmic Dust Have Fallen to Earth," PBS, *NovaNext,* March 13, 2015, http://www.pbs.org/wgbh/nova/next/space/in-the-past-24 -hours-60-tons-of-cosmic-dust-have-fallen-to-earth/.

12. Brian Greene, *The Fabric of the Cosmos: Space, Time, and the Texture of Reality* (New York: Vintage, 2005), p. 19.

13. Swami Nirmalananda Giri, "The Hindu Tradition of Breath Meditation," http://www.ocoy.org/original-yoga/how-to -meditate/the-breath-of-life-the-practice-of-breath-meditation/ the-hindu-tradition-of-breath-meditation/.

14. John O'Donohue, *The Four Elements: Reflections on Nature* (New York: Harmony, 2010), pp. 9, 13.

15. NASA, Global Climate Change, http://climate.nasa.gov.

16. David Ray Griffin, *Unprecedented: Can Civilization Survive the CO_2 Crisis?* (Atlanta: Clarity, 2015), p. 16.

17. Bill McKibben, *Eaarth: Making a Life on a Tough New Planet* (New York: Times, 2010), pp. 27–28.

18. McKibben, *Eaarth,* p. 1.

19. McKibben, *Eaarth,* p. 25.

20. Walter Reid et al., *Millennial Ecosystem Assessment Synthesis Report,* March 23, 2005; quoted in Paul Hawken, *Blessed Unrest* (New York: Penguin, 2007), p. 173.

21. "The Anthropocene: A Man-Made World," *Economist,* May 26, 2011, http://www.economist.com/node/18741749.

22. Jim Antal, personal correspondence, April 2015.

23. Jim Antal, "Why We Divested," *God's Politics,* July 19, 2013, http://sojo.net/blogs/2013/07/19/why-we-divested.

24. Mallory McDuff, *Natural Saints: How People of Faith Are Working to Save God's Earth* (New York: Oxford Univ. Press, 2010).

25. Hawken, *Blessed Unrest.* See also Diana Butler Bass, *Christianity After Religion: The End of Church and the Birth of a New Spiritual Awakening* (San Francisco: HarperOne, 2012).

26. Marcus Borg, *Speaking Christian* (San Francisco: HarperOne, 2011), p. 197.

27. Elizabeth Johnson, "Deep Incarnation: Prepare to be Astonished," paper given at the VI International UNIFAS Conference, Rio de Janeiro, July 7–14, 2010, https://sgfp.wordpress.com/2011/02/15/deep-incarnation-prepare-to-be-astonished/.

28. Jonathan Edwards, "Miscellany no. 108," in *The Works of Jonathan Edwards,* vol. 13 (New Haven: Yale Univ. Press), p. 280.

29. Hildegard of Bingen, quoted in Shane Claiborne, et al., *Common Prayer: A Liturgy for Ordinary Radicals* (Grand Rapids: Zondervan, 2010), September 17 entry.

30. Some cultures add a fifth element to the list: "metal" in China, "void" in Japan, "aether" in ancient Greece.

31. Robert Herrick, "To Find God." May be viewed at Poetry Foundation, http://www.poetryfoundation.org/poem/181049.

CHAPTER 4: ROOTS

1. Maud Newton, "America's Ancestry Craze," *Harper's,* June 2014, pp. 29–34.

2. Bruce Falconer, "Ancestry.com's Genealogical Juggernaut," *Bloomberg Businessweek,* September 20, 2012, http://www.bloom berg.com/bw/articles/2012-09-20/ancestry-dot-coms-genealogical -juggernaut.

3. Historian François Weil explores all these dimensions of genealogy as well as the larger question of what genealogy means through American history in *Family Trees: A History of Genealogy in America* (Cambridge, MA: Harvard Univ. Press, 2013).

4. Many of these themes are nicely explored in Margaret Bendroth, *The Spiritual Practice of Remembering* (Grand Rapids, MI: Eerdmans, 2013).

5. Danièle Hervieu-Léger, *Religion as a Chain of Memory* (New Brunswick, NJ: Rutgers Univ. Press, 2000).

6. That the Bible itself defines the days of Genesis 1 as "generations" makes the entire idea of creation in seven (twenty-four-hour) days not only scientifically ludicrous, but also theologically untenable. "Day" is clearly a literary way of speaking of the "generations" of creation.

7. Andrew Orem was baptized in the Monikie parish church of the Church of Scotland in 1653.

8. In the course of writing this book, I took an ancestry DNA test. The test confirmed the story I had uncovered of my mother's ancestors—that I am predominately of Scottish and English descent; only a small portion of my genetic profile originated in Germany.

9. Barack Obama, *Dreams from My Father: A Story of Race and Inheritance,* rev. ed. (New York: Three Rivers, 2004), pp. 371–72, 376–77, 394, 430.

10. Falconer, "Ancestry.com's Genealogical Juggernaut."

11. Carl Zimmer, "Charlemagne's DNA and Our Universal Royalty," *National Geographic,* May 7, 2013, http://phenomena .nationalgeographic.com/2013/05/07/charlemagnes-dna-and-our -universal-royalty/.

12. Zimmer, "Charlemagne's DNA," emphasis mine.

13. Fritjof Capra, *The Web of Life: A New Understanding of Living Systems* (New York: Anchor, 1997).

14. After writing this chapter, I ran across the idea of the "great web of belonging" in Larry L. Rasmussen, *Earth-honoring Faith: Religious Ethics in a New Key* (New York: Oxford Univ. Press, 2013).

15. John of Damascus, *Treatise on Holy Images,* quoted in *The Green Bible,* ed. Michael G. Maudlin and Marlene Baer (San Francisco: HarperOne, 2008), p. I-101.

16. Barbara Brown Taylor, "Physics and Faith: The Luminous Web," *Christian Century,* June 2–9, 1999, pp. 612–19. Copyright by the Christian Century Foundation and used by permission. This text was prepared for Religion Online by John C. Purdy. A different version of it appears in *The Luminous Web* (Lanham, MD: Cowley, 2000), pp. 47–75.

17. Desmond Tutu, *God Has a Dream* (New York: Image, 2004), quoted in *The Green Bible,* ed. Maudlin and Baer, p. I-113.

18. U.S. Conference of Catholic Bishops, *Renewing the Earth,* 1991, http://www.usccb.org/issues-and-action/human-life-and -dignity/environment/renewing-the-earth.cfm.

19. Sir Walter Scott, *Marmion: A Tale of Flodden Field* (1808), 6.17.

20. Kenneth Gergen, *The Saturated Self* (New York: Basic, 1992).

21. Diarmuid O'Murchu, *Ancestral Grace: Meeting God in Our Human Story* (Maryknoll, NY: Orbis Books, 2008).

22. "Finding Your Quaker Roots," http://www.rootsweb.ancestry.com/~quakers/quakfind.htm.

23. Howard Brinton, in Anthony Manousos, *Howard and Anna Brinton: Re-inventors of Quakerism in the Twentieth Century: An Interpretative Biography* (forthcoming), excerpt found at http://quaker.org/quest/QT-22-Brinton-Biography-Excerpt.html.

24. Brinton, in Manousos, *Howard and Anna Brinton.*

25. Brinton, in Manousos, *Howard and Anna Brinton.*

26. Quoted in Bendroth, *Spiritual Practice of Remembering,* p. 127.

27. M. Kei, from "Chesapeake Country," in *Heron Sea: Short Poems of the Chesapeake Bay* (Elkton, MD: Keibooks, 2007), p. 14.

CHAPTER 5: HOME

1. Laura Ingalls Wilder, *These Happy Golden Years* (New York: Harper, 1943).

2. Philip Sheldrake, *The Spiritual City: Theology, Spirituality, and the Urban* (West Sussex, UK: Wiley-Blackwell, 2014), pp. 117–18.

3. Quoted in Andy Crouch, "Ten Most Significant Cultural Trends of the Last Decade," http://qideas.org/articles/ten-most-significant-cultural-trends-of-the-last-decade.

4. Gaston Bachelard, *The Poetics of Space* (Boston: Beacon, 1994), p. 4.

5. Bachelard, *Poetics of Space,* p. 7.

6. U.S. Conference of Catholic Bishops, *Renewing the Earth,* 1991, http://www.usccb.org/issues-and-action/human-life-and-dignity/environment/renewing-the-earth.cfm.

7. David Marine, "The Origin and True Meaning of Home," http://blog.coldwellbanker.com/the-origin-and-true-meaning-of-home/.

8. Before the early nineteenth century, family patterns were (of course) still patriarchal in much of the West, but were far broader in scope than in later modern families. Most people lived in arrangements that included a vast array of extended relations, servants and slaves, and even trade and commercial relationships that constituted a wide *familia,* one more tribal or feudal than anything most people in Western society would recognize or remember today.

9. An excellent study on shifting family structures in the United States is Isabel V. Sawhill, *Generation Unbound: Drifting into Sex and Parenthood Without Marriage* (Washington, DC: Brookings, 2014).

10. Comparison data for average first marriage statistics in postindustrial countries is available at http://en.wikipedia.org/wiki/Age_at_first_marriage.

11. Kay Hymowitz et al., "Knot Yet: The Benefits and Costs of Delayed Marriage in America" (Charlottesville, VA: The National Marriage Project, 2013), http://nationalmarriageproject.org/resources/knot-yet-the-benefits-and-costs-of-delayed-marriage-in-america/.

12. Sawhill, *Generation Unbound,* pp. 44–46.

13. Hymowitz et al., "Knot Yet." See also Karen Swallow Prior, "The Case for Getting Married Young, *Atlantic,* March 22, 2013, http://www.theatlantic.com/sexes/archive/2013/03/the-case-for-getting-married-young/274293/.

14. Eric Klinenberg, *Going Solo: The Extraordinary Rise and Surprising Appeal of Living Alone* (New York: Penguin, 2012), p. 5.

15. Klinenberg, *Going Solo,* p. 230.

16. Chögyam Trungpa, *Shambala: The Sacred Path of the Warrior,* reprint ed. (Boston: Shambala, 2009), p. 46.

17. Mother Teresa, *A Gift for God: Prayers and Meditations,* comp. Malcolm Muggeridge (San Francisco: HarperSanFrancisco, 1996), p. 18.

18. Dietrich Bonhoeffer, *Life Together* (New York: Harper & Row, 1954), p. 68.

19. Sharon Daloz Parks, "Household Economics," in Dorothy Bass, ed., *Practicing Our Faith: A Way of Life for a Searching People* (San Francisco: Jossey-Bass, 1997), p. 43.

20. For more about the revival of New England wheat and grains, see Molly Birnbaum, "Local Grain," *Modern Farmer,* March 19, 2014, http://modernfarmer.com/2014/03/local-grain/.

21. Rachel Maddow, "Consumer Confidence Is Up, Just Ask New England's Breweries," *Washington Post,* January 25, 2015, http://www.washingtonpost.com/opinions/consumer-confidence -is-up-just-ask-new-englands-breweries/2015/01/25/892d8138 -a324-11e4-b146-577832eafcb4_story.html.

22. Barna Group, "How Many People Really Attend a House Church," August 31, 2009, https://www.barna.org/barna-update/ organic-church/291-how-many-people-really-attend-a-house -church-barna-study-finds-it-depends-on-the-definition#.VMb -Rb4mKBM.

23. Meredith Blake, "HGTV Builds into a Top Cable Network on Foundation of No-Frills Shows," *Los Angeles Times,* July 18, 2014, http://www.latimes.com/entertainment/tv/la-et-hgtv-cable -network-20th-anniversary-20140720-story.html#page=1.

24. Gail Collins, "Hillary's Next Move," *New York Times,* November 10, 2012, http://www.nytimes.com/2012/11/11/ opinion/sunday/collins-hillarys-next-move.html?pagewanted =all&_r=0.

25. What is most intriguing about these shows is that things do not always turn out as expected, offering surprising spiritual morals in the mix: you cannot always purchase the house you want; it is often better to work with what you have; sometimes you have to choose between fixing things you cannot see and

installing gorgeous granite countertops; do not buy too much stuff and let clutter take over your life; if you paint your rooms puce, nobody will buy your house; and when you open up a wall, you never know what you will find. One need not look toward academics discoursing on the metaphysics of "place" or reviewing the latest sociological insights to understand that "home" is a moral universe. Just flip to cable.

26. Shannon Hayes, *Radical Homemakers: Reclaiming Domesticity from a Consumer Culture* (Richmondville, NY: Left to Write, 2010).

27. Emily Matchar, *Homeward Bound: Why Women Are Embracing the New Domesticity* (New York: Simon & Schuster, 2013), pp. 12–13.

28. Diana Butler Bass, *A People's History of Christianity* (San Francisco: HarperOne, 2009), pp. 188–192.

29. Sharon Astyk, *Making Home: Adapting Our Homes and Our Lives to Settle in Place* (Gabriola Island, BC: New Society, 2012), pp. 245–58.

30. Jeffrey D. Long, *A Vision for Hinduism: Beyond Hindu Nationalism* (London and New York: Tauris, 2007), p. 88.

31. Gunilla Norris, "Walking," in *Being Home* (Mahwah, NJ: Hidden Spring, 1991, 2001), pp. 6–7.

CHAPTER 6: NEIGHBORHOOD

1. Lewis Mumford, "The Neighborhood and the Neighborhood Unit," *Town Planning Review* 24 (1954): 256–70 (258), quotation and citation found at http://en.wikipedia.org/wiki/Neighbourhood.

2. Peter Lovenheim, *In the Neighborhood: The Search for Community on an American Street, One Sleepover at a Time* (New York: Perigee, 2010), pp. 221–22.

3. The sources for this collection of versions of the Golden

Rule are drawn from Jeffery Moss, *Oneness: Great Principles Shared by All Religions* (New York: Ballantine, 1969); www.religious tolerance.org.

4. Charter for Compassion, https://charterforcompassion.org/global-compassion-movement.

5. Karen Armstrong, "Let's Revive the Golden Rule," https://www.youtube.com/watch?v=nvusULyhZKI#t=314.

6. "A Message on the Golden Rule from the Dalai Lama," http://interfaith-centre.org/iic-resources/e-learning/global-ethics/the-golden-rule/a-message-on-the-golden-rule-from-the-dalai-lama/#sthash.mlcUMWdj.dpuf.

7. Tenzin Gyatso, "Many Faiths, One Truth," *New York Times,* May 24, 2010, http://www.nytimes.com/2010/05/25/opinion/25gyatso.html?_r=0.

8. Cindy Wooden, "Catholics Must Grow in Love of God, Neighbor," June 13, 2013, http://www.catholicnews.com/data/stories/cns/1302548.htm.

9. Deepak Chopra, *The Third Jesus: The Christ We Cannot Ignore* (New York: Three Rivers, 2008), p. 107.

10. Simon Caldwell, "Prince Charles: We Cannot Ignore the Plight of Christians in the Middle East," *Catholic Herald,* December 19, 2013, http://www.catholicherald.co.uk/news/2013/12/19/prince-charles-we-cannot-ignore-the-plight-of-christians-in-the-middle-east/.

11. Peter Block, *Community: The Structure of Belonging* (San Francisco: Berrett-Koehler Publishers, Inc., 2008), p. 2.

12. "Consideration for Neighbors," http://www.islamreligion.com/articles/1775/#_ftn9256.

13. "Neighbors in Islam," http://islam.about.com/od/familycommunity/fl/Neighbors-in-Islam.htm.

14. I wrote about my experience at St. Stephens in my *Strength for the Journey: A Pilgrimage of Faith in Community* (San Francisco: Jossey-Bass, 2002).

15. Bill Bishop, *The Big Sort: Why the Clustering of Like-Minded America Is Tearing Us Apart* (Boston: Houghton Mifflin Harcourt, 2008).

16. Sue Goss, *Open Tribe* (London: Lawrence & Wishart, 2014), p. 26.

17. Goss, *Open Tribe,* p. 31.

18. Robert Frost, "Mending Wall," http://www.poets.org/poetsorg/poem/mending-wall.

19. Henri Nouwen, *Reaching Out: The Three Movements of the Spiritual Life* (New York: Image, 1975), p. 46.

20. Nouwen, *Reaching Out,* pp. 47–48.

21. David Sherfinski, "Hillary Clinton: 'Smart Power' Includes Showing Respect for One's Enemies," *Washington Times,* December 3, 2014, http://www.washingtontimes.com/news/2014/dec/3/hillary-clinton-smart-show-respect-even-enemies/.

22. David Sherfinski, "Hillary Clinton Hammered for Insisting U.S. Should 'Empathize' with Enemies," December 5, 2014, http://www.washingtontimes.com/news/2014/dec/5/hillary-clinton-empathize-enemies-remark-slammed/.

23. I also wrote about this farmers' market to illustrate the potential of a spiritual awakening in my *Christianity After Religion* (San Francisco: HarperOne, 2012).

24. Paul Sparks, Tim Soerens, and Dwight J. Friesen, *The New Parish: How Neighborhood Churches Are Transforming Mission, Discipleship and Community* (Downers Grove, IL: IVP, 2014), p. 24.

25. "Farmers Markets and Local Food Marketing," http://www.ams.usda.gov/AMSv1.0/ams.fetchTemplateData.do?

template=TemplateS&leftNav=WholesaleandFarmersMarkets &page=WFMFarmersMarketGrowth&description=Farmers+ Market+Growth.

26. http://www.saintstephensrichmond.net/farmersmarket.

27. American Planning Association, *Investing in Place: Two Generations' View on the Future of Communities,* May 2014, https:// www.planning.org/policy/polls/investing/.

28. "Neighborhoods: More Walkable, More Desirable," *RealtorMag,* October 11, 2013, http://realtormag.realtor.org/daily -news/2013/10/11/neighborhoods-more-walkable-more -desirable. Also see America Walks, a web and activist community working on issues of neighborhoods, policy, transportation, and walkability, http://americawalks.org.

29. Kathleen Norris, *Quotidian Mysteries: Laundry, Liturgy and "Women's Work"* (Mahwah, NJ: Paulist, 1998), pp. 15, 23.

30. Thich Nhat Hanh, "A Guide to Walking Meditation," http://www.dhammatalks.net/Books2/Thich_Nhat_Hanh_A_ Guide_to_Walking_Meditation.htm.

31. Alan Roxburgh, *Moving Back into the Neighborhood: The Workbook* (West Vancouver, BC: Roxburgh Missional Network, 2010), Introduction, http://www.wichurches.org/sitecontent/pdf_ files/programs/moving_back_into_neighborhood.pdf.

CHAPTER 7: COMMONS

1. I wrote a book about my experiences in that church post-9/11; see *Broken We Kneel: Reflections on Faith and Citizenship* (San Francisco: Jossey-Bass, 2004).

2. My estimate that morning in church was way off base. The number actually is 500,000 or more in Iraq alone, according to an on-the-ground study conducted by a public health team from the

University of Washington in 2013. See Dan Vergano, "Half-Million Iraqis Died in the War, New Study Says," *National Geographic,* October 16, 2013, http://news.nationalgeographic.com/news/2013/10/131015-iraq-war-deaths-survey-2013/.

3. This shift is discussed in my *Christianity After Religion* (San Francisco: HarperOne, 2012). See also Linda A. Mercadante, *Belief Without Borders: Inside the Minds of the Spiritual but Not Religious* (New York: Oxford Univ. Press, 2014).

4. Heather Menzies, *Reclaiming the Commons for the Common Good: A Memoir and Manifesto* (Gabriola Island, British Columbia: New Society Publishers, 2014), pp. 193–94.

5. In addition to providing outdoor public space, the commons may well have housed visitors to the village (typically those attending church services or political meetings) in temporary shelters known as "warming" or "Sabbath Day" houses during important community occasions. Around these commons, near neighbors and those who lived farther afield could gather either outside on the green or inside the meetinghouse or schoolhouse for celebrations or thanksgivings, to adjudicate disputes or make political decisions. John D. Cushing, "Town Commons in New England, 1640–1840," *Historic New England* 51, no. 183 (Winter 1961), http://www.historicnewengland.org/preservation/your-older-or-historic-home/articles/pdf86.pdf.

6. Martin Luther King Jr., "The World House," in *Where Do We Go from Here: Chaos or Community?* (New York: Harper & Row, 1967), available online at http://www.thinkoutword.org/wp-content/uploads/world-house-MLK.pdf.

7. "Reaction Around the World," *New York Times,* September 12, 2001.

8. The majority does not mean everyone; there are sizable minorities in wealthy, technologically advanced countries who do

not share a global outlook; these are people who purposefully resist or deny the cultural change we are undergoing regarding connection and empathy or who are wedded to alternative patterns of meaning around patriarchy, nationalism, individualism, or certain religion or political ideologies. Rifkin also makes the point that the majority of people in the world's poorer countries remain committed to narrower "survival" views based in tribal-oriented, kin-based cultures. But it is equally the case that a minority of people in those cultures also have empathetic "world house" views. In many cases, I suspect, that minority derives such views from being earth-connected cultures, such as the cultures of Native Americans and First Nations people, whose empathetic worldviews, based on intimate connection with the land and other beings, survived colonization. See Jeremy Rifkin, *The Empathic Civilization: The Race to Global Consciousness in a World in Crisis* (New York: Tarcher/Penguin, 2009).

9. Rifkin, *Empathic Civilization,* p. 176.

10. U.S. Conference of Catholic Bishops, *Renewing the Earth,* 1991, http://www.usccb.org/issues-and-action/human-life-and-dignity/environment/renewing-the-earth.cfm.

11. My own book *Christianity for the Rest of Us: How the Neighborhood Church Is Transforming the Faith* (San Francisco: HarperOne, 2006) explores the ways in which vibrant mainline churches are remaking faith and serving their communities. See also Paul Sparks, Tim Soerens, and Dwight J. Friesen, *The New Parish: How Neighborhood Churches Are Transforming Mission, Discipleship and Community* (Downers Grove, IL: IVP, 2014), p. 95.

12. Slavoj Žižek, "Democracy and Capitalism Are Destined to Split Up," *Big Think,* http://bigthink.com/videos/slavoj-zizek-on-capitalism-and-the-commons.

13. King, "World House."

14. Barbara Erhenreich, *Dancing in the Streets: A History of Collective Joy* (New York: Henry Holt, 2006), p. 14.

15. Ehrenreich, *Dancing in the Streets,* p. 225.

16. Ehrenreich, *Dancing in the Streets,* p. 249.

17. Alexander Schmemann, *For the Life of the World: Sacraments and Orthodoxy* (New York: St. Vladimir's Seminary Press, 1973), p. 112.

18. Martin Luther King Jr., "Remaining Awake Through a Great Revolution," Commencement Address for Oberlin College, June 1965, Oberlin, OH, http://www.oberlin.edu/external/EOG/ BlackHistoryMonth/MLK/CommAddress.html.

19. Some of this discussion follows Karen Armstrong, *Twelve Steps to a Compassionate Life* (New York: Knopf, 2011), pp. 3–24.

20. Jim Wallis, *The (Un)Common Good: How the Gospel Brings Hope to a World Divided* (Grand Rapids, MI: Brazos, 2014), pp. 90, 98.

21. Armstrong, *Twelve Steps,* p. 143.

22. *Charter for Compassion,* http://charterforcompassion.org/ the-charter.

23. Karen Armstrong, "Let's Revive the Golden Rule." TED talk, July 2009. https://www.ted.com/talks/karen_armstrong_ let_s_revive_the_golden_rule.

24. The former president's intentions and true feelings on this subject may never be known. Several of his advisers think the phrase accurately represented Mr. Bush's personal desires, but that others in the White House constantly thwarted him or used them for political gain. See especially David Kuo, *Tempting Faith: An Inside Story of Political Seduction* (New York: Free Press, 2006).

25. George W. Bush, "Bullhorn Speech," http://www .americanrhetoric.com/speeches/gwbush911groundzerobullhorn .htm.

26. Armstrong, *Twelve Steps*, p. 151.

27. This sermon was graciously given to me by the Rev. Oran Warder of St. Paul's Episcopal Church in Alexandria, Virginia, and shared with his permission. For the record, he is a very good preacher.

28. Rifkin, *Empathic Civilization,* p. 6.

CONCLUSION: REVELATION

1. This story is also told in my *Broken We Kneel: Reflections on Faith and Citizenship* (San Francisco: Jossey-Bass, 2004). There, however, I did not give this detail, partly because it was too painful and personal to recount and partly because it did not serve a purpose in the larger narrative of the chapter, which was about children and faith, not about my spiritual journey.

2. Barbara Rossing, *The Rapture Exposed: The Message of Hope in the Book of Revelation* (New York: Basic, 2004).

3. A good, readable book on this subject is Kwame Anthony Appiah, *Cosmopolitanism: Ethics in a World of Strangers* (New York: Norton, 2006).

4. The term "humane localism" comes from Mark T. Mitchell, "Making Places: The Cosmopolitan Temptation," in Wilfred M. McClay and Ted V. McAllister, eds., *Why Place Matters: Geography, Identity, and Civic Life in Modern America* (New York: Encounter, 2014), pp. 84–101.

5. Paul Piff and Dacher Keltner, "Why Do We Experience Awe?" *New York Times,* May 22, 2015. From their study, "Awe, the Small Self, and Prosocial Behavior," available from the American Psychological Association, APA PsychNet, http://psycnet.apa.org/journals/psp/108/6/883/.

6. For more on co-creation, see Venkat Ramaswamy and Francis Gouillart, *The Power of Co-Creation: Build It with Them to Boost Growth, Productivity, and Profits* (New York: Free Press, 2010).

7. Matthew Fox, *Original Blessing: A Primer in Creation Spirituality Presented in Four Paths, Twenty-Six Themes, and Two Questions* (Santa Fe, NM: Bear, 1983).

8. One of the most important theological understandings of co-creation comes from process theology, a tradition influenced by the philosopher Alfred North Whitehead and developed by process theologians such as John Cobb, David Griffin, Philip Clayton, and Catherine Keller. In the United States, Claremont School of Theology in Southern California has been a center of process thought and influenced two generations of mainline pastors.

9. I wrote a small book about my experiences in a congregation where I worked at the time. See Diana Butler Bass, *Broken We Kneel*.

10. Mark Chaves, *American Religion: Contemporary Trends* (Princeton, NJ, and Oxford: Princeton Univ. Press, 2011).

11. It cannot be strongly enough stated that there are many, many secular people who experience wonder, awe, and transcendence in nature, intellectual endeavors, and the arts. Some of these people use the term "spiritual" to describe these experiences, but insist that "spiritual" is not dependent on theism. Others use the term "mystical." Others use descriptive words such as "wonder," "awe," and so on.

12. Quoted in Elizabeth Johnson, *Quest for the Living God: Mapping Frontiers in the Theology of God* (New York: Continuum, 2008), pp. 44–47.

INDEX